The New Gay for Pay

The New Gay for Pay

The Sexual Politics of American Television Production

JULIA HIMBERG

University of Texas Press ◆ *Austin*

Parts of chapter 1 appeared previously, in a slightly different form, in Julia Himberg,
"Multicasting: Lesbian Programming and the Changing Landscape of Cable
Television," *Television & New Media* 15, no. 4 (May 2014): 289–304.

∞ The paper used in this book meets the minimum requirements of ANSI/NISO
z39.48-1992 (R1997) (Permanence of Paper).

Library of Congress Cataloging-in-Publication Data
Names: Himberg, Julia, author.
Title: The new gay for pay : the sexual politics of American television production /
Julia Himberg.
Description: First edition. | Austin : University of Texas Press, 2018. |
Includes bibliographical references and index.
Identifiers: LCCN 2017020579| ISBN 978-1-4773-1359-6 (cloth : alk. paper) |
ISBN 978-1-4773-1360-2 (pbk. : alk. paper) | ISBN 978-1-4773-1361-9 |
ISBN 978-1-4773-1362-6
Subjects: LCSH: Homosexuality on television. | Television and gays—United States. |
Homosexuality and television—United States. | Gender identity on television. |
Television programs—Social aspects—United States. | Television programs—Political
aspects—United States.
Classification: LCC PN1992.8.H64 H56 2018 | DDC 791.45/653—dc23
LC record available at https://lccn.loc.gov/2017020579

doi:10.7560/313596

In loving memory of my mother, Isabel Ann Kip, 1950–2008

Contents

Acknowledgments

While this book bears the name of only one author, writing is far from a solitary endeavor. I have been fortunate to have a great deal of support and assistance over the years it took to bring this project to fruition. I thank the tremendous team at the University of Texas Press, including Nancy Bryan, Sarah Rosen McGavick, Kerri Cox Sullivan, and especially my acquisitions editor, Jim Burr. Jim championed and shepherded this project from its inception to its publication. Thanks also to the external readers, whose thoughtful and encouraging feedback helped me to refine the argument and deepened my analysis of each case study.

The emotional support that writing a book requires often doesn't receive the same credit as intellectual guidance. However, I want to thank the following people for sharing their intellectual as well as their emotional labor with me along the way. I could not imagine better colleagues than those I have in Film and Media Studies at Arizona State University. Aaron Baker, Desirée Garcia, Bambi Haggins, and Kevin Sandler made a concerted effort to shield me from the extensive workload required to run our program so that I could focus my energy on research and teaching. They, along with Christopher Bradley, Daniel Cutrara, Michael Green, Catherine Hartman, Michelle Martinez, and Justin Winters provided a work culture filled with humor and camaraderie. I am especially indebted to Bambi, who offered her friendship, wise perspectives, and activist spirit from the moment I arrived on campus in 2012. I also benefited from the consistent guidance of the English Department, of which the Film and Media Studies program is a part; Jessica Early deserves special thanks for her outstanding mentorship. Over the years, my students have inspired me, providing insights and experiences that have shaped many of the ideas in this book.

My graduate education at the University of Southern California was unparalleled. I had the honor of working closely with Ellen Seiter, Anikó Imre, and Larry Gross throughout my MA and PhD programs. It was Larry's class, "Gays and the Media," that sparked my interest in sexuality studies. Although this book is not a revision of my doctoral dissertation, the research and analytical skills I learned from my dissertation committee provided the foundation I needed to write it. I vividly remember the day Ellen bravely suggested I change my area of study. She was thoughtful and observant enough to suggest that my interests had shifted, and her invitation opened the door for me to pursue a subject that I am endlessly fascinated by and truly passionate about. I was also fortunate to learn from Sarah Banet-Weiser, Ruth Wilson Gilmore, Jack Halberstam, Kara Keeling, Curtis Marez, Tara McPherson, and Michael Renov, whose courses laid the groundwork for my interdisciplinary approach to media studies. I also thank fellow USC graduates Patty Ahn, Christopher Hansen, Jorie Lagerwey, Taylor Nygaard, and Suzanne Scott, whose reassurance and perspective over the years have created enduring friendships. Each of them provided honest feedback and wonderful encouragement, reminding me of the importance of this project during moments of self-doubt. I am especially grateful to Patty and Taylor for long discussions about sexuality, gender, and media as well as for their constant friendship.

Many of the early ideas for this book were borne out of discussions with participants in the 2009 summer doctoral seminar on Queer Media Culture held at Wayne State University. Jackie Byars brought together a fantastic group of graduate students from around the country to study with Amy Villarejo. Amy led us through some of the most productive conversations about sexuality and media I have ever engaged in, and she remains a generous mentor. I am ever grateful for the friendships I formed that summer, which have led to ongoing intellectual dialogues and support as we finished our dissertations and began our careers in academia.

I was also influenced over the years by scholars who took an avid interest in my research. I am grateful for conversations with Benjamin Aslinger, Miranda Banks, Ron Becker, John Caldwell, Norma Coates, David Craig, Hollis Griffin, Hunter Hargraves, Lisa Henderson, Jennifer Holt, Lynne Joyrich, Vicki Mayer, and Mimi White. In their own ways, each of them has influenced this project more than they know.

I will always be grateful to the Film Studies (now Film and Media Studies) program at the University of California, Santa Barbara. I arrived there from the East Coast as a college freshman ready to become a Hollywood director—or so I thought. Through Chuck Wolfe, Lisa Parks, Bhaskar Sarkar, Janet Walker, Constance Penley, Anna Brusutti, Alison Fraunhar, and Cynthia Felando I learned what critical media studies is and fell in love with the discipline. They were, and still are, phenomenal teachers and mentors, and they put me on the path to graduate school. I am also thankful to Anne Kingdon, whom I met when she hired me to work at the campus writing center at UCSB. All these years later, she graciously offered up her keen editorial skills for each chapter.

Writing a book, it turns out, is not just a mental and emotional task but also a physical one. Angee Croxford, a phenomenally gifted and holistic physical therapist, provided me great lessons in health and self-care that were nothing short of transformative.

My life would simply not be the same without "chosen family." Daniel Gilfillan has been steadfast in his care and counsel about all aspects of writing a first book, teaching, and career development. Anikó Imre spent years helping me to make sense of the patterns I observed in popular culture and pushed me to stake my intellectual claims. As luck would have it, Madelaine Adelman and I started writing our books at the same time. Between cafés and kitchen tables, we shared the ups and downs of the process. I thank her for vast amounts of encouragement and feedback from beginning to end.

The bond I share with Heather Bath, Jeff Reynolds, and my beloved Quincy and Simon is like no other, and it has sustained me in myriad ways since we met fourteen years ago. I'm eternally grateful for all of the laughs, tears, home-cooked meals, and philosophical discussions we've shared. I am also tremendously grateful to my love, Dana Moore, and her son, Jacob.

My family of origin is small and spread across the United States, but I am lucky enough to be close with them. My sister, Amy, always seems to find the perfect way to tease me mercilessly and somehow to champion me at the same time. There's nothing quite like a sister, and I adore mine. During my first two years of graduate school, my uncle, Philip, offered me a home with him and his daughter, Fanny. Those years gave us precious time together and a connection that I cherish.

The roots of this project go back to my childhood and the blend of academic and activist spirits instilled in me by my mother, father, stepmother, and stepfather. They each found their own unique ways of encouraging me to choose a career I care deeply about, to constantly crave learning and knowledge, and to fight for my beliefs. I treasure the values they passed on to me: "feminist" was a word shouted loud and proud in my households; equality and civil rights were cornerstones of dinner conversations; and to this day I am nourished by their love, intellect, and principles. My father, Harvey, is a model of intellectual rigor and achievement and the most devoted dad I could have asked for. His love and support throughout my life have meant the world to me. Jamie, my stepmother, has believed in me and championed my every endeavor. She taught me what it means to be a brave, independent woman and I am grateful for her wisdom and kindness. From my stepfather, Mark, I learned the importance of witty banter, a strong work ethic, and dedication to your family, and gained an appreciation for postwar European cinema.

Finally, this book is dedicated to my mother, Isabel Ann Kip. Although she died while I was still working on my PhD, her creativity, thoughtful observations, genuine curiosity about the world, and never-ending love imprinted themselves on me and are, I hope, visible in this book.

The New Gay for Pay

Introduction: The New Gay for Pay

It is February 12, 2016, and President Barack Obama is the guest on *The Ellen DeGeneres Show* (NBC, 2003–), the afternoon talk show hosted by Ellen De-Generes. Ellen profusely thanks Obama for all that he has done for what she terms "the gay community." The studio audience erupts in cheers as Obama responds, "It's one of the things I'm proudest of because my whole political career has been based on the idea that we constantly want to include people and not exclude people. . . . But I will say . . . as much as we've done with laws and with ending 'Don't Ask, Don't Tell,' etc., changing hearts and minds, I don't think anyone's been more influential than you [Ellen] on that, I really mean that." The audience applauds and the camera pans to DeGeneres, seated next to Obama, as tears well up in her eyes. When the applause dies down, Obama says, "You being willing to claim who you were [on national television in 1997] suddenly empowers other people, and suddenly it's your brother, it's your uncle, best friend, your coworkers, and then attitudes shift and the laws followed. But it started with folks like you. I'm so proud of you."

In the early years of the twenty-first century, the notion that "TV changes the way people think about the world" permeated our politics and popular culture.[1] Even in the face of dramatic changes in television programming, for-mats, regulations, economics, and systems of distribution and consumption, the belief remained that television had the power to influence opinions and even to effect change. Such claims were remarkably pronounced in attempts to explain shifts in public opinion and policy about lesbian, gay, bisexual, and transgender (LGBT) rights that took place in the early 2000s. It was in this context that I set out to write this book.

In the following pages I ask how we might productively engage with the deep-seated belief that LGBT representations on television have led to social and political change. More broadly, I ask what role the television *industry*

Figure 0.1. President Barack Obama on the *Ellen DeGeneres Show* (NBC, 2003–), praising Ellen DeGeneres for coming out publicly in 1997.

played in the early twenty-first century in creating and appropriating cultural systems of knowledge about LGBT sexuality and sexual politics amid the wholesale liberalization of the domestic and global media markets.

The Power of Television(?)

In the two decades following DeGeneres's coming out, I watched with fascination as political figures, Democratic and Republican alike, praised openly LGBT celebrities and television content for their incomparable influence. On a 2012 episode of NBC's *Meet the Press*, the longest-running program in US television history (1947–), then–Vice President Joe Biden told the show's host, David Gregory, "*Will & Grace* probably did more to educate the American public than almost anything anybody's ever done so far."[2] Although his claim likely shocked and angered activists, attorneys, educators, and others who had fought for LGBT visibility, recognition, and equality day in and day out for decades, his assertion was part of a larger trend that put television squarely at the center of social and legal change.

News headlines across the nation have regularly attributed public attitudes that increasingly favor LGBT equality to the influence of television characters, personalities, and storylines. In June 2015, on the same day the US Supreme Court ruled that marriage equality was the law of the land, *Time* ran a story about the television shows that "helped shape America's attitudes about gay relationships," expressing a belief that had become standard in mainstream media circles: "Over the decades, TV shows have brought gay couples into viewers' homes and humanized their struggle for equality."[3] Two years earlier, the online publication *Salon* ran a story by Andrew O'Hehir entitled "Did TV Change America's Mind on Gay Marriage?"[4] O'Hehir barely asked the question before claiming it as truth, listing shows that purportedly contributed to the shift in opinion on marriage rights, which over the course of ten years changed more dramatically than similarly charged issues with long-standing and controversial roots.

In 2011, *Entertainment Weekly*'s cover story was entitled "Special Report: Gay Teens on TV."[5] The article offered a direct causal relationship between gay teens in real life, the depiction of gay teens on television, and the impact those images have both on the general public and on the media industries. *Entertainment Weekly* made a connection specifically between LGBT social change and television, rather than another medium or media writ large. The article's lede, for example, reads: "How a bold new class of young gay characters on shows like *Glee* is changing hearts, minds, and Hollywood."[6] This statement is significant for what it says about the perceived influence of television programs in a period variously described as "convergent," "post-network," and "multiplatform" — terms that could be said to speak to a definition of this particular medium as "a complex interplay of sites, screens, technologies, industries, economies, aesthetics, national and global contexts, domestic and public viewing spaces, citizenship and consumer functions, community and fragmentation, as well as new and established production, user, and audience practices."[7] While the advent of the VCR, remote control, and cable television and premium subscription channels in the 1970s, 1980s, and early 1990s affected audiences' viewing habits in significant ways, the changes that happened in the late 1990s and early 2000s drastically altered the medium as a whole. Amanda Lotz writes that these shifts demarcate a new stage in the television industry, what she calls the "post-network" era.[8] In this period, shifts occurred in every aspect of the medium, including ownership, technology, program creation, distribution platforms, advertising methods, viewing practices, and systems of audience measurement.

In light of these wide-ranging changes, Lotz argues, "television" must be redefined: "Television," she writes, "is more than just a technology. . . . It possesses an essence that is bound up in its context, in how the box is most commonly used, in where it is located, in what streams through it, and in how most use it."[9] This reconceptualization — particularly of the qualities of television that fragment audiences and create silos of viewers ensconced in programming that aligns only with their own worldviews — has, for many scholars and critics, challenged the role of television as the voice of the nation, as a unifying force of democracy. Yet in spite of the vast array of choices it offers in programming, methods of consumption, options for user-generated content—among other elements of what Henry Jenkins calls "convergence culture"—claims about television's influence on the change in social attitudes around LBGT issues have never seemed stronger or more prevalent.[10] Television programming itself reflects on this dynamic; in HBO's 2013 documentary *The Out List*—a series of interviews with LGBT celebrities about their experiences in Hollywood—actor Neil Patrick Harris says,

> It's such an interesting time now . . . because gay visibility is so prevalent, you can watch *The Amazing Race* and see a gay couple fight, argue, and win. General, normal, mainstream, Middle America that doesn't get out and witness a lot of diversity, I feel like they get that diversity through television. Now there are so many examples that you can't just put the gay in the little gay box anymore.[11]

Harris's assessment of the influence of television's LGBT representations is significant not only for what he says but because of who he is; Harris is America's darling, Doogie Howser, who grew up to be a "good gay." He is a multitalented, married father who can entertain audiences with a wink. He is also a gay, white man who embodies stereotypes while breaking boundaries. His remarks represent the themes that circulated in popular culture about LGBT television representation at the time: television images were numerous, diverse, and powerful.

"Television Effects" Matter

Although television programming forms the basis of many everyday discussions about LGBT rights, little in the way of sustained academic work has taken seriously the idea that the medium of television has been a driver of broad-based change. Despite the fact that a great number of critical media studies have debunked this belief or advised against debating it, the notion has maintained a remarkably strong hold in popular thinking. I do not want to revisit these arguments or stake a claim for the value of what has been called "television effects," the idea that what audiences see directly influences their values, opinions, and behaviors.[12] The relationship between television and its viewers is far more complex and thus cannot be reduced to the assertion that viewing multidimensional and relatable representations of LGBT people on television can produce a change in attitudes and opinions across the nation. However, I do want to argue that the *belief* in "television effects" matters.[13]

This is where this book makes its central intervention into studies of television and sexuality; my primary goal here is to understand how television constructs and reinforces beliefs—specifically, what I call "commonsense ideas"—about sexuality and identity-based politics. The notion of "commonsense ideas" refers to informal or popular thinking about television's influence on public opinion and debates;[14] for, even in the post-network era, television remains embedded in the routines, rituals, and institutions of everyday life.

My main argument begins from the assertion that as simplistic, limiting, and even dangerous as these commonsense beliefs may be, turning away from them is not productive. As Richard Dyer writes of lesbian and gay media stereotypes, "Thinking about stereotypes needs to go beyond simply dismissing them as wrong and distorted—doing so does not make them go away, and tends to prevent us from learning just what they are, how they function, and why they are so resilient despite strong rejection of them."[15] The resilience Dyer writes about also applies to popular thinking about sexuality, representation, and politics: regardless of accuracy, commonsense beliefs shape public discourse and often contribute to rhetorics of political change. Indeed, I argue, sexuality and LGBT politics offer ideal subjects for unpacking the dynamics of television production, because sexuality and mediation are so deeply interwoven and because of the seismic shifts in US culture's treatment of LGBT issues and identities—shifts that many attribute, in great part, to television.

Mixing Methods

In order to engage with these ideas, I combine approaches that are usually (but I argue not usefully) kept separate, developing a methodology that reveals arenas of struggle, tension, and negotiation within the television industry. The narrative moves between and integrates methods and subdisciplines, including textual analysis, industry studies, social analysis, studies of branding, and political-economic analysis, while also incorporating ethnographic work.

In its attempt to elucidate the relationship between television production and popular ideas about sexuality and sociopolitical change, this book examines the day-to-day operations of media development, production, distribution, and promotion. It features interviews with television producers, network executives, market researchers, media advocates, political consultants, and public relations experts.[16] This approach has been described variously as "mid-level" research, "studying up," and "studying sideways."[17] In this mode of analysis "agency," or power, lies in the experiences and interactions of industry workers, who are far more than cogs in the wheel of Hollywood's vast empire. This approach responds to calls for research in "localized zones," as Graeme Turner and Anna Pertierra describe them, which are spaces that contain the routines and practices of the television industry.[18] In other words, the book examines the "micro-politics" of everyday meaning-making, revealing industry workers negotiating production processes in ways that can't be seen through macroanalyses (such as those undertaken from the view point of political economy) or by looking at television representations themselves as finished products.[19]

Of the different ways this type of research has been described, I found the anthropological tradition of "studying up" to be the most useful. It seeks to investigate individuals and institutions in positions of power precisely because of the cultural influence they wield. This mode of analysis is relevant to the interviews I conducted, because almost all interviewees were well-educated, highly paid, gay, white men. In May 2015 the ACLU requested that state and federal agencies investigate the hiring practices of major Hollywood studios, networks, and talent agencies over concerns of pervasive and rampant gender and racial discrimination.[20] The homogeneity of the individuals I encountered, then, is not surprising, but rather has been characteristic of the media industries throughout their history.

By taking into account that the ideologies, experiences, and business practices of most industry players are marked by racial, gender, and class privilege, "studying up" allows me to go beyond the critique that Hollywood lacks diverse leaders. There are too many white men running television for sure, and despite granting agency to industry workers, I am nevertheless critical of them and the very institutions they work in. At the same time, these are the people making important decisions about cultural representation every day. As Laura Nader writes about "studying up," "There is a certain urgency to the kind of anthropology that is concerned with power . . . for the quality of life and our lives themselves may depend upon the extent to which citizens understand those who shape attitudes and actually control institutional structures."[21] "Studying up" informs citizens about how institutions work, ideologically and practically. The intended result of "studying up," then, is to enable citizens to actively and responsibly participate in a democracy. Rather than letting interviews speak for themselves, I critically analyze them, delving into the beliefs and practices of industry workers as revealed through their words, particularly in the context of commercial imperatives, industrial structures, and activist agendas.

Using this approach, I discovered surprising configurations of activism, advocacy, and capitalism in the television industry. Many openly lesbian and gay workers in positions of power have been able to navigate and operate within the corporate media industry space in explicitly political ways, accruing agency and authority through the patient building of relationships, coming out, and taking their own personal risks. Through this strategic maneuvering, industry workers do create opportunities for LGBT political change by taking advantage of and exploiting resources that are available to them at higher levels of power.

On the basis of these findings, I propose in this book that cultural workers serve as mediators of sociopolitical life: they embody contradictory lives, as advocates and expressive creators on the one hand, and as business leaders on the other. As John Caldwell writes, "leaving issues of 'identity' at the level of audience . . . ignores the strategic importance that identity activities now play in modern media corporations."[22] Undoubtedly, however, my interview subjects' identities and responses are coded and managed strategically to present a selective image of themselves and the subject matter at hand. This is especially true for "above the line" workers who are well versed in the art of spin. In media industries scholarship, "above the line" workers include producers, directors, and showrunners, in other words, those individuals in charge of departments, budgets, and a program or network's creative vision. Therefore when I analyze each interview I conducted—the interview experience itself and the content of the interview—I pay close attention to both what is said and what is not said, offering polysemic interpretations of each interview.[23]

Another component of "studying up" for me was getting an inside view of some of the institutional structures of LGBT television production and reception. I attended events sponsored by civil rights organizations, such as GLAAD and the National Association for the Advancement of Colored People (NAACP), and market research firms, such as Community Marketing, Inc., that addressed LGBT television production, evaluation, audiences, and consumers. To gain a more sustained view of the practices of LGBT media organizations, I volunteered to be a member of GLAAD's Television Jury (in that period "GLAAD" was an acronym for the Gay and Lesbian Alliance Against Defamation, but the organization changed its name to GLAAD in 2013). My two years as a jury member, attending monthly meetings where, as a group, we debated and ranked the merits of programs with LGBT characters or plotlines, familiarized me with the discourses that circulate within this mainstream organization.[24]

Built into my analysis, then, are my experiences as a participant-observer. Rather than studying production at a distance, through media reports and industrial documents alone, I witnessed firsthand industry workers' efforts to generate meanings about LGBT sexuality. My interpretations of these experiences are informed by my knowledge of decades of LGBT, queer, gender, and feminist studies, which have long since demonstrated that concepts of gender and sexual identity categories, such as "lesbian" and "gay," "male" and "female," "masculine" and "feminine," are historically situated and socially constructed.[25] I therefore reflected on the patterns I observed at these events while also integrating my understanding that these labels are not innate or acquired and then simply embodied in real life or on the screen; rather, they are constantly being shaped, performed, and reconfigured.[26]

Why Now? The Cultural Context of the Twenty-First Century

The choice to use this methodological approach is both the result of and a reaction to a set of conditions that permeate US popular and academic discourse about sexuality and post-network television. First, there has been a noticeable shift in discussions of identity, whether about sexuality, race, or gender; US culture seems dominated by the belief and/or aspiration that it has entered an era of "post-identity" wherein discrete categories such as lesbian, gay, black, white, and so on are deemed less relevant and intrinsic to one's life experiences and opportunities. Popular culture tends to celebrate this notion, seeing it as a symbol of progress. The term "post-gay," like "post-racial" and "post-feminist," supposedly indicates that society has evolved to a place where the politics of identity categories have been transcended. One's "choice" to be "out" as LGBT, for example, is usually couched in personal terms, dominated by the mantra "to be one's true and authentic self." In this configuration of sexuality, coming out does not determine the entirety of one's identity. On television, this means that sexual orientation does not define the character or her or his motivations on a show; rather, she or he "just happens to be gay."

The belief that society has reached a post-gay moment is pervasive in television programs; for example, in MTV's scripted series *Faking It* (2014–2016), high school best friends are mistakenly outed as a lesbian couple. Instead of correcting the misinterpretation of their relationship, they use it to boost their popularity, even allowing themselves to be elected Homecoming Queens. Although *Faking It* received criticism from within and outside LGBT communities for featuring characters who pretend to be lesbian, the show's premise suggests that MTV's millennial audiences not only accept LGBT people but actually celebrate, praise, and even idolize them. There are other programs like the political thriller *Scandal* (ABC, 2012–), which in its sixth season features an openly gay white man who is on the verge of becoming the next US president. He is married to a much younger man, a former prostitute, and they are raising his adopted black daughter together. The show, however, focuses on whether Cyrus Beene (Jeff Perry), a manipulative political monster who will stop at nothing to become the leader of the free world, assassinated the presidential candidate he was running with as a vice-presidential candidate. Underscoring the dominance of post-gay representations, *Scandal* barely touches on the fact that if he becomes president, Beene would achieve the unimaginable: becoming the first openly gay president, who is also married to a man and who has a young black daughter.

From the vantage point of cultural critics, post-gay rhetoric is tied up with a host of worrisome implications. As part of a broader neoliberal system, it reflects a shift from a focus on collective consciousness about sexuality and sexual identity to an individualism that emphasizes the free market and consumption as the route to social and political equality. Critics raise concerns about how this shift away from community and collectivity separates the personal from the political, presenting one's "choices" to identify with certain belief systems or lifestyles as a matter of preference rather than based on convictions or political principles. Amin Ghaziani describes how "the rhetoric and reality of the post-gay era resonates most with those lesbians and gay men" whose behaviors and styles of dress adhere to traditional norms of gender and sexuality and to conventional ideas about love, monogamy, and marriage.[27] Connected to Ghaziani's observations are troubling qualities of post-gay culture that equate it to a form of assimilation that highlights the ways LGBT people are the same as heterosexuals, seeks limited reforms to the existing social and political structure, and embraces cultural inclusion rather than radical rebellion. As Nikki Sullivan writes, "the aim of assimilation was (and still is) to be accepted into, and to become one with, mainstream culture."[28] Assimilation does not result in change to a society when new groups are included. As opposed to the function of true integration, which fundamentally alters society as a result of the diversity that comes with including different identities, assimilation simply adds groups to the existing social structure. When assimilation has occurred, television depictions of sexual minorities often become classed, raced, and gendered to match the expectations of white, gender-conforming, heterosexual middle-class representations.

Scholars argue that this particular form of representation on television tokenizes LGBT characters, ultimately generating more insidious forms of homophobia. As Suzanna Walters observes, "more and more, and particularly in shows that position themselves as 'hip,' the new homophobia takes the form of a 'gloves off' approach that many mistakenly see as the true sign of inclusion and integration."[29] For Walters, and many other critics of LGBT visibility politics, assimilation is a "trend that threatens to engulf gay difference."[30]

The push for visibility, a topic I address throughout the book, has been a long-standing battle cry of activists fighting for cultural recognition. Out of the dark history of LGBT discrimination and oppression, visibility emerged — especially after the Stonewall Riots of 1969 — as a strategy for making identity evident on a broad scale.[31] Calls for visibility in the United States are tied to notions of sexual orientation and gender identity as experiences that revolve expressly around the "closet" and "coming out." The logic of this experience is that one "discovers" her sexual orientation or gender identity and then must "come out of the closet" in an act she hopes will be empowering, freeing, and accepted. While scholars problematize the construction of the "closet"—as perpetuating binary oppositions between homosexuality and heterosexuality, and therefore non-normativity and normativity—the closet and disclosure dominate the contemporary Western experience of being a sexual minority.[32]

Television, established as a domestic medium associated with the intimacy of the home, the family, and private space, has been at the heart of calls for LGBT visibility. Just as early television focused on unifying the heterosexual nuclear family in the post–World War II era, many contemporary television advocates have focused on LGBT visibility because of the contention that images have the power to influence and to change public opinion.[33] In other words, in US society, media representation is a form of cultural currency, providing validation to social minorities that they are seen as part of the nation-state.[34] Being left out of the culture of representation is equated with exclusion, or what Larry Gross terms "symbolic annihilation."[35]

Because of the power afforded television representation, critics worry that homonormative representations — images that mimic stereotypical heterosexuality and heterosexual relationships, especially norms of gender, femininity, and masculinity as well as race and class — might function to divide LGBT communities from within, making it impossible to form a united front to fight for equality for everyone across intersectional lines of difference. As Heather Love says, "One may enter the mainstream on the condition that one breaks ties with all those who cannot make it—the nonwhite and the non-monogamous, the poor and the genderdeviant, the fat, the disabled, the unemployed, the infected, and a host of unmentionable others."[36] Homonormative representations are problematically presented as natural rather than as constructed, thereby imposing an unrealistic set of norms on LGBT individuals, couples, and communities. The costly consequences of these homonormative images, critics argue, include a demobilized LGBT constituency and a privatized, de-politicized LGBT culture, as well as a hierarchy of worthiness and authenticity built around whether certain individuals, such as those in relationships that mirror heterosexual marriage, may be deemed more or less entitled to legal rights than others.[37]

Despite the range of viewers' responses to and interpretations of television content, which have been extensively documented in cultural studies, queer studies, fan studies, and reception studies, homonormative representations dominate programming. Simply put, television is still darn good at representing and reifying dominant norms—of gender, sexuality, class, race, ethnicity, age, region, religion, and so on. As a result, "Those who are gender or sexually nonnormative become" symbols of difference and targets of exclusionary policies.[38]

The final cultural context that inspired the approach of this book is the prevalent notion that full LGBT equality is inevitable and even achieved, largely because of the Supreme Court's rulings on marriage rights.[39] The *New York Times*'s Frank Bruni adeptly articulates how firmly entrenched in both popular and political culture this narrative is in an op-ed titled "The New Gay Orthodoxy":

> Something remarkable has happened—something that's mostly exciting but also a little disturbing. . . . And the development I'm referring to isn't the broadening support for same-sex marriage, which a clear majority of Americans now favor. No, I'm referring to the fact that in a great many circles, endorsement of same-sex marriage has rather suddenly become nonnegotiable. Expected. Assumed. Proof of a baseline level of enlightenment and humanity. Akin to the understanding that all people, regardless of race or color, warrant the same rights and respect. Even beyond these circles, the debate is essentially over, in the sense that the trajectory is immutable and the conclusion foregone. Everybody knows it, even the people who still try to stand in the way. The legalization of same-sex marriage from north to south and coast to coast is merely a matter of time, probably not much of it at that.[40]

Bruni's article is critical of thinking of marriage equality as a victorious endpoint and urges the reader to endeavor to understand the patterns in entertainment and in politics that create and reinforce this ready-made container for progress and that infuse it with a naturalness that makes it seem commonsensical.

The fait accompli narrative has triggered a vigorous critical response that problematizes and undoes the sense of inevitable triumph, calling attention to the dangers of what Michelangelo Signorile calls "victory blindness" and

Walters calls "the tolerance trap."[41] Both phrases capture the spirit of this critique: that neither is the fight for LGBT equality over nor is a strategy of inclusion an effective or guaranteed path to full equality. Walters says, "Tolerance is a trap precisely because it offers up a rosy *myth* in place of rough-hewn *history*. It cuts corners on liberation, producing a far shoddier and cheaper product than originally desired. And worse: we all think we got a bargain."[42] Moreover, these and other cultural critics cogently warn of the "heady whirl of a narrative of victory, a kind of bedtime story that tells us we've reached the promised land, that can make everything else seem like a blur."[43] The dangers of this "blur" are far-reaching and long lasting, including the further marginalization of those who voluntarily or involuntarily fall outside the narrow boundaries established by assimilationist politics. This approach to working toward equality privileges only some LGBT people (especially gay, white men) and reinforces systems of exclusion, particularly for LGBT people of color and gender nonconformists. As Yasmin Nair succinctly asks: "But who gains 'equality' . . . ? And at what cost?"[44]

These critiques point to the dominance of a narrow brand of LGBT politics that is overwhelmingly white, male, gender-conforming, middle-upper class and that features marriage as the single battle cry of the movement. They are also part of a larger critique of what is termed "neoliberalism." Discussed in many contexts and by an even greater number of scholars, neoliberalism can be broadly defined as the dominant global policy since the late 1970s. It promotes individualism over community, the privatization and deregulation of industries traditionally the purview of the government, and the belief that market-driven ideologies and logics can be successfully applied to all aspects of human life, including areas of social and cultural life typically theorized as outside of the market such as identity, everyday activities, and personal relationships.[45] President Trump's 2016 election, I would submit, reflects the ultimate triumph of neoliberalism, embodying each element of neoliberalism's ideologies and policies. Television programming and changing ownership structures reflect and reinforce neoliberal tenets, exemplified in shows like *Judge Judy* (CBS, 1996–) and *Intervention* (A&E, 2005–), which take on the role of the state in matters of the law and addiction, respectively.[46]

Along with other critics, I can identify with the anger that queer scholars and activists have experienced for decades over a once-radical movement that sought broader and far more complex definitions for sex, love, commitment, and family. Nowhere in the stories reported by magazines like *Time* or programs like *Meet the Press*, mentioned earlier, is there mention of the uneven and contested spaces of LGBT or queer life outside of media or outside of the political and electoral realm. Nowhere are the histories that meticulously document the disparate lives, loves, and politics of America's sexual minorities, particularly feminists, queer women, and queers of color.[47]

By exploring the contingent nature of television production, however, I hope to push beyond the critique of LGBT television representations as only commodified, homonormative, and assimilationist, in order to identify spaces of contradiction and intervention. I resist the tendency to lump mainstream LGBT television representations into the ever-growing pile of texts and institutions that have fallen prey to the forces of neoliberalism. By many accounts, neoliberal ideologies and policies have become so naturalized that they are now part of the fabric of American culture. Too often for my liking, these critiques also assert that neoliberalism is a single, totalizing, and overdetermined system and that consequently, short of a complete overthrow of capitalism, there is no solution. To be clear, I do not intend to simplify this work or suggest that it is reductive; to the contrary, this scholarship points out and renders visible problematic structures that are so ubiquitous it is nearly impossible to see where they begin and end.

Yet it is no secret that capitalism co-opts creativity and that neoliberalism dictates that markets drive social change. These two positions tend to become binary choices that trap the conversation in an echo chamber. As Walters writes, "those oppositions (between assimilation and the ghetto, between radicalism and the tepid embrace) always miss out on something, always tell a story that is just too simplistic to capture the complexity of how minorities move through majority populations."[48] It is this "miss[ing] out on something" that I react to in critiques of popular culture. I argue, power operates on multiple levels of industry practices and that it is not so pervasive as to allow for complete domination on any one level. After all, consensus does not spontaneously erupt; rather, it is the product of a series of negotiations and contradictions.

My goal is to go beyond the argument that television corporations apolitically and exploitatively appeal to LGBT demographics simply for the sake of profit. Rather, this book's title, *The New Gay for Pay*, is a reference to an updated and more complex definition of the phrase, which conventionally describes a straight actor who performs same-sex sex acts in pornographic films solely for profit as well as companies who try to appeal to LGBT consumers for the sake of financial gain. In this updated version, the US television industry acts broadly as an intermediary or an interpretive space between the co-optation and the facilitation of LGBT politics.

Rather than call for a return to the radical queer politics of earlier decades or bemoan the normalization and commodification of LGBT identities that offer up sameness as the only route to equality and political inclusion, I intend to show that television neither limits LGBT identities or politics (making them "invisible") nor simply encourages them via increasing visibility. Television production and marketing do not just respond to (whether exploiting or liberating) presumably preexistent identities and politics; rather, I argue, the television industry participates—in complex and multifaceted ways—in the very production of sexuality, sexual identities and communities, and sexual politics.

The Chapters to Follow

The book focuses on four concepts that are embedded in belief systems about sexuality and that have long played a role in television representations of social minorities: visibility, advocacy, diversity, and equality.

Chapter 1, "Visibility: Lesbian Programming and the Changing Landscape of Cable Television," highlights the rise of lesbian programming on cable television in the early 2000s, a time when demographic research claimed lesbians as a newly prized consumer group. This research set the stage for how lesbian characters and consumers have developed since that time. Against this backdrop I focus on the basic cable network Bravo and the premium network Showtime in case studies intended to investigate the relationships among network branding, promotional logics, cable industry structures, and program development. As part of this study, I explore how market research operates, which is a key factor in how audiences are defined, how politics generally are linked to the market, and how specifically LGBT cultural politics are avowed and disavowed. For all of its importance across sectors of television, market research is surprisingly underdiscussed in media studies. Combining this analysis with interviews I conducted with executives and producers at Bravo and Showtime as well as specialists in LGBT market research, I identify a thread in cable television that seeks to explain the rise in lesbian representation as more than an "edgy" marketing strategy or the resurgence of 1990s "lesbian chic": what I call "multicasting," targeting several distinct audience demographics, reflects the investment of individual industry workers in politically progressive social values, which they incorporate into network culture through complex branding practices.

In chapter 2, entitled "Advocacy: Hitching Activism to *Modern Family*'s Gay Wedding," I address the role of television advocacy in support of lesbian and gay marriage equality. *Modern Family* (ABC, 2009–), a broadcast program that has earned critical and popular acclaim, was the basis for two national political campaigns in favor of same-sex marriage rights, one by the

Human Rights Campaign (HRC) and the other by the American Civil Liberties Union (ACLU). My analysis of *these* marriage equality campaigns insists on connecting discourses (sexual politics and television "effects") to industries (television and LGBT advocacy), getting at the complicated and contradictory relations between them. These complications and contradictions become visible when the campaigns are examined from the outside (publicity, public response, and the like) as well as from the inside (how they were conceived, executed, and evaluated by those working at HRC and the ACLU). This approach addresses three areas of research—institutional, organizational, and individual—as a means of treating each aspect as part of everyday social struggle rather than as a reflection of it.[49] *Modern Family*'s marriage campaigns, and their conditions of cultural production, illustrate a provocatively gray area; rather than seeing television advocacy in stark opposition to progressive social politics, this case study opens the door to a recognition of the complementary intersections of commercialization, advocacy, and visibility.

Chapter 3, "Diversity: Under-the-Radar Activism and the Crafting of Sexual Identities" moves beyond the critique that televisual diversity is confined to a narrow version of difference that amounts to a form of assimilationist politics. Rather than assessing the well-established nature of representational diversity, in this chapter I identify spaces where openly lesbian and gay media professionals have agency within a range of social and institutional power structures. A series of interviews illustrates the ways that industry workers have subversively helped advance progressive LGBT politics through their everyday media practices, whether in advocacy, public relations, or corporate social responsibility. The key theme to emerge from the interviews I conducted for this chapter was how much work remains strategically kept out of public view, and even out of the view of corporate leaders.

What I describe as "under-the-radar activism" proves to be progressive and in the service of often-marginalized LGBT communities. It is also work that in other ways meets the profit-based demands of business. This finding brings into stark relief the competing demands on individual industry workers and the precarious balance required to meet those expectations. The experiences and insights of the interviewees are intriguing illustrations of spaces of intervention and agency that exist even when (or maybe especially because) they tend not to be expected.

Chapter 4, "Equality: Proposition 8 and the Politics of Marriage on Television," turns to traditional politics, examining California's 2008 controversial ballot initiative, Proposition 8 (Prop 8), a statewide ballot initiative that limited marriage to the union of one man and one woman. In a surprising defeat in the liberal state of California, the measure passed by a slim margin on the same day that Barack Obama was elected the first black president of the United States. I center my analysis on the television commercials aired in the run-up to the election as well as the 2014 HBO documentary *The Case against 8*, examining the content, production, and distribution of both television texts in addition to data from polling and focus groups, as well as interviews with the lead media consultant who designed the "No on Prop 8" television commercials. The stories behind the "No on Prop 8" campaign demonstrate that representation alone is far too simplistic a mode of analysis for ascertaining the state of cultural politics. The nature of political campaigns produces numerous clashes of strategies and beliefs, which I argue define, rather than undermine, them.

In the conclusion, entitled "The Personal Is Still Political (and Profitable)," I bring together the book's main themes with a discussion of identity politics since the election of Donald Trump as US president. I stake a claim for the future on the basis of both emerging LGBT representational patterns and the spaces where industry workers intervene in overdetermined narratives about LGBT rights and television visibility. I argue that these spaces offer evidence that there is significantly more agency among individuals than is attributed to a wide swath of industry workers in US television culture. As a result, this final chapter offers an activist claim of its own: from a multitude of positions within entertainment and politics, there are powerful ways to effect change and to do so from within the system. My hope is that this book offers insights that might be the basis for doing just that.

CHAPTER I

Visibility: Lesbian Programming and the Changing Landscape of Cable Television

Community Marketing researchers are often asked, "What's new in lesbian and gay market trends?" This year, the most important insights come from new significant research findings into lesbian consumers. Based on this new wealth of research and analysis, we are calling 2008 "The Year of the Lesbian."

COMMUNITY MARKETING, INC., PRESS RELEASE, FEBRUARY 14, 2008

In 2008, researchers at Community Marketing, a US lesbian and gay market research firm, claimed to have found a goldmine in lesbian consumers. They, along with members of the press, treated the Lesbian Consumer Index as exciting and surprising news. It said, among other things, that US lesbian consumers had higher incomes and better educations, and spent more time online and watching TV than advertisers had ever dreamed possible. The upscale lesbian lifestyle magazine *Jane and Jane* wrote that the Index "breaks stereotypes. . . . [The] buying habits of lesbians rival those of gay men."[1] *The L Word's* (2004–2009) creator, Ilene Chaiken, cited this research when she announced in August 2008 that the final season of the Showtime series would use more product integration; the Lesbian Consumer Index reported that 39 percent of lesbian respondents watched Showtime, compared to 18 percent of gay men.[2] Like gays in the early 1990s, lesbians in 2008 were hailed as untapped wealth, promoted as a promising discovery for advertisers to target with a world of goods and services.[3]

This new attention to a "lesbian consumer market" coincided with a rise in lesbian representations on cable television, which in turn resulted from fundamental shifts in modern media industries, including multiplatform applications, digitization, and branding.[4] In this environment, sexuality became an especially prominent marketing tool to draw audiences.[5] *Lesbian* sexuality, in particular, has emerged as a significant topic for creating "edgy" programming and attracting a wide range of viewers to US cable television. This strategy, which I call multicasting, represents a calculated approach to attracting viewers to cable programming that is based on demographics constructed and refined by market research. Since 2008, there have undoubtedly been substantial and influential changes in the fictional and real lives of sexual minorities in the US, and these are reflected in patterns of marketing, branding, and television production practices. However, the events of those first years of the twenty-first century set the stage for these subsequent shifts.

In the early 2000s, lesbian sexuality on cable television began to offer viewers what Ron Becker argues gay sexuality on 1990s broadcast television offered straight audiences: "gay material wasn't only useful for network executives . . . but also for many viewers for whom watching prime-time TV with a gay twist spoke to specific political values and offered some a convenient way to establish a 'hip' identity."[6] Lesbian cable programming in the first years of the 2000s, I argue, represented industry structures that appealed to politically progressive social values at the level of audience, but that also revealed and underscored the incongruities of practices of producing, branding, and marketing. My discussion of multicasting then is not an argument about the commodification of lesbian sexuality. Rather, I argue that multicasting shows that what is quickly marked as either progressive or co-opted actually serves as an intermediary or an interpretive space between the co-optation and the facilitation of LGBT politics.

Drawing on interviews with industry practitioners and market researchers, in this chapter I examine the role of institutional beliefs and practices in the production of lesbian programming appearing on a basic and a premium cable television network, respectively, Bravo and Showtime. Although these networks differ in their financing structures and content regulations, basic and premium cable channels are arguably more alike than different in their methods of branding and targeting audiences. Both are built on the logic of seeking small, specific audiences, and began the twenty-first century by using lesbian programming as a strategic approach to attracting multiple audience segments.

As an entry point into this analysis, I begin by exploring Bravo and Showtime's brands, emphasizing recent shifts in methods of production, distribution, and marketing. In the sections that follow, I examine two themes that emerged from the interviewees' descriptions of their networks' brands and target audiences. I also look at interviewees' emphasis on post-gay ideology, which is at odds with cable's relentless focus on "diversity" when conceptualizing lesbian characters and consumers. I also incorporate a discussion about the integral role market research plays in the post-network era, using Bravo's "affluencer" campaign as a case study. Together, these key parts of the interviews reveal industry workers' subconscious interpellation into systems of sexual privilege, the functions of lesbian programming, and the changes they indicate about basic and premium cable's audiences and branding strategies.

Rather than evaluating these images in terms of their representational politics, I situate lesbian-themed US cable television programs within the rapidly changing worlds of media and marketing. In doing so, I foreground the history of a predominantly white, upper-class Los Angeles lesbian culture that emerged in the 1970s as a way of making an argument about the crucial role class plays in lesbian televisibility. This is a partial history, one that does not include the diverse groups of women who either could not afford to be part of this culture or actively rejected it. However, I do not intend to marginalize the vibrant communities and media cultures created by these women or to suggest that they did not play a vital role in producing lesbian representations. I also do not intend to reinforce a narrative that puts white, upper-class lesbians at the center of US lesbian history; it is the foregrounding of white lesbians on television that Renee DeLong observes has "overshadowed the classed and raced elements of marriage law, and [that continues] to separate LGBTQ activism from race, class, and immigration concerns."[7] The history I tell, though, purposefully focuses on a narrow context—based on what Rosemary Hennessey calls "class affiliations" of lesbian visibility—because, I argue, it is a history that laid a foundation with often-overlooked fractures and contestations.[8] Multicasting draws on this history and updates it for twenty-first-century ideologies and logics of the cable television market, and indicates how cable television is dealing with an expanding media landscape.

Branding Cable Networks: "Brace yourself"

In the media landscape of the early twenty-first century, where digital convergence is a central concern and defining feature of industry operations, television networks (and programs) are branded consumer products designed to distinguish themselves from the competition by creating connections with their consumers. Shifts at every level of the industry—including ownership, technology, program creation, distribution platform, advertising method, and systems of audience measurement—require that each network single itself out so that it can compete in this environment.[9] Cable television is particularly significant to the story of the modern media industries; as Jennifer Holt writes, "In the years just before [the 2009 proposed Comcast/NBCUniversal] merger, NBCUniversal president Jeff Zucker repeatedly celebrated cable as the strongest component of the company, saying that the core cable networks represented over 75 percent of the company's profits."[10] In the modern deregulated media environment, then, cable networks often provide the biggest streams of revenue for the major media outlets.

Yet as Catherine Johnson notes in her introduction to *Branding Television*, "the adoption of branding by the television industries is by no means straightforward or uncontested."[11] One of the difficulties with applying branding to television networks is the nature of television as a medium; it is an *experience* of viewing and consuming, whether in the traditional program schedule, which Raymond Williams famously defined as television's "flow," or in twenty-first-century practices of time- and place-shifting.[12] Consistent with a convergent media landscape, television branding is more than simply an element of design and packaging added to a product; rather, it is a form of mediated and dynamic communication that constantly frames and reframes the relationships between producers, products, and consumers. This is especially true in late capitalism, where advertising remains dominant but individuals organize their lives within what Sarah Banet-Weiser calls "brand culture."[13] Brand culture defines how consumers are connected to the commercial world through daily living and individual identities, going beyond the simple application of economic branding to culture. Crucially, Banet-Weiser argues that brand cultures are "ambivalent" in that they are embodied and constructed in different ways and that they are sometimes politically progressive and liberatory and other times reactionary and exploitative.

Brands are, then, dependent on interactivity between the consumer and producer. This interactivity, however, is not necessarily open or equal; branding attempts to shape, control, and manage the values attributed to products and the uses to which they are put. In her 2000 manifesto *No Logo*, Naomi Klein establishes the extent to which culture has become branded, charting an elaborate schema of corporate global branding and resistance. A decade later, Melissa Aronczyk and Devon Powers expand Klein's argument, describing the myriad ways in which global branding operates and tracing the movement away from citizenship and toward consumerism, the steady corporatization of public spaces, and the pervasiveness of promotional practices. They argue that examining twenty-first-century branding requires more than recognizing that everything in our lives has been marketed and commodified. Instead, we need to look at branding in light of the fact that we live in what they call "promotional culture," which for the purposes of this analysis acts on both television and audiences.[14] Within this context, cable network branding functions as a means of creating identities, communities, and lifestyles, rather than simply audiences.

Both Bravo's and Showtime's marketing materials indicate that they are branded niche cable networks, putting forth particular types of shows that seek specific types of audiences. In the early 2000s, after it was acquired as a division of NBCUniversal, executives transformed Bravo to focus on pop culture, creating its own brand of fashion, makeover, and celebrity shows, including *Project Runway* (2004–), *Top Chef* (2006–), *Queer Eye for the Straight Guy* (2003–2007), and the wildly successful *Real Housewives* (2006–) franchise. To promote its shows, Bravo uses the tagline "by Bravo," invoking the advertising language of companies that sell material goods ("by GE," "by Mattel"). The tagline highlights that the network owns and produces its own content. Emblematic of post-network ownership structures under increased deregulatory practices, "by Bravo" also illustrates that the development of original programming has become central to a cable network's brand identity. With its consistent use of dramatic and character-driven shows, Bravo solidified its image as what Jane Feuer calls "the 'quality' reality cable service."[15] Aside from a commitment to the cultures of food, beauty, and fashion, Bravo's signature is upscale reality shows that are ideal vehicles for spin-offs, cross-promotions, and media convergence.

In reinventing itself, Bravo aggressively embraced online revenue. Ahead of many cable network competitors, Bravo established a website for its shows that includes cast blogs, special "webisodes," entire show episodes, social networking sites for fans, and even online stores that sell brands worn by the characters to generate additional advertising profits. The network also took advantage of deregulation that permitted broad consolidation, purchasing a host of online outlets such as indie website Television Without Pity (defunct as of early 2014). Lauren Zalaznick, network president at the time, described the purchase of the site as broadening "the scope of our sites to create a community where smart people with something to say about their favorite shows . . . can get together."[16] Zalaznick also outlined a strategy mandating that all programming extend to digital media. Positioning the digital as intrinsic to the identity of each Bravo show, Zalaznick said, "It's a concerted effort to make each of the projects have a legitimate digital DNA to them from the get-go."[17] Under this directive, show creators have to pitch ideas to the network that include a detailed picture of the show and its online components.

This emphasis on digital aspects of programming was part of the network's aggressive appeal to affluent, educated, and tech-savvy adults with high levels of disposable income, who the network calls "affluencers." In a 2007 interview, Zalaznick described "affluencers" as "consumers who spend just as much time blogging about their favorite shows as they do watching them."[18] Erin Copple-Smith's study of "affluencers" parses the ways Bravo discursively constructed "affluencers" as an audience brand. She argues that it was primarily the network's use of cross-promotions that operated as a means of establishing "the bounds of the target audience, to create them, and to hail them into being."[19]

Bravo has been unusually transparent about its brand, widely publicizing a separate website dedicated to the "affluencer" campaign, unabashedly flaunting the network's hunt for wealthy, high-tech consumers hungry for the latest trends. On the site, users can access (for free, with no login/account) an assortment of quantitative and qualitative information about Bravo's audiences intended to court potential advertisers. Affluencers.com is divided into five sections: "Current Opportunities," "Programming," "Brand Profile," "Insights," and "Passion by Bravo." Within each, one can view statistical breakdowns about Bravo's audiences, their purchasing habits, and demographic details displayed in colorful and easily digestible form.

Showtime's recent branding has focused equally on crafting a specific audience image and developing original content. As a premium cable network, Showtime's business model requires the network to focus solely on drawing audiences. Like its larger competitor, HBO, Showtime has distinguished itself as a "quality" network defined by programming that is original, groundbreaking, and compelling, with high production values and superb writing and acting.[20] Through complex characters and narratives, its programming—both scripted and documentary—pushes the boundaries of television content, exploring controversial and taboo issues such as addiction, mental illness, and serial murder as well as social lightning rods like racism, sexism, and homophobia.

In 1997 Showtime premiered its new slogan, "No Limits," which it used until 2005. During this time, the network made a name for itself with its adaptation of the British show *Queer as Folk* (1999–2000), which featured gay and lesbian sex and sexuality with abandon, as well as with niche dramas such as the African American series *Soul Food* (2000–2004) and the Latino drama *Resurrection Blvd* (2002–2004). Promoting these shows far more than the network's library of acquired films and pay-per-view sports, Showtime established itself as a network that offered programs no one else was producing. Shortly after the 2004 debut of *The L Word*, the first show to feature an ensemble cast of lesbian characters, the network changed its slogan to "TV. At Its Best." This slogan differentiated Showtime from HBO, which had successfully established itself as the preeminent site of "quality" tele-

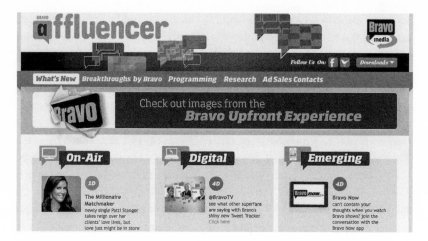

Figure 1.1. Bravo's "affluencer" website is dedicated to advertisers but accessible to anyone online.

vision, encapsulated in its declaration to not be television at all—"It's Not TV, It's HBO." Against the HBO brand, Showtime staked its claim as a proud purveyor of both television and "quality." During this time, Showtime produced critically acclaimed programs such as *Huff* (2004-2006), *Brotherhood* (2006-2008), *Sleeper Cell* (2005-2006), *The Tudors* (2007-2010), *Penn & Teller: Bullshit* (2003-2010), and *Secret Diary of a Call Girl* (2008-2011). In 2011, the network changed its slogan once again, this time to "Brace Yourself." This slogan suggests Showtime's continued investment in programming that takes up controversial issues and offers complex stories that invite audiences on narrative adventures filled with shock, excitement, and unexpected twists and turns. This programming engenders loyal subscribers who appreciate the shows and the fact that they cannot be found on other television networks.

A particular version of lesbian sexuality lends itself to the cutting-edge distinction that networks like Bravo and Showtime believe their audiences seek out on cable television. Since 2000, amid the changing economics of television markets, deregulation of the media industries, and the expansion of inexpensive genres and celebrity branding, the prevailing lesbian woman on US television has been stereotypically feminine, fashion-conscious, and upper-middle class. This image is simultaneously the product of a mainstream media culture that relentlessly reinforces a postfeminist sensibility; although there is little agreement about what postfeminism is—the term is used variously, even contradictorily, to signal an epistemological break with second-wave feminism, a backlash against feminist principles and politics, and as a historical shift to a new incarnation of feminism—stable features define it, including the notion that femininity is a bodily property and the result of an empowered personal choice, completely cut off from any political stakes or broader sense of community.[21]

While the women of *The L Word* have garnered the most attention in both academic and popular discourse, lesbian characters and personalities on cable shows including *The Fosters* (ABC Family, 2013-2015; Freeform, 2016-), *The Real L Word* (Showtime, 2010-2012), *Faking It* (MTV, 2014-), *Pretty Little Liars* (ABC Family, 2010-), *Nip/Tuck* (FX, 2003-2010), *Work Out* (Bravo, 2006-2008), *Top Chef* (Bravo, 2006-), *Queer as Folk* (Showtime, 2000-2005), *South of Nowhere* (The N, 2005-2008), *Sex and the City* (HBO, 1998-2004), *American Horror Story* (AMC, 2011-), and *White Collar* (USA, 2009-) have presented equally feminine, voguish lesbian women, most of whom are white. The notable exceptions to this pattern are lesbian characters on *The Wire* (HBO, 2002-2008), *Transparent* (Amazon, 2014-), *Sense8* (Netflix, 2015-), and *Orange Is the New Black* (Netflix, 2013-).[22]

Throughout its six seasons, Showtime's promotions for *The L Word* used lesbian sex and sexuality to define the show's identity and support the network's overall brand. The initial ad campaign for *The L Word* promoted the show as a lesbian version of *Sex and the City*, using the tag line "Same sex. Different city." Utilizing fashion photography lighting and runway poses, billboard and print ads featured the show's cast dressed in elegant gowns and feminine suits, foregrounding their looks above all else. The show's cast stood alongside one another, looking directly at the camera, lights accentuating their lean, female figures against a sleek backdrop. Subsequent promotions followed from this visual style, featuring the cast either in black or pink form-fitting, feminine outfits or with bodies "tastefully" nude, arms and legs wrapped around each other to conceal the most private parts. Framed this way, lesbian sexuality becomes a marker of "quality" programming, ideally suited to the edgy, liberal, and sophisticated tastes of Showtime's subscribers.

Like Bravo, Showtime promotes itself to a high-tech audience demographic. In 2000, to keep up with needs for revenue and audiences, Showtime launched a series of online ventures aimed at broadening its viewer base by creating a series of original and fan-produced content for the Internet. Audiences could rate and review featured works and participate in technology forums. Showtime's aggressive targeting of wired audiences earned it the reputation of being "the premier next-generation entertainment destination featuring original content created exclusively for the web."[23] The network also launched multiplex channels, including Showtime Too, Showtime Beyond, and Showtime Extreme, as well as channels exclusively for digital cable, such

Figure 1.2. A promotional photo for the sixth and final season of Showtime's series *The L Word* (2004–2009).

as Showtime Family Zone, Showtime Next, and Showtime Women. Multiplexing allows Showtime to increase its value to subscribers with little additional cost to the network because the content airing on the other channels is usually not new (aired originally on the main Showtime channel) or is already in Showtime's library.[24] Subscribers feel that they are getting more for their money, and Showtime does not accrue substantially higher costs. Reacting to the popularity of Apple's iTunes, Showtime established a library of programs available for instant purchase and download on the site. The availability of the network's shows online not only increases revenue but also raises public awareness about Showtime's original programs. In 2011, Showtime premiered "Short Stories," a set of short films that the *New York Times* describes as "not [looking] out of place at some high-toned European festival."[25] Accessible for free on Showtime's homepage, on its dedicated YouTube channel, and as podcasts on iTunes, the short films target audiences who use the Internet, rather than television, as their primary viewing source for media texts.

With *The L Word*, the network reached out to a high-tech demographic by holding fan fiction contests where the winner's scenario would be used as an episode's opening sequence. The show also launched two social networking sites. First, the show's team was said to have bought an island on Second Life, which is an online virtual world launched in 2003. Second Life users create avatars, or digital representations of themselves, where they interact with others' avatars. A decade after its launch, Second Life had approximately one million regular users, according to the site's developer Linden Lab. *The L Word* also created OurChart.com, an offshoot of the fictional chart on the *The L Word* (the chart connects lesbian characters on the show that have either been in romantic relationships with each other or had a one-night stand). OurChart.com allows audience members to interact with it, creating a web of lesbian connections both within and outside the narrative of the show. In her analysis of the show's chart and the public OurChart.com, Julie Levin Russo notes that "this vision of a web platform driven by relationships was prescient for its time (these episodes aired in January 2004, just before the inception of Facebook) and already signals the harmony between *The L Word*'s rendition of sexual community and the development of digital social networking."[26] OurChart.com, while certainly a logical marketing strategy in the context of media convergence, is also emblematic of Showtime's use of the Internet to appeal to a wired "quality" audience.

Classifying Representation: "A more . . . successful version of most lesbians' lives"

Although the race, ethnicity, and femininity of many of these characters have been cause for both criticism and celebration in the popular press, their class status is arguably more significant to an examination of their visibility and marketability.

Television images today correspond to a legacy of lesbian-themed films that privilege images of classy women. Early films such as *Rebecca* (1940, dir. Hitchcock) and *Queen Christina* (1933, dir. Mamoulian) depict upper-class women born into the strictly regulated worlds of the ruling class, which provides a degree of protection in the form of access to wealth. Tracing the roots of these images in Hollywood films, Patricia White examines the types of lesbian images that appeared in films of the Production Code era, from 1930 through 1968, and details how lesbian characters were made visible. In the films she discusses, lesbian visibility "is veiled in the feminine display that is the cinema's primary dream language rather than embodied in the cross-gender identifications offered by the invert or the butch."[27] More recent films, such as *Desert Hearts* (1986, dir. Deitch), *Claire of the Moon* (1992, dir. Conn), *High Art* (1998, dir. Cholodenko), and *Loving Annabelle* (2006, dir. Brooks), carry on these early cinematic traditions, depicting lesbian women as stereotypically feminine, educated, and refined.

One of the most instructive ways to see how class is embodied in cable television shows is to look at their marketing campaigns and title sequences, which are often the first glimpses viewers have of a show and are meant to reveal key information to attract audiences. As Jonathan Gray argues, promotional materials like these are "paratexts" that play an important role as wholly industrial entities.[28] Paratexts not only make extra money for television programming but are crucial to transmitting the meaning and value of the shows themselves, as the information they convey determines whether someone chooses to watch a show.

Work Out (2006–2008), which premiered following Bravo's success with reality programs like *Project Runway* and *Queer Eye for the Straight Guy*, is a lifestyle reality show that stars openly lesbian gym owner and personal trainer Jackie Warner, and follows the personal and professional lives of Warner, her entourage of trainers, and their clients. In 2016 Bravo aired the first season of *Work Out: New York*, returning to the show's themes of gym drama. Both versions of *Work Out* present lesbian sexuality within the context of a glamorous beauty culture, where high-end fashion, healthy food, and physically fit bodies are the norm. In the original version, *Work Out*'s title sequence immediately draws the viewer into an elite world, first showing street signs marking the entrance to Beverly Hills and to Rodeo Drive, followed by quick cuts of Warner and her trainers in the gym and of the gym equipment, and shots of well-toned bodies. Along with the images, the show's theme song establishes a tone of fame, voyeurism, and exhibitionism that comes from the worked out body: "You can really work it out / Beverly Hills where the rich keep it sexy, work hard, play hard, turn into celebrities / whatever drives your passion, Jackie keeps you motivated, top of your game, your lifestyle will change." Opening with Beverly Hills culture establishes the ambiance of an elite world of fitness and beauty that only few attain. There are no overt signifiers of Warner's sexuality; the show's title sequence is code that associates it foremost with social and aesthetic markers of wealth and beauty.

The show's montage editing and extreme close-ups of well-toned, beautiful bodies focus visual attention on the athletic female body. Warner's representation in this opening sequence and throughout the show draws on a long tradition of athletes in sports. Women have long faced uphill battles in professional sports, where female athletes have been associated with failed heterosexuality and eventually with lesbianism. As Martha Gever notes, lesbianism has been "the danger awaiting women who ventured into this masculine domain."[29] Films like *Personal Best* (1982, dir. Towne) and *The Gymnast* (2006, dir. Farr) capitalized on associations between athleticism and lesbianism, appealing to a wide variety of social tastes and attitudes. In her review of *Personal Best*, Linda Williams notes that "in box office terms, the combination of sports and sex was a stroke of genius. Those who would normally be shocked or at least irritated by a lesbian relationship in any other context find it quite 'natural' among female athletes."[30] Twenty-five years later, *Work Out* recalls this association, aided by Warner's firm and chiseled body, and her strong, savvy, and exacting personality.

Marking class as central to the show's identity, Showtime advertised *The L Word* in upscale women's publications like *Elle* magazine, which targets consumers interested in "fashion, beauty, and style—with a brain" who are looking for "high-end inspiration."[31] *Curve* magazine's Lya Carrera writes,

> What was lesbian chic in the 1980s has come full circle with the emergence of *The L Word* and it has put lesbian fashion back on the map. . . . The image of lesbians that was prevalent in the media—two words: flannel shirts—has been replaced with something more positive, as gay women are now seen as being fashion-conscious.[32]

"Flannel shirts" signifies lesbian women's rejection of conventional femininity, "rendering them less desirable or recuperable within a model of ideal consumption."[33] Traditional addresses to women as consumers appeal to their roles as wives, mothers, and caretakers of the home and family. But the publicly visible lesbian woman that emerged in the 1960s and 1970s refused the heterosexual contract, both ideologically and practically.

During the 1990s, the rhetoric of "lesbian chic" helped to diversify the public lesbian image.[34] In popular discourse, "lesbian chic" was proof that lesbians were no longer associated with feminist, anti-consumption stereotypes but instead were seen as apolitical, postfeminist consumers. In addition, an unprecedented number of female celebrities and personalities have come out since that time, including k. d. lang, Ellen DeGeneres, Rosie O'Donnell, Martina Navratilova, Melissa Etheridge, Suze Orman, Wanda Sykes, Rachel Maddow, Robin Roberts, Ellen Page, Maria Bello, Jodie Foster, Portia de Rossi, and Cynthia Nixon. Danae Clark's widely cited 1991 essay, "Commodity Lesbianism," argues that the intensified marketing of lesbian images that began in the 1990s is less indicative of a growing acceptance of lesbianism, or homosexuality more broadly, than of capitalism's appropriation of lesbian styles for mainstream audiences. She examines the marketing strategy called "gay window advertising" that allows lesbians and gays to "read into an ad certain subtextual elements," deciphering queer elements that heterosexual consumers are unaware of.[35] As Clark observes, "If heterosexual consumers do not notice these subtexts or subcultural codes, then advertisers are able to reach the homosexual market along with the heterosexual market without ever revealing their aim."[36] This strategy lands marketers in the best of two worlds, keeping heterosexual consumers in the dark and safely multiplying their consumer base.

Closely examining the concept of the "lesbian consumer," Katherine Sender's research confirms Clark's assertions about the functions of lesbian advertising. She notes that "lesbians and, especially, lesbian feminists are not easily allied with either image of consumption; imagined to be hostile to the family and to fashion, they are neither the 'fish' of heterosexual women, nor the 'fowl' of gay men."[37] Moreover, she says, "the whole lesbian chic thing has been largely a media event rather than reality."[38] In light of this research, it can be said that contemporary lesbian cable programming does not suggest a breakthrough in television's ability to cater to lesbian consumers, a resurgence of "lesbian chic," or the increasing acceptance of US lesbians in social, economic, and political life. Rather, I contend it is cable's use of high-class, in conjunction with feminine, lesbian characters that has allowed for the rise in representation.

It is not surprising that, on their own, these high-class characters are used to create a consumer market for television; after all, US television has always been a fundamentally commercial enterprise, financed predominantly by advertising revenue. Its main objective has been to attract substantial audiences so that it can sell their attention to advertisers seeking to promote their products and services. Indeed, as Sut Jhally and Justin Lewis note, "television in the United States is notable in creating a world that shifts the class boundaries upward."[39] Yet the need for profits does not mean that the television industry operates as a straightforward supply-and-demand system. Rather, as Philip Napoli explains, "media industries (ad-supported industries, in particular) are unlike most other industries in that they operate in what is perhaps best described as a dual-product marketplace."[40] This structure makes the economics of the television industry unique compared to traditional economic approaches because it makes and sells two things at the same time: it sells content to audiences and it sells audiences to advertisers. In this context, the construction of lesbian representations is a matter of negotiation based on multiple, and often contradictory, economic forces.

Also, while early broadcast history established television as a medium of the masses, dependent on broad-based appeal for financial success, close analyses of audience measurement practices show, as Eileen Meehan says, that "the general population and the individual television viewer is irrelevant to the market for consumers."[41] Rather, advertisers demand high-quality consumers—consumers who have disposable income, desire, and retail access (physical and online) to buy brand names often and loyally. Put another way, while Nielsen claims "Everyone Counts," commercial broadcasters are gener-ally interested in only two things: the size of the audience and its composition (i.e., the amount of disposable income its audiences have and how willing they are to spend money rather than save it). As Meehan explains, "Advertisers' demand for such high-quality consumers means that highly rated programs that attract a broad range of consumers across the Nielsen sample may earn lower revenues or be canceled while lower-rated programs that deliver the most valued demographic earn higher revenues and get renewed."[42]

Cable television is ideally suited to this demand for high-quality consumers because of its financial structure; premium cable networks like Showtime rely entirely on subscribers for revenue, which frees them from advertisers' de-mands and FCC restrictions. Basic cable networks such as Bravo receive some of their funding from fees paid by MSOs (multisystem operators) for the right to include the channel in their lineup. These retransmission fees vary and are negotiated by the MSOs and individual cable channels based on demographic research. According to the FCC's website, "local franchising au-thority (LFA) legally may (but is not required to) regulate the rate your cable TV provider can charge for basic cable service."[43] Under the current system of channel "bundling," the cable industry guarantees monthly income from tens of millions of subscribers. Unlike premium networks, basic cable channels rely on advertising to supplement those fees. Although basic cable channels can afford to target smaller audiences than the mass demanded by broadcast networks, they must maintain a ratings level high enough to keep them on Nielsen's charts and to bring in the advertising revenue needed to sustain and promote themselves.[44] This dynamic forces cable networks to walk a fine line between targeting small, loyal audiences and appealing to a big enough audi-ence to keep advertisers invested.

Moreover, to reduce costs, cable networks air original reality programming as well as reallocated shows. "Reallocation" is when programs that were de-veloped for broadcast networks but lack sufficient ratings are transferred to cable channels in the hopes that they can succeed with niche audiences. "Re-allocation," Amanda Lotz says, "consequently decreases the risk inherent in program development; it also encourages programmers to pursue shows that would otherwise be deemed too uncertain by offering an additional opportu-nity to recoup production expenditures."[45] Moreover, as a financial practice, reallocation offers networks a means of sustaining themselves and amortizing costs for parent companies. Interconglomerate reallocations, however, often come under scrutiny because they foreclose opportunities for independent television productions.

On one hand, constructing lesbian characters within this environment represents the commodification of yet another social minority, continuing a pattern of exploitation that scholars such as Arlene Dávila, Esteban del Río, Lisa Duggan, Rosemary Hennessy, Lisa Henderson, and Jose Muñoz have noted about sexual, racial, and ethnic minorities.[46] On the other hand, as Lynne Joyrich argues in "Epistemology of the Console," "there is no pure space of gay self-disclosure uncontaminated by relations of consumerism and commodification, just as there is no pure space of consumerism uncontaminated by what we might see as closet relations."[47] In this context, the trope of lesbian characters with cultural and economic capital fits seamlessly with cable's demands for valuable audiences and with its corresponding need to brand networks in the competitive, fragmented media era. Showtime's 2010–2012 reality series *The Real L Word* is arguably one of the most explicit examples of a television show making use of this trope under the auspices of addressing lesbian femininity and realism. Throughout the six-year run of *The L Word*, critics and audiences alike fumed that the show's representations were inaccurate; fans, bloggers, and journalists described the show's characters as too beautiful, thin, and unrealistic. In response to the criticisms, Chaiken developed a reality series with Showtime that sets out to "prove" that lesbian women really do look like the characters on the show. The casting call for the show reads: "Are you and your friends proof the *The L Word* exists in real life? Do you want to be part of groundbreaking television? *The L Word* was a runaway iconic hit, affecting millions of lives—imagine what the real life version will do!"[48] Drawing on critiques that the fictional show was unrealistic in its depictions of hyperfeminine and fashion-forward lesbian characters, the reality spin-off version reveals a deep investment in creating evidence that these lesbian representations are accurate, enumerable, and waiting to be discovered by television producers.

In addition, for shows like *The Real L Word*, *The L Word*, and *Work Out*, lesbian sexuality is presented in the context of Los Angeles's public lesbian culture. Often overlooked by historians who describe gays as party-going, sex-crazed, big spenders, and lesbians as domestic, rural, and financially marginal, women's bars and clubs began to spring up all over Los Angeles in the late 1970s and 1980s. According to Lillian Faderman and Stuart Timmons, "by 1983, there were more than forty lesbian bars in Los Angeles . . . that aimed to be much more upscale."[49] The women who frequented clubs such as the Palms, Cinema Lady, and Executive Suite styled themselves after Hollywood stars of the time.

In *Gay LA: A History of Sexual Outlaws, Power Politics, and Lipstick Lesbians* Faderman and Timmons provide a detailed account of the history of Los Angeles's lesbian and gay cultures from the beginning of the twentieth century until the early 2000s. Working from primary source documents and extensive interviews, they write, "In L.A., thanks to a tolerant cultural climate, lesbians could finally step out of the shadows and indulge openly in their pleasures."[50] However, this history leaves out the class conflict has long figured into lesbian social groups, community organizing, and calls for public visibility. As Amin Ghaziani explains,

> Over the long course of gay history, but especially from 1950s homophile organizing onward, the gay imagination has routinely oscillated between, on the one hand, a narrow, single-interest vision, rooted in conventional identity politics, that seeks an end to discrimination against gays, and on the other hand, an expansive, multi-issue, coalition view that is grounded in a political philosophy of intersectionality and social justice.[51]

For example, the Daughters of Bilitis (DOB), founded in 1955 and considered the first lesbian organization in the country, divided over whether to become a publicly visible organization; Martin Meeker describes how class conflict — between working-class women who wanted the group to remain secretive and private and middle-class women who wanted to publicly counteract popular lesbian images—created a rift in the organization; he says that "as a result, gender-transgressive, or butch, women . . . were dissuaded from joining . . . unless they modified their self-presentation along the lines suggested by the DOB."[52]

This higher-class lesbian culture became tightly enmeshed in glamorous Hollywood styles and a sense of professionalism in 1970s Los Angeles. In her analysis of *Work Out*, Dana Heller reminds us of California's unique place within the national imaginary, one that "represents the pre-eminent locus of self-recreation, opportunity, and youthful experimentation."[53] Based on this mythology, it is a place that provided safe haven in the twentieth century "as young gays and lesbians from the nation's more culturally conservative heartland sought refuge in politically and socially progressive locations such as San Francisco in the 1950s and 1960s, and West Hollywood in the 1970s and 1980s."[54] Influenced by feminism (second wave and radical) and anti-discrimination legislation, some formed clubs and organizations invested in promoting images of affluent, stylish lesbian professionals. For example, in 1976 Betty Berzon founded Southern California Women for Understanding (SCWU) in response to other organizations' focus on gay men. According to Faderman, with SCWU, Berzon "hoped to establish what had never existed — a political group made up exclusively of upper-middle-class lesbians."[55] The

SCWU set out "to change the [public] image of lesbians by presenting our membership as successful, achieving women."[56]

The organization's efforts were fueled by the fierce debate around California's Briggs Initiative, a 1978 statewide proposition that would have banned lesbians and gays from working in public schools. Although the measure ultimately failed, the SCWU began trying to combat so-called negative stereotypes, including butch–femme couples as well as what Faderman describes as "the poorly dressed and ill-mannered lesbian feminists."[57] Instead, the organization sought out successful, high-achieving women who conformed to upper-middle-class norms of style and dress.[58] Current organizations such as Power Up, founded in 2000 to provide resources, networking opportunities, grants, and awards for lesbian industry workers, build directly on past groups such as the SCWU. In light of this history, cable television's lesbian representations are not new or unusual; rather, they are rooted in twentieth-century sociopolitical approaches to gaining visibility and equality. Yet this part of lesbian culture is, underneath its smooth veneer, deeply contested. The sections that follow address how branding, audiences, market research, and post-gay ideology produce this contested landscape of lesbian television visibility.

Branding Post-Network Audiences: "I don't really think about the audience that much"

Despite Bravo and Showtime's well-defined brands, executives at both networks described their audiences to me in general terms. Andy Cohen was the openly gay executive vice president of original programming and development at Bravo for a decade and has written two best-selling books. He is probably most famous as an on-camera host on Bravo's popular late-night show *Watch What Happens: Live* and as host of the reunion episodes of the *Real Housewives* franchise. I got a direct office phone number for him through *Work Out*'s executive producer, and for our interview Cohen spoke with me by phone from his New York City office. I asked him questions about the network's branding, its casting of lesbian contestants on its reality shows, and how he conceives of the network audience given the extensive and precise market research done for the "affluencer" brand.

According to Cohen, Bravo sees two main groups as its target audience: "women in cities . . . who are the trend-setters in their community. We also have gay guys and their best girlfriends . . . and then I think it's just anybody who's interested in food, fashion, beauty, design, and pop culture."[59]

Robert Greenblatt, president of entertainment for Showtime at the time of my interview, who also is openly gay, talked about Showtime's audience in more imprecise terms. When I asked him whom he considers the network's target audience, he replied: "I don't really think about the audience that much aside from a very general parameter, which is we tend to be an adult network. It's thirty-five plus mainly, which isn't that unusual when you consider that you have to pay extra to get us."[60] As network executives, Cohen and Greenblatt probably do not have to think about or track audiences; television networks have entire divisions devoted to audience analysis. However, premium cable channels' need to attract subscribers means that their branding and programming strategies focus on audiences. Because Showtime conceives of its "quality" audience as a liberal, sophisticated group of upwardly mobile professionals, the question of who watches Showtime is the most important factor when it comes to defining its brand, even more so than how many viewers the network has.

In response to these broad descriptions of target audiences from Cohen and Greenblatt, I brought up the topic of brand identity with them, hoping to gain a better understanding of the connections between the two. Cohen and Greenblatt used contradictory language, defining Bravo and Showtime as unique brands whose programming could not be categorized. Cohen barely answered my question about Bravo's brand, only describing the network as committed to audiences who are interested in "food, fashion, beauty, design, and pop culture," a line plastered all over the network's website. Greenblatt, with whom I had an hour-long interview in his Los Angeles office, spoke at length about the process of developing original programming in an effort to brand Showtime. He talked about HBO's success with original series like *Oz* (1997–2003) and *The Sopranos* (1999–2007) and how Showtime quickly followed suit: "[We said] let's be premium, let's be quality, and let's try to figure out our own little niche, which we ultimately did."

Although Greenblatt described Showtime's brand as its "own little niche," he went on to clarify that "it wasn't like we made a list of ten things every show had to be and the shows fit into some arbitrary box." As a result of this method of program development, he said "none of [our] shows are really that directly similar to any of the others. . . . They're all different but they have some common threads, which I think are now seen by people as 'Oh I get why that's on Showtime,' . . . and I'd rather have the audience define the brand for me than for me to define the brand for them." As we continued to talk about Showtime's programming, Greenblatt used his own personal experience to articulate his ideas about branding. He said:

I've been doing this long enough to know that you can sit around and go to marketing research firms and do focus groups and do all kinds of scientific work and come up with what you thought was a brand that you should adopt, and the odds are you'll never be able to figure that out because the creative process is elusive and it's impossible to pin down.

Cohen and Greenblatt's descriptions of audiences and brands reveal a tension at work in the contemporary cable marketplace; despite their different sources of revenue, both basic and premium cable are at once defined by the concept of niche marketing and operate through the practice of multicasting to draw audiences. *The L Word*, for example, was hailed as the first show about lesbian characters for lesbian audiences. Yet the show self-consciously acknowledged that it served a range of viewers during its six seasons. In a discussion with former *Los Angeles Times* television critic Howard Rosenberg, creator and executive producer Ilene Chaiken said that the network's research showed that *The L Word*'s core audience was women, straight and lesbian. She also openly conceded that heterosexual men watched the show for the pleasure of seeing sex between two women. For Chaiken, this is the reality of making a television show: "We can't afford to give up audiences."[61] As a show runner, she considers the business needs of television inevitable; at the same time, she feels that meeting those needs does not hinder the authenticity of *The L Word*'s lesbian representations.

The L Word in fact directly addressed criticism that it catered to the straight male voyeur in its content. During the first season, critics such as the *New York Times*'s Alessandra Stanley contended that while femme images may challenge traditional viewers' sense of what being lesbian looks like, these same images were constructed for the pleasure of the straight male. Stanley's review of *The L Word* calls the show "a manifesto of lesbian liberation and visual eye candy for men."[62] Such criticism was concerned with the way that the television industry as a business commodifies images for the mainstream public, without regard for political implications, and is particularly ignorant of the content's connection to pornography.[63]

In the second season, the show introduces Mark, an aspiring filmmaker who moves in with two of the main characters, Shane and Jenny. His new project involves "putting his finger on" how lesbians work, especially in the bedroom. Mark's role in the show centers on Shane, Jenny, and their friends, whom he pays twenty dollars an interview to discuss their sex lives on camera. Mark's friend persuades him to install hidden cameras in the house in order to further capture his "objects of study." With nine "strategically and respectfully placed" cameras (placed everywhere but the bathrooms) Mark becomes obsessed with Shane's bedroom practices, envious of her ability to seduce any woman she wants. He goes so far as to pay a woman to masquerade as a delivery girl and sleep with Shane, because, he says, "reality just needs a little help sometimes."[64]

Mark's character, however, addresses concerns that parts of the series pander too much to the viewing preferences of its voyeuristic straight male audience. Through representing a projected audience of straight men "getting off" on depictions of lesbian sex, the show problematizes their voyeurism. In addition, the visual effects in the episodes intersperse Mark's grainy, black-and-white surveillance footage with brightly lit color shots of the show—an acknowledgment that viewers are also in the position of voyeurs. By offering two perspectives, *The L Word* reminds viewers that a lens always mediates the show itself. Thus, while Mark offers a negative image of a voyeuristic, heterosexual man, his character is an implicit admission that the producers of the show consider this demographic necessary to drawing an audience large enough to make it successful in business terms.

A similar argument can be made about Bravo's lesbian programming. For my research on Bravo, I interviewed Amy Shpall, executive producer of *Work Out*. Shpall told me that when casting the show's trainers, Bravo executives requested that they cast several "very straight" men to balance Doug and Jesse, two gay male trainers.[65] *Work Out*'s physically attractive core cast, which includes the openly lesbian Warner, two openly gay male trainers, and several straight trainers, provides eye candy for a variety of audiences. The multicasting for this show thus tries to appeal to straights and gays (females and males) on the premise that there is someone for everyone to identify with and to desire.

In the case of both Bravo and Showtime, then, their branding strategies position the networks as arbiters of taste and "quality" for their audiences, yet their methods of program development and production suggest that they simultaneously seek to offer a broad range of shows that appeal to incongruous tastes. With lesbian-themed shows like *Work Out* and *The L Word*, cable networks are multicasting to a diverse group of "quality" audiences.

Market Research and the Making of Demographics: "Markets drive social change"

In the focus on branding, market research has become indispensible to television networks looking to expand their audiences across multiple platforms and to capitalize on synergistic media practices. Despite Greenblatt's claim that it is impossible to forecast television's success, market research does play a vital role in quantifying consumers' viewing and buying habits. In its attempts to measure television audiences, market research seeks to strengthen networks through a set of metrics that identifies the uniqueness of each network as a brand. As a result, market research looks at audiences as consumers, using quantitative and qualitative methods to determine a brand's position in the market and its relationship to its competition. In this process, the first objective is to establish the brand's strength by finding where its defining features overlap with perceived consumer needs and competitor weaknesses. The next step is to determine specific strategies for maintaining the brand's distinctive edge while also offering methods for expansion.

For cable television, in the effort to maximize a network's ratings opportunity, market research constructs audience segments based on such qualities as "capturability" and economic potential. Crucially, sustaining and expanding a brand creates a high-wire balancing act that relies on the principles of narrowcasting and multicasting; in order to stay relevant and retain its market status, a brand must broaden its appeal yet cannot stray from the core qualities that define it and distinguish it in the marketplace. Through market research, then, cable networks establish brands and target audiences that rely on a tenuous balance between niche appeal and calculated expansion.

Although market research is a key component of television branding, it rarely figures into discussions about how the industry operates. Scholarship about audience demographics tends to focus on Nielsen ratings and the ways that audiences are commoditized through this standard measurement system.[66] This is equally true for digital media scholarship that addresses the intersections of television and newer methods of measurement such as "Nielsen Twitter TV Ratings," which were announced in October, 2013.[67] Indeed, there are overlaps between Nielsen and other forms of market research; Sender writes, "audience and market research share the underlying aim of transforming subjects into taxonomic collectives for reasons of profit."[68] Yet as a dual-product marketplace, television audiences are a source of conflict within the industry: advertisers are interested in keeping prices low and thus in underestimating audience numbers, but network owners, seeking the highest possible profits, are interested in overestimating audiences. In order to operate efficiently—audience measurement and advertising rates are, after all, a permanent and constant element of television industry operations—they must have a single method that is the basis of ad rate negotiations. "This means," Meehan says, "ratings are not the same as a research institute conducting social scientific studies of television viewers."[69]

Perhaps one reason market research goes largely un(der)examined in television studies is because it remains a hidden aspect of development, production, and distribution; its significance to making a "hit" or to predicting a show's failure is not publicized or made part of any broader narrative. More often than not, successes and failures in television are attributed either to "genius" creators, intangible qualities, or unpredictable audience tastes. Market research techniques are also proprietary, which is why specific information is not publicly available. Data from Nielsen is available for purchase but at significant cost. In 2010, I was researching the financial advice guru Suze Orman (also openly lesbian) and requested a set of demographic data about *The Suze Orman Show* (CNBC, 2002–2015) from a contact I was referred to at Nielsen. In order to receive a price quote on the data, I had to explain how I would use it. The information I received worded the permissible uses this way:

> The Data may be used solely to conduct an academic study examining the effects of audience composition among select talk shows on social and political topics featured by the program's host. The Data may be used to determine the political potential of select women talk show hosts. Limited excerpts of the Data may be used in an academic paper summarizing the results of the study, to be submitted for publication in academic journals or included in academic presentations on this subject. The Data shall not be used for media buying, planning or selling, or for any other purpose.[70]

Based on the request I made, the price for a one-year agreement for use of the data within the "Permissible Uses" outlined in the above statement was $3,355.00. In addition, the price for biannual averages of the same data from 2008 through 2010 was $3,200.00. Given that I was a graduate student at the time, these fees were cost prohibitive, but they provide a sense of the difficulty in accessing this type of data source.

Market research is particularly important to the production of lesbian television programming because Nielsen does not track numbers of LGBT viewers. Despite the problematic nature of ratings, without Nielsen numbers for LGBT audiences, lesbian viewers remain an enigmatic television demographic. Market research, then, provides some of the only quantifiable information about lesbian consumers. As this chapter's opening epigraph notes, the results of the Lesbian Consumer Index prompted researchers to proclaim 2008 "The Year of the Lesbian." Subsequent annual reports about lesbian consumers indicate equally high levels of education, disposable income, and interests in media products and services.

While 2008 was the first year that market researchers offered up data suggesting that lesbian women were a desirable target market, advertisers had begun reaching out to the broader "gay market" in the late 1980s. The beginnings of marketers' concerted efforts to reach LGBT consumers resulted from a series of surveys indicating that lesbians and gays were unusually affluent and well educated. Those results, released by the Simmons Market Research Bureau and later by Overlooked Opinions, encouraged mainstream advertisers to buy space in lesbian and gay publications. But they also put forth an image of a mythical gay consumer: white, wealthy, educated, and ready to spend money. Subsequent research revealed that initial surveys were based on a limited pool of consumers, made up mostly of the readers of lesbian and gay publications such as the *Advocate* and openly lesbian and gay people who volunteered to be interviewed at pride events. These surveys were thus skewed toward lesbians and gays who were already purchasing LGBT publications, could afford to be out and not lose their jobs, and had enough free time to travel to pride events, local and national. The data also skewed heavily toward men, not women.

M. V. Lee Badgett, considered by many to have done the most systemic research in the United States on the economics of lesbians and gays, reviewed a series of books published in the 1990s that asserted the affluence, good taste, and high education levels of America's LGBT consumers. Of the books, she writes, "Their collective focus on middle- and upper-middle-class gays and their concerns unfortunately reinforces the stereotypes of affluence." She attributes this focus on the high end of the economic spectrum partly to "market forces in the publishing world," implying that almost all the books published on the topic were not intended to be scholarly explorations of the economic status of LGBT citizens. Rather, they were published by mainstream commercial presses and made available at major bookstore chains, whereas scholarly books tend to be available only by special order. Based on these facts, Badgett concludes, "The logical market for such guidebooks would be actual and aspiring gay members of the managerial class. They are the ones with the motives and money to buy expensive books, to redirect their investment and consumer dollars, and to use these books to guide their management of their sexual identity in the workplace."[71]

While Badgett and other economists have explained in detail why early research on LGBT consumers was inaccurate and newer research has made significant corrections to the way studies are conducted about LGBT consumers, marketers ignore most of the updated information. According to Sender, the more accurate research "is inconvenient to marketers not only because it challenges the ideal image of the 'gay market,' but because it undermines the notion of the taxonomic collective upon which market segmentation rests."[72]

This ideal "gay market" is envisioned as a single enumerable and desirable consumer population. Market researchers construct this image based on three interrelated assumptions: homogeneity, separation, and essence.[73] Together, these assumptions form a taxonomic collective, or a group that is the result of institutional attempts to neatly classify and organize a population according to one distinguishing feature, in this case, homosexuality.

To develop the "affluencer" concept, for example, Bravo worked with the consulting firm Sterling Brands and with Lieberman Research Worldwide, an international market research company. Through surveys and focus groups, these firms identified three key audience segments, which were referred to internally at Bravo but were not publicized: "Wills & Graces," "PTA Trendsetters," and "Metro Climbers."[74] These audiences were considered to be among the most affluent and influential consumers watching TV. According to a 2009 press release from the Advertising Research Foundation's annual David Ogilvy Awards, where Bravo was the Silver award winner, "The key objective [with these data] was to identify the commonalities of programming affinities."[75] In a 2012 presentation at the University of Southern California, representatives from Lieberman Research Worldwide—Jeff Reynolds, president and CEO, and Teddy Kerman, research director—described their company's research process, during which they identified eight programming-affinity groups. The three groups chosen by Bravo shared media preferences, which easily translated to consumer qualities valued by high-end advertisers. The commonalities emphasized singled out audience groups who were brand conscious and interested in trends, used digital technologies to enhance their experiences of media, and had more purchasing power than average consumers. According to the report from the Advertising Research Foundation, Bravo's "affluencer" campaign was highly successful; Nielsen's report on viewer engagement announced that in 2007 Bravo's audience was more engaged than any cable network they tracked. A year later, Bravo's engagement levels surpassed that of all broadcast networks. By 2013, NBCUniversal reported, Bravo had "+69% higher user interaction rates on average" than other networks.[76]

These reports reveal that market research investigates in detail the qualities of consumer groups that make them the most attractive to advertisers. In a phone interview from his San Francisco office, the founder and president of Community Marketing, Thomas Roth, told me that to produce what they consider accurate representative samples, market researchers use US census data as their reference.[77] This methodology, however, produces deeply flawed information. The US census began counting same-sex couples in 2000, but it includes only lesbians and gays living in the same household who specify the relationship between them as "partner" and therefore doesn't keep records for single lesbians and gays, lesbian and gay couples living in separate households, or same-sex couples who interpret their relationship as something other than "spouses" (in instances where same-sex couples need or choose to stay closeted or where same-sex couples choose alternative family structures). While it quantifies categories such as age, race, and gender, the US census does not seek information on an individual's sexual orientation. As a result, market researchers' representative samples are as accurate as the limited data provided by the census.

In addition, the promotion of findings in studies such as the Lesbian Consumer Index suggests the following question: what drives market researchers to conduct specific studies at particular times? That is, Community Marketing has conducted an annual survey of LGBT consumer behavior since 2000, but began creating a separate lesbian index only in 2008. In the case of the Lesbian Consumer Index, researchers culled the data from Community Marketing's annual LGBT survey. From this single survey, market researchers perform what they call "subgroup analysis" within various identity groups; the Gay Consumer Index drew data from surveys in which respondents self-identified as "male" and "gay," while the Lesbian Consumer Index drew from respondents who self-identified as "female" and "gay." Market researchers assert that this methodology guarantees accurate comparisons among "subgroups," because in using a single survey for all respondents, researchers can precisely compare consumer behaviors of different niche markets.

In response to my question, Roth told me, "We had a gut feeling that lesbians weren't . . . buying anything, [and] the research was able to prove that." While he acknowledged that market researchers "observe and influence trends," Roth maintained that influence occurs at the level of advertising, not in the research itself. He went so far as to insist that "markets drive social change," thereby explicitly espousing neoliberal ideology. Despite some pushing on my end, Roth refused to address the fact that Community Marketing always had the means to produce materials like the Lesbian Consumer Index but did not use them.

His comments also reinforce the belief that market researchers discover preexisting consumer markets. However, the lesbian consumer market is what Ien Ang describes as a discursive construct, which works in the service of an institutional control that is never actually met, and that, as Ang says, "has to be continuously pursued by accumulating ever more information."[78] Falling prey to the idea that their studies uncover a niche market that was already there, market researchers do not acknowledge the ways in which their research helps to construct consumer demographics; researchers, in fact, shape images of consumers to make them identifiable and sellable to advertisers.

In her study of gay marketing practices, Sender details the rhetoric that embodies the dominant model of market research; she quotes market researchers who in varied forms express the belief that "preformed markets are simply waiting to be roused." She adds, "This model assumes not only that there is a preexisting gay market, but that sexual identification functions as an incontrovertible marker to distinguish a taxonomic collective of gay consumers from their heterosexual counterparts."[79] Although not explicitly stated, Sender's argument builds on the work of Stuart Ewen, who argues that consumers are not simply found; rather, advertising creates them. He says, "The functional goal of national advertising was the creation of desire and habits."[80] Ewen sees the underlying dynamics of the system of needs as being based not on the interests of consumers but rather on the historic needs of capitalist production and overproduction. Applying his theories about consumer markets specifically to the LGBT market, Sender explores the ways marketers and media makers construct meaning rather than simply represent it.

In my own research on the "gay market," I saw this logic at work in some of the operations of market research firms. In 2009, amid increasing public attention to lesbian consumers, I attended the Gay and Lesbian Market Symposium. At the symposium, market researchers presented a set of data from their most recent polling and focus groups about LGBT consumers to a range of human resources personnel in businesses such as banks, hotels, airlines, magazines, law firms, film festivals, building contractors, and nonprofit organizations. Roth and David Paisley, senior research director at Community Marketing, detailed the ways their company's findings could help specific types of businesses court LGBT consumers in the most efficient and effective ways.

Roth and Paisley, both white, well-educated, openly gay men, stressed that the 1990s had one "gay market" but the twenty-first century has many "gay markets" to tap into. Businesses must understand, they insist, the different LGBT niches and cater to the one(s) most appropriate to the products or services they want to sell to consumers.[81] Community Marketing considers itself an activist-oriented company "built on market research and education." However, because the company partitions lesbian and gay consumer groups into commodifiable markets, in reality, just as television executives and producers do, the company tries to disprove negative or inconvenient images of lesbians and gays.

Market research also tends to conceal lesbian and gay communities' participation in the construction of these markets. As I discuss elsewhere in this book, for LGBT citizens, representation and participation in the consumer marketplace and in mainstream media have often been regarded as an essential route to social acceptance and political inclusion. In broad terms, Jeffrey

Escoffier describes how an urban subculture formed by stigmatized and invisible lesbians and gays evolved into a public community with an activist political agenda and an influential position in contemporary American culture. Detailing what he calls the "political economy of the closet," Escoffier argues that the market process often played a crucial role in the emergence of lesbian and gay communities, and conversely, that these communities have significantly affected the American marketplace.[82] Rather than something imposed on LGBT citizens, the "gay market" was engendered partly by members of the LGBT community who saw access to and representation in the consumer marketplace as a means to gain both financially and in terms of public visibility, recognition, and cultural influence and authority.

As a market research firm dedicated to LGBT consumers, Community Marketing considers itself uniquely positioned to meet the needs of this particular population. Yet, through the practices of market segmentation which market research relies on, researchers shape images of lesbian consumers to make them identifiable and sellable to advertisers. Particularly because it draws on cultural knowledge about lesbian identity, market research data ends up reproducing assumptions about sexuality. Closely examining the 2008 Lesbian Consumer Index, for example, I learned that one of the ways this data gathering and manipulation works is through sponsored survey questions. After the Los Angeles symposium, I approached Roth and told him about my research. He said he would be happy to answer any questions I had with him, and we scheduled a phone interview for later that week. In advance of the interview, I requested a digital copy of the surveys Community Marketing used to create the Lesbian Consumer Index so that I could ask specific questions about it as well as about the firm's research theories and methodologies.

In my interview with Roth, I asked him why the survey referenced specific brands, such as Michelin Tires and Absolut Vodka. He explained that advertising agencies approach Community Marketing each year and pay for their brands to appear in its surveys. Roth described this strategy as mutually beneficial: Community Marketing receives revenue from the agencies sponsoring questions and the agencies receive what is called "third-party validation" for their products. In other words, companies like Absolut use consumer surveys to find new and profitable market opportunities for their products.

Absolut, as well as other companies that sponsor questions in Community Marketing's surveys, has a long history of advertising in LGBT publications and sponsoring LGBT events; for instance, in 1979 Absolut Vodka was the first mainstream company to advertise in the *Advocate*. At the time, the vodka was just being imported from a Swedish producer and was virtually unknown, and the executives' choice to advertise in an LGBT publication did not pose a significant risk to sales of the product. In what Dan Baker calls the "domino effect," once the product was successful other companies began advertising in LGBT newspapers and magazines.[83] Because Absolut Vodka already knows it has a loyal LGBT customer base, sponsoring questions in consumer surveys reinforces its role in constructing niche markets. That is, by incorporating questions about Absolut Vodka consumption into a survey about consumer behavior, Community Marketing reinforces the belief that lesbian consumers, because of their sexual orientation, are likely to drink that particular brand.

Post-Gay Ideology: "We're gay without necessarily having to come out of the closet"

The consumer groups molded by market researchers also contribute to television industry workers' ideas about sexuality. Another consistent theme among interviewees was a strong belief in post-gay ideology. This term signifies how lesbian identity functions in television narratives. Few lesbian characters and personalities in contemporary television programs come out in the course of a show. In early 2008, I contacted Meredith Kadlec, the openly lesbian senior vice president of original programming and feature film development at Here Media. Here owns the Here! television network (now HereTV), which is the only US subscription cable network dedicated to LGBT programming. I spent several hours interviewing Kadlec in her office in Westwood, California. She was relaxed during our interview and interested in discussing trends in lesbian programming and representation. Acknowledging that industry workers are active agents in the production of cultural knowledge, she said, "I'm not opposed to coming out stories, I would say that I'm not doing them because I feel like there's so much other stuff to be done. . . . Anything that I do with a coming out element is going to have other layers of stuff going on because that's what to me is missing. It's not enough for me it to be like, 'Now know I'm gay.'"[84] Arguably, this sentiment evinces the primary distinction between lesbian representations of the late twentieth century and early 2000s. In 2007, making the case for what he calls "post-closet television," Becker says, "In recent years . . . gay men (and to a much lesser extent lesbians) have been seemingly (and at times seamlessly) integrated into the landscape of US television . . . with little to no fanfare."[85] While programs such as *All in the Family* (CBS, 1971–1979), *Roseanne* (ABC, 1988–1997), *Ally McBeal* (Fox, 1997–2002), *ER* (NBC, 1994–2009), and certainly *Ellen* (ABC, 1994–1998) broke new ground with lesbian characters, their storylines revolved around heterosexual struggles to come to terms with lesbian identities, preventing the

story from moving beyond this "single cataclysmic moment."[86] While scholars note how these representations position heterosexuality as central to the
narrative and make lesbian sexuality peripheral, my interviewees—Kadlec,
Cohen, Greenblatt, Shpall, Roth, and Paisley—framed this post-gay rhetoric
as a popular and progressive form of representation, one that accurately reflects people's lived experiences in early twenty-first-century America.

Since the mid-2000s, the press has frequently referred to Bravo as the
"de facto gay channel" because of the style of its shows and its consistent incorporation of lesbian and gay people in its reality programming.[87] Yet the
network disagrees with this label; rather than being a "gay channel," Cohen
said, Bravo has a "gay sensibility": "I would say we're gay without necessarily
having to come out of the closet." He used himself as a metaphor for the network's identity; Cohen said he looks at Bravo "in the same way that I view
my sexuality. I wouldn't put gay at the top of the list of who I am. I would
say that it's something about me, and that's how Bravo is." When I asked for
an example of how this philosophy operates in the network's programming,
Cohen answered, "We've had a lot of gay female chefs on *Top Chef* over the
last four years and that's just because a lot of talented gay women have come
and auditioned for the show." For him, constructing lesbian television show
contestants as coincidentally lesbian was a more accurate depiction of viewers'
lives; he described Bravo as wanting "to reflect life around," which involves
including lesbian and gay characters, but not featuring their sexual identity
in the shows. Rather than make a political statement, Cohen says he tries "to
represent every color of gay, and there are good gays and bad gays, just like
there are good gays and bad gays in life." Incorporating a lesbian or gay character into a show for the sake of diversity, Cohen said, "is sort of a ten-years-
ago sensibility," because it creates a focus on how that person is portrayed and
how her or his sexuality comes across to viewers. For Cohen, Bravo's bottom-
line philosophy is to look for successful shows, ones that will be popular, bring
in advertiser support, and increase Bravo's audience.

Before Bravo began incorporating a significant number of lesbian personalities into its reality program lineup, Sender addressed the characterization of
Bravo as the "de facto" gay channel. She argues that "dualcasting" can provide
the network's required audience base of women (18–49) and still appeal to a
niche audience of gay men. With its programming choices, Bravo draws on
what Sender describes as "long-standing associations between gay men and
heterosexual women in order to appeal to a sizeable female audience."[88] Tap-
ping into the image of gay men as the stylish, classy, trendsetting best friends
of heterosexual women, Bravo uses gay-themed programs as an integral component of its strategies for attracting media audiences.

With the development of *Work Out*, as well as other Bravo shows that feature lesbian contestants, the network was able to multicast to an even broader audience. In my interview with Amy Shpall, she reiterated Bravo's claim that sexuality is not a central concern of the network. For her, Jackie Warner's lesbianism was purely coincidental. Shpall told me that she interviewed gym owners of all kinds for *Work Out*, never specifically seeking out one who was lesbian or gay. Once she found openly lesbian Warner, her goal was to represent lesbians and gays as "completely normal." For her, the show was a reflection of her own reality, in which lesbians and gays surround her in her personal and professional lives.

The press has similarly described Showtime as a network that caters to LGBT audiences with ensemble shows such as *Queer as Folk*, *The L Word*, and *The Real L Word*. Robert Greenblatt agreed that the network has established a loyal LGBT following with its original programming; he called *The L Word*'s viewers "super loyal," even during seasons when the show's plot-lines generated harsh criticism from fans for being unrealistic, insufferable, and aggravating. Greenblatt noted that with shows like *Queer as Folk* and *The L Word*, there was no doubt they would attract LGBT audiences. But he added that he does not think there will be future shows with ensemble casts of lesbian or gay characters. Rather, "as the world evolves," he said:

> You're seeing gay characters just part of the fabric of lots of shows and I actually think . . . it may be more reflective of the world . . . and may ultimately raise the consciousness of the world if they start to see gay characters in these worlds as just part of the world and not "oh look there's the gay character."

Cohen and Greenblatt's comments not only reflect post-gay rhetoric from openly gay people but at times even distance the networks from any association with LGBT identities or communities. These conversations suggest that industry workers are unaware of their own interpellation into television's systems of sexual privilege. On one hand, their notions about a post-gay America are rooted in their own high levels of education, thorough understanding of liberal politics, and strong belief that television images undeniably hold the power to increase awareness and acceptance. On the other hand, their extolling the virtues of post-gay representations highlights how removed they are from the realities of most sexual minorities, particularly sexual minorities of color, of lower economic status, and in rural and conservative parts of the country. Suzanna Walters notes that "in this new era of 'tolerance,' homophobia in public realms such as television more often appears in ambiguous form, hidden under a veneer of liberal acceptance."[89] Arguably, my interviewees' post-gay ideology runs the risk of ignoring and even perpetuating contemporary forms of homophobia and heteronormativity.

However, there is another way to look at the idealization of post-gay television among industry workers. Coexisting with these other perspectives is a certain political progressiveness masked as commercial utility. Granted, it is a narrow, normative progressiveness, but I contend that Cohen's use of the word "sensibility" in describing Bravo's incorporation of lesbians (and gays) can be read as a savvy understanding of his need to meet the industry's requirements but still exert his own power within his role as an executive. Greenblatt articulated a similar concept when I asked him about Showtime's LGBT audience. He said, "brand is over-used," Showtime's programming "is more like a feeling." On the surface, these descriptions support research on the affective nature of branding discussed by scholars such as Henry Jenkins and Sarah Banet-Weiser.[90] They also communicate inclusiveness and openness, marking cable networks as forward thinkers. They suggest on the one hand an investment in quantitative and qualitative methods of branding and market research and, on the other, an effort to naturalize this same investment. In pointing out this dynamic, I am not arguing that industry discourse simply attempts to conceal its operations or that industry workers have a false stake in the politics of representation. Rather, what seems noteworthy is the way that empirical practices are transformed by industry workers' discourse into a form of politics. Against rhetoric in popular and academic circles that, for example, makes claims about the artfulness of cable television programming, this research suggests that liberal political values play a vital role in the production of cable's lesbian programming. Although as Sender writes, "Marketers and critics alike have tended to characterize the lipstick lesbian as the newer, apolitical or postfeminist lesbian consumer,"[91] the logics of branding, market research, and industry discourse reveal a politically motivated representational practice (albeit a narrow, liberal one) that relies on high-class and feminine lesbian characters to multicast to a range of audiences.

Multicasting: "It's just getting on board with the sensibility"

Multicasting complicates prevailing assumptions within television studies about the operations of the cable industry and the construction of brands and audiences. With the proliferation of cable channels, television scholars have concentrated on the structures and implications of narrowcasting and niche audiences. In this work, the dominant model of cable television is one of segmentation that targets narrow groups of audiences. Where once television audiences were defined by the principles of reaching the largest audience possible, Lotz describes the post-network television audience as "more accurately understood as a collection of niche audiences."[92] With the continued expansion of cable television and the convergence of multiple media forms, scholars have identified the ways that terms like "customization" and "personalization" define the industry's approach to targeting audiences, often critiquing the claim that viewers have more agency and power over media products as a result of the financial value of niche demographics. This scholarship tends to address the ever-narrowing focus on segments, which, Turow argues, produces a "fractured society" in which individuals are hindered from learning about other identities and social categories, which ultimately erodes attitudes of acceptance, tolerance, and interdependence.[93]

Against this perceived turn toward narrower audience segments, scholars such as Alisa Perren, Cynthia Chris, Katherine Sender, and Beretta Smith-Shomade have challenged the dominance of the narrowcasting model, arguing that cable programming is "increasingly pursuing the same 18- to 49-year-old demographic long sought by broadcasters" in order to remain competitive and profitable.[94]

Multicasting, by contrast, neither rejects narrowcasting nor embraces a general audience appeal. Rather, it is a strategy for drawing audiences to cable programming based on demographics shaped and refined by market research. The interviews presented in this chapter embody what I argue is a commonsense understanding of the ways that targeting, multicasting, and market research operate in contemporary cable television. While interviewees—particularly Cohen and Greenblatt—articulated polished and public relations–laden statements about television brands and audiences, their comments simultaneously offered a nuanced conception of the post-network industrial landscape. In particular, their descriptions of network identities, audience demographics, programming development strategies, and marketing practices shed light on the inner workings of the cable marketplace as it is simultaneously driven by a strong sense of panic (defined as an era of uncertainty, instability, and change) and ranked as a new "golden age" in the medium's history.

Although they do not necessarily engage directly with the topic of market research and, even in the case of Greenblatt, deny its key role in developing network brands and cultivating desirable demographics, interviewees gave glimpses of systems of knowledge about the industry that in fact underscore the significance of measurement and market research to the production of programming, brands, and audiences. In the case of lesbian programming, measurement is packaged politically and capitalizes on progressive social values.

Because market researchers work with cable networks to build their brands and then to successfully maintain them, they must continually try to sustain and expand brands so that they remain culturally visible and financially viable. Arguably, we see this dynamic play out most clearly in interviewees' discussions of post-gay television, where lesbian audiences do not define the target audience of such network programs as *Work Out* and *The L Word* but rather are one of several quantifiable and desirable demographics that the networks are seeking to engage. Multicasting thus represents cable networks' desire to simultaneously target a niche audience and operate under the aegis of post-gay ideology.

This chapter has uncovered theories and practices about the television and market research industries that help us better understand how images of lesbian characters and personalities on cable networks serve as marketing and programming tools; Greenblatt succinctly defined the multicasting approach: "It's just getting on board with the sensibility and hopefully we continue to offer things that are going to keep [viewers] engaged." I thus urge critics and scholars to see cable's lesbian programming at the intersection of industrial practices, branding strategies, and market research. The interviews and analysis presented here are crucial indications of how cable television is grappling with demands for audiences and brand differentiation. The phenomenon of lesbian programming suggests that multicasting has become a significant method of network branding and program production in the contemporary cable marketplace. In the next chapter, I turn to a broader topic—both for television and LGBT culture—by examining the role of broadcast programs in marriage equality campaigns.

CHAPTER 2

Advocacy: Hitching Activism to *Modern Family*'s Gay Wedding

On an episode of *Entertainment Tonight* (CBS, 1981–) in August 2012, Ann Romney, wife of the Republican presidential contender Mitt Romney, professed her love for the hit sitcom *Modern Family* (ABC, 2009–). The darling of ABC's comedy lineup, the show follows the lives of an extended family in Los Angeles who are connected through patriarch Jay Pritchett (Ed O'Neill) and his adult children, Claire (Julie Bowen) and Mitchell (Jesse Tyler Ferguson). In this "modern" family, Mitchell (Mitch) is gay, and in the series premiere, he adopts a baby from Vietnam with his partner, Cameron (Cam, played by Eric Stonestreet). In response to Ann Romney's comments, the show's co-creator Steven Levitan took aim at candidate Romney's stance against marriage rights for lesbians and gays, sarcastically Tweeting that he was "thrilled Ann Romney says ModFam is her favorite show. We'll offer her the role of officiant at Mitch & Cam's wedding. As soon as it's legal" (2012).

Only weeks after Romney and Levitan's comments, the Human Rights Campaign (HRC), the largest LGBT rights organization in the United States, launched a video fundraiser called "HRC's Modern Family Sweepstakes."[1] Distributed online, the video makes a special offer: donate to the HRC before October 24, 2012, and win a chance to dine with the stars who play Mitch and Cam. In a written message that accompanies the video, attempting to entice fans of the show, especially fans of "America's favorite gay TV couple," the HRC promises, "Your donation will help millions of loving, committed same-sex couples across the country fighting for equality." In the video, Ferguson and Stonestreet are on the *Modern Family* set, sitting in the same chairs they use for the show's mockumentary interviews. Capitalizing on the sexual orientation of both actors—Ferguson is openly gay and Stonestreet is straight—the video parodies the fears of straight actors playing gay roles: that audiences will assume they are gay in real life and that they will be forever typecast in gay roles. Out of character, they introduce themselves and Ferguson says, with a smile on his face, "and we are lovers." Stonestreet corrects him: "Uh, we are lovers *on TV.*" Still smiling and seemingly delighting in Stonestreet's exaggerated discomfort, Ferguson continues, "On TV, we are lovers, yes. So, whether you are gay or straight, the family that we portray might remind you a little of your own" (here he exaggerates the "we," waving a hand back and forth between Stonestreet and himself). Stonestreet, seemingly unable to help himself, interjects "on TV" once again after Ferguson says, "the family we portray." In this 105-second video, there is yet a third instance in which Stonestreet adds "on TV" to Ferguson's earnest but humorous plea for contributions to the HRC in the run-up to the presidential election. Notably, the election of 2012 saw marriage initiatives on ballots in Maryland, Minnesota, Maine, and Washington.

The video parodies not only concern over straight actors playing gay characters but also the notion that, as Ferguson says, "whether you are gay or straight, the family that we portray might remind you a little of your own." Before he can finish the sentence, two makeup artists walk into the frame and begin fussing over the two men. While Stonestreet insists that their "TV family" is just like any other family, he asks one of the makeup artists to fix the "flyaways" in his hair. This portion of the video reminds viewers, ironically, that Ferguson and Stonestreet are on a television set, with dozens of people just on the other side of the camera working to create this nonfictional advocacy message for the HRC.

Watching the HRC's *Modern Family* sweepstakes initiative, I was struck by how the script replicates the relationship between Mitch and Cam on the show; although Ferguson and Stonestreet are out of character during the video, they interact as they do on the show. Viewers familiar with the show will immediately recognize their facial expressions, mannerisms, and reactions to each other, especially their signature bickering. Interested in how LGBT television advocacy works, I wanted to know: how did the HRC come up with the idea for this fundraiser? Who wrote the script? How was the HRC able to use the *Modern Family* set for filming? Who involved the actors and got them to agree to go to dinner with a complete stranger in the name of political fundraising? In other words, I wanted to look at this fundraiser from behind the scenes to learn how the development and production *process* works, and what that process reveals about the nature of modern LGBT television advocacy. As I describe in the introduction, my research has convinced me of the value of what anthropologists call "studying up," because this method acknowledges the significance of those in positions of power, given that their power matters on multiple registers.[2]

"Studying up" allows a look at the markedly ambivalent structure and culture of LGBT television advocacy. As the largest national LGBT lobbying organization, the HRC has an extensive base of supporters as well as a broad range of critics from both the right and the left. While critics from the right simply oppose their mission, many critics from the left oppose their mainstream approach to social change. Rather than evaluating the positions the HRC takes, or the goals it pursues for LGBT people, my focus is to examine how advocacy organizations such as the HRC contribute to cultural production.

The ambivalence I refer to involves experimentation with television advocacy tools, contested political relationships between popular discourse and advocacy work, and attempts to rebrand large nonprofits to better appeal to younger generations. Here, I use examples of two *Modern Family* marriage advocacy campaigns, one by the HRC and the other by the American Civil Liberties Union (ACLU). I have highlighted these initiatives not to privilege *Modern Family* as a superior text or to label the show as more culturally and historically relevant than others, but rather because it has been both a central site of critical commentary and a visible mechanism of television advocacy work in support of marriage equality.

This chapter rejects the cynical notion that LGBT television advocacy has been so co-opted by partnerships and alliances between industry players and moderate advocacy organizations that it has been rendered politically useless or meaningless—a mere cog in the capitalist machine of marketable LGBT identities and narratives. Neither does this chapter embrace a return to an imagined space of "outsider politics" where LGBT activists are "queering" television with the help of a few good, insider Hollywood gays. Indeed, as Roopali Mukherjee and Sarah Banet-Weiser write, "acknowledging that one can no longer—if one ever could—stand outside the system to critique it" is vital to assessing the state of LGBT television advocacy.[3]

Below I detail the conflicting and contingent alliances that define contemporary television advocacy by examining each campaign, including interviews with the staff that produced the HRC's *Modern Family* fundraiser. Rather than celebrate or defend *Modern Family* to its critics or parse out moments of queer potential in the show's narrative, characters, production, or marketing, I will argue that the HRC and the ACLU both deploy their power in more dynamic ways than either supporters or detractors might believe. In addition, this chapter incorporates an analysis of an interview I conducted with Joe Solmonese, who was not involved with the campaign but was president of the HRC from 2005 until 2012, a period in which LGBT television representation increased, as did public opinion in favor of marriage equality.[4]

To contextualize the campaigns and the interviews, I review the history of LGBT television advocacy, describe the ways digital media, deregulation, and marketing alter the foundations of advocacy, and ground these discussions in my own experiences as a member of the GLAAD television jury, where I evaluated LGBT representations for the organization's annual awards. Brought together under a single lens, these historical, cultural, economic, and political elements make visible emerging patterns in LGBT advocacy that are built around paradoxical definitions of sexual identity.

Modern Family Mania

Since its debut in 2009, *Modern Family* has established itself as a popular and award-winning staple of the television landscape. As the *New York Times* notes, "In a rare concurrence, the darling of the critics is one of the highest rated comedies on television, and is the 20th rated show overall this season."[5] Echoing satirical sitcom successes such as *The Office* (NBC, 2005–2013) and *Parks & Recreation* (NBC, 2009–2015), the show is a single-camera mockumentary that includes stylistic signatures of the genre such as knowing nods to the camera and interviews with an off-screen filmmaker. The show has earned consistently high ratings and ad revenues, and has won a bevy of industry awards.[6]

The show has also received kudos from LGBT advocacy organizations, who praise the show for its inclusive characters and narratives.[7] *Modern Family* regularly ranks in first or second place among prime-time network shows for adults 18–49 years of age, the most desirable demographic for television advertisers.[8] Finally, as another testimony to this show's appeal, USA, the highest-revenue-earning cable network on the air, purchased episodes of *Modern Family* for an average of $1.8 million an episode in 2013.[9] Anticipating its spillover effect, the *Hollywood Reporter* announced, "After giving *Modern* some time to establish itself with viewers on a new network, USA will debut two originals, Denis Leary's *Sirens* and *Playing House*, from *Best Friends Forever* duo Jessica St. Clair and Lennon Parham, in 2014."[10] Following the lead of other basic cable channels—such as TBS, which has found great success with the purchase of CBS's *The Big Bang Theory* (2007–)—USA hoped to capitalize on the popularity of *Modern Family* to draw younger, more upscale viewers to the network and launch their own comedy lineup after a decade of building a brand around character-driven dramas.[11]

As the 2012–2013 network television season came to a close, *Salon*'s Daniel D'Addario noted, "'Modern Family' has been, in its first four seasons, an unusual cultural flashpoint. Both Barack Obama and Mitt Romney have both claimed the show as a favorite."[12] *Modern Family*'s popularity—with both Democratic and Republican presidential candidates—along with its mass and critical appeal, reflects the show's symbolic power to bolster mythic notions of a unified nation in an era of social, political, and economic fragmentation. Even after the reelection of President Obama in 2012, the show continued to shine as an award-winning and popular sitcom.

I witnessed this level of praise for the show at the 2014 Flow Conference, hosted by the Department of Radio-Television-Film at the University of Texas at Austin. There, the Pulitzer Prize–winning television critic Howard Rosenberg told a large group of professors, students, and independent scholars that the show has had an "enormous impact on the thinking of America."[13] He was speaking at one of three "Core Conversations" facilitated by the conference "in the interest of encouraging greater consideration of the links between the present state of television and TV studies and its past."[14]

In this forum, attended primarily by television scholars, *Modern Family* was hailed as a watershed moment in television, especially in the history of network television. These celebratory—even self-congratulatory—statements, proclaimed by Rosenberg and his fellow panelists as incontrovertible facts, elicited a collective, albeit polite, groan from the audience; the friend I was sitting with, a queer television studies scholar, squeezed my hand in frustration. He, like many others in the room who had been trained to be critical and wary of simplistic claims about "television effects," was tired of hearing the show lauded as the twenty-first century's most popular and progressive network sitcom, and one that was unquestionably responsible for driving social change. Frustrated by the seeming naïveté of Hollywood elites who routinely distance themselves from any activist impulses and then make bold claims about the impact of content on cultural norms, many scholars in the room reacted to what Alexander Doty calls "the limits of television liberalism." In this critique, Mitch and Cam are '"good' gays who keep their 'place at the table' by striving to be just like their straight middle-class counterparts, living in a monogamous relationship and building up a (mildly dysfunctional) family with children, a stay-at-home 'mom,' and a working 'dad.'"[15]

I do attribute much of the show's popularity with both critics and viewers to the fact that it has not often challenged the status quo; although the basic makeup of the family is refreshingly attuned to some of the realities of American life—divorce, blended families of stepchildren and stepparents, international adoption, age differences in marriage, interracial marriages, and women returning to the workforce after raising children—it does little to question, let alone problematize, stereotyped norms of gender, race, ethnicity, class, immigration, and sexuality. Bolstering Doty's critique, Mitch and Cam *are* "good gays"—white, middle-upper class, gender conforming in a heteronormative way, and marriage seeking. Mitch is the more masculine, breadwinner of the family and Cam is the effeminate, "maternal" stay-at-home dad who worries about all the things that "moms/women" worry about (e.g., what school his daughter will be accepted to, what his partner and daughter will wear to social events, and how to host the perfect party). In later seasons, as their daughter Lily grows up, Cam returns to his love of acting and football, teaching and coaching at the local high school. These narrative choices, some argue however, make use of stereotypes in order to turn them on their heads, further complicating representations of social minorities.[16]

Beyond the show's gay representations, *Modern Family*'s female characters began the series exclusively as wives, mothers, and homemakers who were economically dependent on their husbands. Beginning in season 3, Claire decides to reenter the workforce, first by running for city council and then eventually by creating a successful career for herself that continues throughout the following seasons. At the same time, however, critics of the show point to the frequency with which episodes revolve around female characters as the butt of family jokes or as overreliant on men to learn how to use technology.

In addition to these sexist tropes, the show relies on regressive racialized representations of immigrants. Since its debut, racial plotlines have centered on the character of Gloria (Sofía Vergara), the much younger, second wife of Jay Pritchett, the family patriarch. Gloria is a stereotypical fiery Latina from Colombia. She has a child from a previous marriage, and her voluptuous body is fodder for many plotlines and punch lines. Isabel Molina-Guzmán argues that Vergara's character, "as a contemporary Latina spitfire, . . . is ultimately coded as ethnically safe through her ability to serve as an intercultural bridge and comedic foil to her white upper-middle-class second husband and his family."[17] Through her thick accent, which Vergara publicly acknowledges enhancing for comedic effect, Gloria's linguistic mishaps are the source of comedy within and outside the narrative. As a result, Molina-Guzmán writes, "the narrative of the show always concludes by recuperating the normative and nostalgic values of whiteness and US heterosexual family life." At the same time, though, Gloria is frequently several steps ahead of Jay, often outsmarting and outwitting him.

The reaction from the Flow conference audience, then, embodies a perfectly logical—indeed, an important—critique to make of *Modern Family* and network television more generally. As a broadcast program, *Modern Family* occupies a specific place in the television landscape. Broadcast networks are the oldest in the history of television; they are aimed at reaching the widest possible audience, earning enormous sums of money in advertising revenue, and attracting viewer interest by paying extremely high production costs for big-budget shows. In recent years these networks have struggled to compete with the edgy and niche-oriented content of cable and streaming programs but have gone to great lengths to adapt to the time- and place-shifting behaviors of audiences. As Lynn Spigel and Jan Olsson write, "The rise of multichannel cable and global satellite delivery, multinational conglomerates, Internet convergence, changes in regulation policies and ownership rules, the advent of HDTV . . . all contribute to transformations in the practice we call watching TV."[18] For broadcast networks, the goal is for audiences to use any one of these "interconnected parts" to access a program, treating it as a franchise with elements that speak to a range of interests. Yet, because of its populist origins and its role as a domestic medium, broadcast television, more than any other media, has been the embodiment of dominant ideology, creating and perpetuating a common set of typically gendered, raced, xenophobic, classed, and homophobic values. *Modern Family* lies at the intersection of the medium's history and its changing structures and uses in the digital era.

However, I find it worrying when scholars dismiss the use of a popular and homonormative broadcast show in advocacy work as just another problematic example of the assimilationist and normalizing drives of a once-radical movement that never would have considered marriage a central goal. First, the quick dismissal of TV as a tool for social change overlooks the productive role that sitcoms have historically played in popular culture.[19] Efforts toward social change have long been tied to comedy, which, as Bonnie Dow says, "becomes a vehicle for social discussion. The portrayal of social conflicts and their resolution through comedy can lend guidance to a culture that faces adjustment to social change."[20] Stephen Tropiano puts *Modern Family* in a category he calls "gaycoms"—a gay-centered situation comedy, which includes earlier shows such as *Ellen* and *Will & Grace*.[21] According to Tropiano, these programs contribute to LGBT social and political change: "Television shows, and sitcoms in particular, are often undervalued for their power to open up people's minds and influence the way they view the world."[22] While he acknowledges that the images that "influence the way [audiences] view the world" often do depict a narrow set of normative personalities and relationships, they also situate LGBT people squarely within the cultural landscape of the national imaginary.[23]

Secondly, an examination of *Modern Family*'s use as a mechanism of advocacy via other sources—publicity, press reports, and the details of the marriage campaigns' development, production, and online public response—positions the story of the campaigns within the broader operations of television advocacy in the twenty-first century. I use the ACLU's and the HRC's campaigns as case studies because of how much they differ from traditional television advocacy. Both campaigns are examples of LGBT rights organizations choosing one television program as a mechanism of advocacy without the official involvement of the show or network it airs on; advocates have not historically used this strategy to make a case for equality. Rather, since the late 1960s, advocates have sought influence over LGBT television content though direct involvement with networks, advertiser boycotts, and use of the mainstream press to generate support from straight society. Before I analyze the development and production of the campaigns, I describe the traditional form LGBT media advocacy has taken since activists began to see television as a site of broad cultural influence in the mid-twentieth century.

Looking Back: The History of LGBT Television Advocacy

Early advocates fought for increased LGBT media visibility on the basis of pervasive *invisibility*. John D'Emilio notes, "Ending the silence and shedding invisibility have been goals from the beginning of an organized movement; pre-Stonewall activists used progress in these directions as their measuring rods for success or failure."[24] When advocates turned their attention specifically to television in the post-Stonewall era (after 1969), they also focused on changing what were perceived to be "negative" portrayals of sexual minorities. Although 1950s and 1960s television included some sexual minorities, those who did appear were usually the victims or perpetrators of crimes, suffered from severe mental illness, or were incapable of healthy social relations. For example, ABC's *The Asphalt Jungle* (1961) and NBC's *The Eleventh Hour* (1962–1964) were two of the first shows to feature individual episodes with lesbian characters, but they depicted lesbianism as a horrifying mental illness.[25]

In Kathryn Montgomery's 1990 book *Target: Prime Time*, she looks at how LGBT advocates learned to effectively use strategies of coercion, subversion, and persuasion, and sought out mutual, shared interests (as opposed to oppositional critique and condemnation) to gain influence over television development and programming.[26] These strategies were a way of seeking an active role in the creation of LGBT images and to publicly praise and condemn them.[27]

By the late 1960s, advocacy efforts were concentrated in two organizations: the Gay Activists Alliance (GAA) and the National Gay Task Force (NGTF). The GAA ultimately dissolved but was replaced in 1985 by the Gay and Lesbian Alliance Against Defamation (GLAAD).[28] It quickly became *the* national organization both for television networks to work with on behalf of sexual minorities and to call public attention to noteworthy images, positive and negative.[29] The NGTF still exists, although in 2014 it changed its name to the National LGBTQ Task Force.

Initially early organizations like the GAA faced unique problems that set them apart from other advocacy groups; the Federal Communications Commission (FCC) did not provide legal assistance to sexual minorities in the same way it did to women and racial minorities, for example. In addition, as Montgomery writes, "Many people still viewed homosexuality as sinful, deviant behavior rather than a legitimate life-style."[30] After all, homosexuality remained a mental illness according to the American Psychological Association (APA) until 1973.

Despite these difficult—sometimes hostile—conditions, advocates worked relentlessly for LGBT television representation. Viewing TV as uniquely positioned to be a simultaneously entertaining and creative force for democracy, advocates prioritized increasing the number and quality of LGBT characters and storylines. As Montgomery describes it, "Through trial and error, gay activists learned which tactics were most effective in dealing with the networks. They learned how to adapt their tactics to fit network strategies. . . . In time the gay activists gained a reputation within the industry as the most sophisticated and successful advocacy group operating in network television."[31]

In particular, the concept of "realistic" representations became an enduring battle cry of LGBT television advocates. "Realistic" representations are LGBT characters who are as multidimensional as their heterosexual counterparts. The attention to "realistic" images on television relates to its origins as a domestic medium, with characters appearing regularly in viewers' homes, creating an intimacy that film does not. John Ellis explains that television programming's repetitive and ritualized nature makes its actors famous precisely because "their notoriety results from their fairly constant presence on the medium rather than their rarity."[32] In other words, television characters become a regular part of viewers' routines and lives. Even in an era of binge-watching and the online release of an entire season at once on outlets like Netflix and Amazon, the intimacy and regularity of television characters continues to encourage a sense of familiarity and closeness. The "fairly constant presence" Ellis describes often gives audiences the feeling that characters are their friends, sharing in daily struggles and life events.

Stressing the importance of "realistic" representations, advocates worked with television networks to influence how sexual minorities appeared on screen. Describing the history of 1970s activist organizations, Larry Gross notes, "If the activists were to succeed, they had to encourage positive images and not imply flight against negative stereotypes."[33] However, this approach led to a variety of outcomes that established normative patterns of representation. For example, in calling for "positive," or "sympathetic" images, television representations have often framed LGBT stories as a defense of normality and a right to equality. As Suzanna Walters observed in 2003, in most shows, "gayness is seen through the eyes of confused heterosexuals, struggling with their own actions and feelings" rather than featuring stories about fully realized LGBT characters.[34]

Between the 1960s and the 1990s, Gross writes, the number and scope of LGBT (mostly lesbian and gay) representations increased greatly, on shows across television markets. But, he says, "those appearances are almost invariably in the context of some controversy centering on our right to pursue lives in ways that heterosexuals take for granted."[35] This type of story and character development primarily came from the overall ideology of organizations like the GAA. Michael Bronski says that the GAA (which by the 1970s was the central organization working on television content) had a single-issue approach to politics that "became the template for the contemporary gay rights movement, which works to change, not overthrow the system."[36] In other words, the liberal-oriented GAA sought access to the rights and obligations accorded to heterosexual citizens rather than challenging the foundations of normativity. This approach extended to the organization's work with television networks, and consequently, the majority of representations were limited to depictions of mostly white, male, gender-conforming, and middle-upper class sexual minorities. Especially pronounced were boundaries reinforced between definitions of heterosexuality and homosexuality and a racial hierarchy in which sexual minorities of color were seen as "abnormal" in comparison to white LGBT characters.

Although Montgomery's research shows that "the movement itself was not monolithic, and from time to time there were serious disagreements among the various divisions within it," these representations had an undeniably narrowing effect on the landscape of advocacy politics.[37] The legacy of this type of advocacy is evident in contemporary programming, including in shows like *Modern Family*—particularly in the gendered, raced, classed, and heteronormative aspects of the show discussed earlier. However, there are also crucial differences that go beyond debates about whether these representations are liberating or limiting. The sections that follow reveal the intricacies of how television advocacy works within national LGBT organizations in the era of "convergence culture."[38]

Happily Ever . . . : Advocacy Campaign Endings

In May 2013, several months after the launch of the HRC *Modern Family* fundraiser, the ACLU announced a campaign to see Mitch and Cam get married. Trying to raise support for marriage equality, the nonprofit launched ModernFamilyWedding.com, a petition designed to let the show's producers know that viewers wanted to see Mitch and Cam tie the knot on national television. The ACLU's online petition was designed as a wedding-themed invitation, with figurines of Mitch and Cam arm-in-arm, dressed in tuxedos atop a white wedding cake. In a press release, the ACLU writes:

> We're doing this not just because we love *Modern Family*, but because we are at a watershed moment when the Supreme Court is considering two cases regarding the freedom to marry; when states are passing marriage equality laws with increasing frequency; and a majority of Americans sup-port marriage equality. And the freedom to marry is being advanced in American living rooms as much as in courtrooms.[39]

To indicate support for the initiative, each person had to "RSVP" as if accept-ing a formal invitation to an actual wedding. Next to the RVSP link, the invi-tation reads: "Tell the producers: if Cam & Mitch get hitched, I'll be there!" The ACLU shows a keen understanding of broadcast television's need for live audiences in an era of audience fragmentation and time- and place-shifting practices; in press announcements, the ACLU said they intended to deliver the "guest list" to co-creators and executive producers Steven Levitan and Christopher Lloyd in order to prove the episode would be a ratings hit. In its original announcement about the wedding campaign, the ACLU noted that "TV characters help to shape public consciousness," citing events including Ellen DeGeneres' coming out in 1997 and the long-running and culturally influential series *Will & Grace*: "For many, Mitch and Cam are the gay couple with whom they interact with [*sic*] the most," the ACLU noted. "Inviting 13 million people to Mitch and Cam's wedding will only bring more people into the push for marriage equality."[40]

The ACLU's announcement makes clear that the timing of this campaign was not coincidental: it launched its campaign while the US Supreme Court

AMERICA WANTS TO SEE

CAM & MITCH GET HITCHED

ON MODERN FAMILY

The freedom to marry is spreading. So it's time for America's biggest, red-beard-iest prime-time couple to get hitched in front of millions of American viewers.

That's how we keep fairness moving forward. We just need to convince Modern Family's writers and producers to script a Cam and Mitch wedding by all "RSVPing" to watch it, below.

TELL THE PRODUCERS:
IF CAM & MITCH GET HITCHED, I'LL BE THERE!
By completing this form, I agree to receive occasional emails per the terms of the ACLU's privacy policy.

| Email * | First Name * | Last Name * | Zip Code * | RSVP ≫ |

Figure 2.1. One of the pieces produced by the ACLU's campaign to pressure *Modern Family* producers to marry Mitch and Cam on the show.

was considering two major decisions: whether section 3 of DOMA (the Defense of Marriage Act) was constitutional (it prevented same-sex couples whose marriages were recognized by their home state from receiving federal benefits) and whether backers of California's Proposition 8 (passed by voters in 2008) had standing to defend the measure and contest lower court rulings that Prop 8 violated the state's equal protection clause. In the *Huffington Post*'s report on the ACLU's marriage campaign, Amanda Terkel writes, "Besides just rooting for a new plot development, the ACLU wants Americans to remember what's at stake as the country awaits the Supreme Court's decisions in the Defense of Marriage Act and Proposition 8 cases."[41] In a statement provided to the *Huffington Post*, the ACLU's executive director, Anthony Romero, reiterated this connection: "As we wait for the Supreme Court to rule, we want to keep this issue on the minds and screens of Americans everywhere."[42]

Six weeks after the ACLU launched the *Modern Family* wedding campaign, the Supreme Court ruled in favor of marriage equality, both striking down section 3 of DOMA and upholding the lower courts' rulings on Prop 8, invalidating the measure.[43] These rulings opened the door for a legally recognized same-sex wedding on *Modern Family*, which is set in California.

After the Supreme Court rulings, the ACLU quickly revised its strategy; the announcement for the new campaign reads:

> As Cam from *Modern Family* might say, "Ding dong, Prop 8 is dead." That means same-sex couples are now free to marry in California. And DOMA is dead too, which means those marriages and those of tens of thousands of others will now be recognized by the federal government. And wouldn't getting married in front of 13 million TV viewers be a great way to celebrate? That positive example in front of millions of Americans could help break down barriers to marriage in other states, where the fight for the freedom to marry is now turning. So let's give the show's producers a bit of encouragement. After you watch this fun, short video, share it with everyone you know, so it goes BIG online! (And if you haven't already show the producers how much you want to see this happen by RSVP'ing to the wedding at www.modernfamilywedding.com.)

The day after the Supreme Court rulings, the *Hollywood Reporter* wrote, "20th Century Fox Television confirms . . . that a marriage for gay couple Cameron and Mitchell is being considered for season five storylines."[44] Indeed, *Modern Family* opened its fifth season in the fall of 2013 with the highly anticipated engagement of Mitch and Cam. Writers wove the storyline throughout the entire season. The season culminated in a two-part episode titled "The Wedding, Part I" and "The Wedding, Part II," representing a marked contrast from the extensive measures taken to conceal Ellen DeGeneres' coming-out episode in 1997 on *Ellen*.

When the engagement and then the wedding episodes finally happened, however, the ACLU was nowhere to be found; they didn't publicize the engagement or wedding or make a connection between their advocacy efforts and the show's decision to have the characters marry onscreen. Although including a same-sex wedding has been a common tactic in television programming to save a waning show or to extend its longevity and, as Walters says, "are more often than not the place where heterosexual ambivalence is addressed and homophobia redressed," it was surprising that the ACLU did not take advantage of the fact that part II of "The Wedding" had an audience of 10.45 million in its original US broadcast.[45] Those ratings made it the most viewed episode finale of the five seasons of the show that had aired up to that

point. In an unusual move, ABC announced that on May 12, 2014, in antici-
pation of Mitch and Cam's wedding, the network would pay the $35 fee for
marriage licenses at the City Clerk's office of New York for that day only. The
offer served as a useful marketing tool to advertise the episode in a city unlikely to react negatively, providing a unique chance for the ACLU to bask in
the glory of the network's choice to make a direct connection between legal
marriage equality and a fictional television wedding—the blurring of fiction
and reality that visibility politics relies on.

The ACLU seems to have abandoned an activist strategy that easily lent
itself to an ideal use of visibility politics and the possibility of capitalizing on
donations and signing up new supporters, forgoing an opportunity to increase
the capacity and efficacy of the organization. Ultimately, both *Modern Family*
campaigns fizzled out, disappearing from public view. The ACLU's campaign
completely vanished, leaving only traces of its existence on old websites and
digitally archived news reports.

What does it mean when a well-established organization like the ACLU
seemingly—"seemingly" because there is no available press on it—drops an
activist campaign that offered a plethora of opportunities for fundraising and
self-promotion? The HRC's fundraiser raises a similar question. When the
sweepstakes ended, there was little fanfare about the winner; the HRC's website featured one brief notice about the winner, a woman named Sharon Adler,
"a retired software developer and grandmother from New Hampshire."[46] The
announcement included a photo of her with her daughter, Ferguson, and
Stonestreet. Charlie Joughlin, the HRC's former national press secretary, describes Adler's evening: "Jesse and Eric were incredible hosts, and could not
have been more gracious. Coincidentally, *Glee*'s Jane Lynch [openly lesbian]
was seated at the table next to them and stopped by for a quick chat!"[47]

That both campaigns petered out despite the momentum of the marriage
equality movement lead me to inquire about their production and the larger
patterns they represent. Although case studies are sometimes provocative examples of unique or unusual circumstances, the themes that define these *Modern Family* marriage campaigns arguably reflect broader patterns in the work
of LGBT advocacy organizations amidst the changing landscape of television,
a landscape that sees "digital alternatives . . . as the most important drivers
of economic growth."[48] In the following sections, I analyze interviews I conducted with leaders at the HRC. Their perspectives on contemporary visibility
politics, organizational branding, and activist strategies reveal a great deal
about the inner workings of LGBT advocacy, something typically hidden and
not well understood by those outside the organization.[49]

Inside Advocacy: "She needs those benefits *now*"

Critics have been troubled by myopic visions of advocacy organizations based on narrow conceptions of privacy, equality, and freedom. Lisa Duggan, for example, writes that advocacy organizations that define equality as "access to the institutions of domestic privacy, the 'free' market, and patriotism" represent a "homonormative gay politics."[50] In this argument, advocacy groups seek the inclusion of LGBT people in the dominant paradigm instead of attempting to subvert it. Consequently, Duggan argues, mainstream advocacy initiatives fail to challenge the very systems of power that oppress sexual minorities to begin with, particularly leaving the needs of sexual minorities of color and poor sexual minorities out of organizational priorities.

Thus, by attempting to be included in heteronormative society, mainstream advocacy organizations have created over time a hierarchy of LGBT issues (with white, wealthy gay men at the top) that has marginalized individuals and communities. Urvashi Vaid, the former director of the National Gay and Lesbian Task Force, the oldest LGBT civil rights organization in the nation (now the LGBTQ Task Force), has more generally argued that the top–down approach of most civil rights organizations reflects an investment in a culture of assimilation and normalcy. Vaid writes, "We consciously chose legal reform, political access, visibility, and legitimation over the long-term goals of cultural acceptance, social transformation, understanding, and liberation."[51]

In practical terms, this has meant that organizations, especially during the 1990s and into the 2000s, directed their financial resources toward causes like marriage equality and away from causes like housing and employment non-discrimination, protections that arguably affect more people than marriage does.[52] As the previous chapter argues about cable television executives and market researchers, LGBT advocates are pulled into normative systems of race, class, gender, and sexuality. Each of my interviewees echoed dominant ideas about LGBT identities, television, and politics. For example, in my May 2015 interview with Joe Solmonese about his time as president of the HRC, he articulated an unwavering belief in the power of business to effect social change. Speaking about the "religious freedom" bill then Indiana governor, and future Republican vice president, Mike Pence, signed into law in March 2015, Solmonese said, "Corporations taking a stand makes a bigger difference [than activists] . . . The strongest and most impactful voice was Tim Cook, [the openly gay] CEO of Apple."[53] He expressed these views on free-market politics in response to my comment that many in the LGBT community were angry that groups like the HRC weren't visible in the protests against Pence.

Solmonese went on to explain that what LGBT activists overlooked was that any statement large and successful corporations could make to an anti-gay, pro-business Republican governor would be more powerful and persuasive than LGBT advocacy groups could ever make to Pence, who would have viewed them as purely self-interested. Further, Pence didn't consider their criticisms to be legitimate constituent concerns. Corporations like Apple, as well as Angie's List, which threatened to halt a $40 million expansion in Indianapolis, were "our strongest asset," Solmonese said. Solmonese was no longer working with the HRC at the time we spoke. As he put it in an email: "as a 'former head of something' I really am liberated to say whatever I want!" His comments, although steeped in neoliberal logic, are not those of an LGBT leader regurgitating organizational publicity mantras. Rather, they reveal the depth of Solmonese's surrender to the belief that the free market is the most efficient and effective means of securing long-term social change.

However, another comment Solmonese made shifted my initial interpretation. In our discussion about the HRC's critics, we touched on accusations that the organization had lost sight of the radical politics of early gay liberationists. I expected Solmonese to mount a defense of organizations like the HRC, making a case for the value of measured efforts to work within the system—the ever more intertwined world of politics and business—rather than trying to challenge or take down the system. Surprisingly, he offered a series of examples of projects he had spearheaded at the HRC that focused on small, local changes that affected a wide range of LGBT people. For instance, Solmonese said that he was criticized during his tenure for advocating for and securing "incremental tax benefits on the way to marriage." Colleagues told him, "You should refuse anything else but marriage." He said these arguments incensed him because of the number of people who could benefit from incremental measures. He said, "What about the seventy-eight-year-old lesbian who survives on her partner's Social Security benefits? She needs those benefits *now*."

Although Solmonese would still be defined as an assimilationist—because of his ultimate desire to secure access to the rights and resources accorded to non-gay people by the state—his strategies for that assimilation are marked by an awareness of the need to push for legislation that assists as many, or the most marginalized, LGBT people as possible and not just those in already privileged positions. Solmonese thus sensed that the image from the outside of the organization was drastically different from what he saw on the inside. He was specific about this difference: "I think the general public has a greater appreciation for our work than within the LGBT community." Considering that the critiques of the HRC come primarily from openly LGBT people, this comment was especially poignant, even fitting.

We also talked at length about the role of television in political change. I told him I was writing about the HRC's *Modern Family* marriage campaign and that I was interested in his take on how television programming fits into the organization's political work more generally. Other advocacy leaders I spoke with mentioned the importance of representation to attract hearts and change minds. Solmonese, however, drew a direct link between politically active gay television producers, executives, and showrunners and politically accurate and effective television content. He said that programs like *Modern Family* and *Will & Grace* are made by "people inside of those shows who are connected to the movement." Listing the names of several highly successful white, gay men in the television industry—Alan Ball, Robert Greenblatt, John Wentworth—Solmonese said, "there's a whole bunch of them, all HRC members, involved with the movement." While developing characters and storylines, Solmonese told me, they wanted to use their platform—TV—to present LGBT-themed programs that "helped the cause." "Organizational involvement," he explained, "is what helped them to have the resources to tell the stories in the right way." Solmonese talked extensively about Ryan Murphy's long-standing and intentionally provocative and inclusive work in television, calling it "transformative," with genuine reverence in his voice.[54]

Solmonese's claims about the direct involvement of openly gay television creators and executives run counter to industry rhetoric in the popular press, which reveals a set of contested political relationships. In an interview with *Entertainment Weekly* about the launch of the ACLU's campaign, for example, *Modern Family* co-creator Christopher Lloyd commented, "The ACLU had their heart in right place, but there was a silliness to the whole thing. . . . They [Mitch and Cam] don't exist, you know! They really are fiction."[55] Denying the history of visibility politics and its standing as a common understanding of how culture and politics are related, Lloyd dismisses the campaign, even adding that the production team "didn't want to make an overt political statement" with the characters.

Similarly, when HBO premiered *True Blood* (2008–2014), critics argued that the vampire story was a metaphor for gay rights in the United States; in the show, vampires and humans coexist but vampires are treated as social outcasts. However, Alan Ball, the show's openly gay executive producer, denied this connection. On a press tour for the show, he said, "I really don't look at the vampire as a metaphor for gays. . . . For me, part of the fun of this whole series is that it's about vampires, so it's not that serious."[56] Such de-politicizing by television industry insiders is common, even among openly LGBT media makers. It reflects Hollywood's competing interests, where showrunners like Ball and Lloyd constantly struggle to satisfy drastically different audiences, network executives, and financial imperatives. At the same time, according to Solmonese, many in the television industry quietly maintain an investment in LGBT politics and work hard to incorporate that investment into the stories they create.

Creating the Campaign: "It's all a great idea in theory"

The *Modern Family* marriage campaign illustrates how the HRC utilized the show as a vehicle for raising public awareness, fundraising, and drawing new members to the organization and to the LGBT rights movement more generally. Anastasia Khoo, the marketing director for the HRC who oversaw the *Modern Family* marriage campaign, told me that the fundraiser began as a typical tale of the power of connections but soon developed through a combination of convenience, access, and serendipity. Speaking over the phone while attending a conference in Miami, Florida, she explained: "Jesse Tyler Ferguson was a longtime supporter of the organization and personal friend of our president, Chad Griffin," she said, "so, Chad had approached Jesse about doing it and he said 'great.'"[57] Griffin, hired by the HRC in 2012, has strong ties to Hollywood, which have only fueled criticisms of his and the organization's too-cozy relationship with corporate America and reliance on corporate activism. Even the conservative gay pundit Andrew Sullivan laments that "Griffin, after all, is a product of Hollywood—a former agent and prodigious fundraiser."[58] The American Foundation for Equal Rights (AFER), established in the wake of California's Proposition 8, was started and run by PR consultants, including Griffin, and partially funded by celebrities like Rob Reiner, Dustin Lance Black, and Bruce Cohen.

However, the story quickly veered from the standard scenario. When Khoo said, in her interview with me, that Griffin approached Ferguson "about doing it," she did not mean conducting a *Modern Family* fundraiser. Rather, she and her marketing team were looking for a celebrity to agree to be part of a sweepstakes-style fundraiser. Khoo described the idea as coming "on the heels of the Obama campaign doing a lot of good tactical fundraising events, . . . saying, 'We'll fly you to DC or Chicago and meet Michelle or see Barack,' and so that at the time . . . there were a lot of those contests happening and we had always wanted to do this with a celebrity but couldn't really find the right one." While Griffin's friendship with Ferguson undeniably offered a convenient opportunity for the sweepstakes, it did not inspire or even initiate the event that focused on *Modern Family* itself. Moreover, the hype about *Modern Family*'s central role in shifting public opinion as well as its success and broad appeal was not the basis for the fundraiser. As I learned more about how the HRC's marketing team put together the fundraiser, it became clear that this was not the preplanned and controlled event that I had imagined.

Eric Stonestreet's involvement was as unplanned as was Jesse Tyler Ferguson's. According to Khoo, Stonestreet agreed to participate because he is "really good friends" with Ferguson. She told me that when Griffin asked Ferguson to help with a fundraiser, he happily accepted, and added, "I'd love to have my costar join us as well." Celebrity events like these rarely fall into place so easily; Khoo said, "It's sort of rare in the celebrity world to have someone be all in and willing to do whatever you ask."

Similarly, when I asked her how the HRC had managed to use the show's set to film the fundraiser—a crucial factor in drawing fans of the show accustomed to seeing Mitch and Cam side-by-side, bantering back and forth—Khoo replied, "It was born of their schedule." Filming on the set would seem essential to creating an effective fundraiser aimed at *Modern Family* fans and supporters of LGBT equality, yet Khoo called it "a happy accident." The show was filming at the time the HRC was producing the sweepstakes: "The producers had generously offered the set so that we could just use it." She noted how helpful this was, especially considering that the set was already lit and staffed with a professional crew. Without the set, the HRC would have needed to scout and secure a location, get the actors to that location, arrange for a crew to film it, and pay for all the expenses that come with such a shoot.

When I asked Khoo about the fundraiser's script, which captured Mitch and Cam's characters individually and the dynamic between them, Khoo laughed and thanked me. She laughed, she said, because "they banter like that in real life." Given that television writing is an art form, though, undertaken in "writers' rooms" where teams of professionals work together on a script, I still wanted to know about the process of writing the script (even though some of it was ad-libbed, according to Khoo).[59] Because the fundraiser had happened three years earlier, Khoo said, her memory was hazy on some of the details: "The script, if I recall correctly . . . it was a combination of us having input . . . we wrote a draft and then shared it with the writers and producers on the show and then certainly their agents and the talent themselves to make sure they were comfortable with it." My sense was that because I had spoken highly of the script, Khoo wanted to take a certain amount of credit for it, perhaps more than the HRC deserved. What is most significant in all of this was the ease with which the script came together to fit the themes of the HRC's fundraising efforts; it embodied the public perception of television advocacy as opposed to its actual operations.

Although the production process for this fundraiser went so smoothly, the

HRC has not completed others like it. Khoo sighed, "No, we haven't." She attributed this in part to the fact that this was a one-off event and to the organization's no longer having "the right sort of person or timing . . . so not for lack of wanting." Another reason involves the behind-the-scenes work such an endeavor requires. She discussed the pressures and the significant amount of labor involved in working with celebrities. She told me that she had been unprepared for the amount of time it takes to "figure out a day that works for them, making sure they're really comfortable with the process and with bringing them along on it, answering any questions they may have."

Extensive legal issues further complicate a sweepstakes dinner like this one. Khoo explained:

> For us, on our side, it's actually kind of intense to pull off something like this. . . . It's all a great idea in theory, but the pieces that you have to put together are making sure that it all runs from a legal perspective, because there's these weird state-by-state gambling issues and it's much more complicated from a legal perspective than I had ever thought and so [I] had to do a lot of due diligence so that the winner wouldn't be compensated in any way or all of these things that you have to work out with the lawyers, which is intense.

Beyond the legal issues, she said, "When you pick the winner [you have to] do a little research about them, making sure they're not some creepy mass murderer, you just never know. When you work with high-caliber and high-profile individuals, you want to make sure that it's a positive experience for everyone and is not putting them in an uncomfortable situation and so that all takes time to do."

For many reasons, then, this type of advocacy work is difficult to successfully execute, even for an organization with significant financial and human resources. The remainder of my conversation with Khoo helped me to see this fundraiser as part of a larger effort to draw new members to the HRC and to rebrand the organization for millennial voters.

Rebranding Advocacy for the Twenty-First Century: "Relevant and resonant"

I asked Khoo who the HRC had had in mind as an audience for the *Modern Family* sweepstakes, especially because the video appeared only on the HRC's website, on YouTube, and on social media sites like Facebook. She replied that given the mainstream crossover appeal of the show, "we were looking for individuals both who may support the issues but that also really love the show and likely had no connection with the organization that would be like 'yeah, I would like to meet them and have that opportunity.'" Drawing on the popularity of the show and on the data showing increasing support for marriage equality among American voters—and younger voters in particular—this fundraiser was about reaching potentially new supporters and donors. These were *Modern Family* viewers who, in Khoo's words, "might not know much about the issue or may not be ready to sign a petition or something like that, but . . . this is a nice entry point for building a relationship with them and the organization."

My conversation with Khoo about the target audience for the fundraiser was at its core about branding, an ever more pervasive strategy for competing in both media and marketing; the HRC utilized *Modern Family* in much the same way that cable television networks "multicast" to several groups of audiences to build and reinvent brands, or what Michael Curtin calls "matrix media."[60] This example is part of a broader pattern in which advocacy organizations use individual television programs to define their brands for new groups of citizens.

Unlike the HRC's *Modern Family* sweepstakes, the ACLU's campaign was much more explicit about its efforts to rebrand for a new demographic—a younger, more technologically engaged, and savvy one. Their *Modern Family* campaign existed exclusively online, launched as part of the ACLU Action Center, which focuses on Internet-based advocacy, making use of social media and other online outlets popular with younger voters.

In an opinion piece for the *New York Times*, "'I Do' and the ACLU," Frank Bruni describes the organization's brand as "somewhat musty" and sees the *Modern Family* campaign as a transparent effort to attract new members (read: donors). Bruni writes, "A vital and storied player in this country's political life and intellectual debate over many decades now, the ACLU needs to shore up its relevance, and that's acknowledged by its decision simultaneously to focus on a bit of mainstream culture; to underscore the ACLU's ongoing involvement in a political issue (marriage equality) with special appeal to voters under 40; and to ally itself with social-media platforms."[61] Bruni quotes ACLU executive director Anthony Romero, whom he interviewed for the story: "We've got to find new ways of being relevant and resonant with a new generation. . . . The idea of getting direct mail in a third-rate bulk-reply envelope and sending in a check is not going to work for this generation. In twenty years, that business model goes the way of the horse-drawn carriage."

When news outlets announced the ACLU's campaign, however, it was clear many readers were unaware of the organization's involvement in LGBT rights over time. In comments posted online, some expressed shock and public disapproval that the organization would spend any of its time or resources promoting politics through a television sitcom. Their reactions point to the belief that the ACLU works exclusively on "direct" civil liberty issues, such as litigation and lobbying, and that media advocacy falls outside its purview. By extension, many of these reactions make a judgment about using television as a vehicle for addressing a civil rights issue like marriage equality; they seem to view this as an illegitimate or inappropriate way to create social change.

Yet the ACLU has a long history of supporting LGBT media advocacy in addition to working on direct civil liberties issues through lobbying and litigation. Leigh Ann Wheeler writes, "The ACLU's first interventions on behalf of homosexuals often involved neither the courts nor the law. Instead, they counseled individual victims of discrimination, and chastised media outlets that rejected advertisements submitted by homophile organizations."[62] Moreover, despite debates during the 1950s and 1960s among ACLU leaders about the troubling divide between public and private, the organization nonetheless took a strong stance on what, at the time, were called "homosexual rights." Wheeler notes, "by January 1966, *Newsweek* identified the ACLU as the only group 'apart from the homophile organizations' that actively opposed laws against homosexual acts."[63] The organization's long and steady engagement with the protection of the civil rights of sexual minorities, including making use of the media in challenging discrimination, puts the *Modern Family* campaign within its historical record but also embodies a new way of reaching out to younger voters as demographics shift.

In its revised statement following the Supreme Court's 2013 decision—quoted earlier—which uses phrases such as "Ding dong, Prop 8 is dead" and that emphasizes the "positive example" Mitch and Cam's on-screen marriage would set, the ACLU draws on stereotypes of gay men's love for Judy Garland and *The Wizard of Oz* (1939, dir. Fleming), reiterates an unquestioned belief in the power of visibility politics, and reinforces the meaningfulness of television ratings in the broader culture. When Romero discussed the *Modern Family* campaign, he said, "The ACLU has been working since 1936 to guarantee the rights of lesbian and gay people, and we see sending Cam and Mitch down the aisle before 13 million American viewers as the perfect next step."[64] It would be easy to interpret this statement as either a sign of an advocacy organization's lack of knowledge about the realities of television audiences today (i.e., naïveté), or a rhetorical technique used simply to capitalize on the success of the show in a time when two major decisions were before the Supreme Court (i.e., strategic denial). However, I understand it as exploiting television programming as it has existed both historically and in the twenty-first century.

Advocates use television's intrinsically multiplatform, convergent qualities to rebrand organizations and find a wider base of donors, and also take advantage of broadcast ratings, which although lower than those earned in the past, represent a large swath of the population. In political terms *Modern Family*'s average weekly audience of "13 million viewers," according to the ACLU, matters a lot. Political scientists and communication scholars who study campaign advertising note that the total expenditures on direct-targeting activities such as mailings and phone calls represent only a small fraction of what is spent on television advertising. As political campaigns become more and more expensive to run (thanks in large part to the era of super PACs and the rolling back of campaign finance reforms), spending on broadcast television advertising has increased in conjunction with rising costs.

In addition to targeting young, tech-savvy citizens, media advocates focus on broadcast programs because those audiences tend to correlate to desired voter groups. In October 2014, prior to midterm elections, the *Washington Post* reported that "live television viewing was down 13 percent for all age groups with the exception of viewers 55 and older, who are steadily watching their shows at their scheduled broadcast times, according to Nielsen."[65] While television producers and advertisers try to impress shrinking and fickle audiences, broadcast television is still the largest medium to reach voters and it remains politically valuable.

Romero's comment about being "relevant and resonant with a new generation," however, refers not only to the aging membership of the ACLU, but also to a bigger question facing LGBT advocates across the nation: what's next? In other words, with marriage rights secured for same-sex couples in Supreme Court decisions handed down in 2013 and 2015, how do organizations like the HRC and the ACLU convey the importance and urgency of the next set of battles facing LGBT citizens? Joe Solmonese, whom I spoke with two months before the Supreme Court's 2015 ruling, anticipated that the Court's decision would mean a "massive rebooting of the movement." He said, "As you consider what's next, you also have to consider this inaccurate sense that I think a lot of people are going to have that the work will be done at the end of June." From an advocacy perspective, he said, the road ahead would be difficult for several reasons; first, over the years, attorneys and activists established organizations exclusively dedicated to achieving marriage equality. "What happens to those organizations now? The staff that work for them? The donors who fund them?" Second, the kinds of goals that potentially lie ahead—including legislative protections in housing, accommodations, and employment for both sexual orientation and gender identity at the national and international levels—require different types of engagement. Solmonese described this type of advocacy as "asking more people for less [money]."

Marriage equality was a highly marketable goal—one that drew wealthy supporters and deeply moving publicity campaigns, culminating in the Twitter hashtag "#LoveWins." Hollis Griffin writes, "These nine characters operate as an abbreviation that invokes more intimacies than it can contain, a feat it accomplishes by charting a narrative in which the politics of sexuality get reduced to a binary between those who are 'for' this thing called 'love' and those who are 'against' it."[66] The new goals are less glamorous than and more grounded in daily life. Where you live and work don't have the same appeal as idyllic and magical weddings. The question, Solmonese said, will be "how do you get these things to matter to other people?" In this context, LGBT nonprofits and their leaders are rebranding their work for a different type of advocacy, in which the multiplatform television industry, dominated by viewer choice and control, is a principal player.

For both the HRC and the ACLU—in a state of flux as their agendas began to shift dramatically in response to marriage equality and to the Trump administration's challenges to LGBT rights—the campaigns demonstrate that advocacy organizations increasingly see scripted television as a tool of change.

Television Advocacy in a New Era

The proliferation of television channels and digital media outlets has created a significant shift in the industry, one that is largely the result of the deregulation of the media industries; between the mid-1980s and early 2000s, 90 percent of television regulation was done away with. One of the most significant of these deregulatory moves was the Telecommunications Act of 1996. As the first significant reform of the Communications Act of 1934, it marked a dramatic shift in the industry as a whole. Jennifer Holt notes that it was also the "last piece of legislation necessary to solidify the blueprint for new millennium entertainment empires."[67] As critics have observed, when President Bill Clinton signed it into law on February 8, 1996, the press barely paid attention, yet its provisions allowed for drastic changes to the rules of media ownership, facilitating a culture of "merger mania."[68] Holt explains, "The net effect of the Telecommunications Act in terms of media ownership was that one company could now own significantly more broadcast stations than ever before, and cable systems were legally permitted to combine with broadcast networks and phone companies."[69] In this climate, media corporations dramatically increased their in-house profits and began to produce a variety of media content, distributing and cross-promoting it across company holdings while localism and minority ownership dwindled.

Although the rise of digital media, especially the Internet, engendered a plethora of claims that television was in a death spiral, the results of digitization reflect a different reality. Critics often claim that twenty-first-century media in all their forms have never been better, and scholars document the extent to which television has remarkably reinvented itself despite declining audience numbers and panic among advertisers, who for decades have relied on this platform to reach mass audiences with a single thirty-second commercial. Describing the myriad ways television networks have changed with technology, audiences, culture, and marketers, Jennifer Gillan writes about what she terms "must-click TV," a model that "emphasizes continual circulation of the interconnected parts of a TV franchise in a network's (and media conglomerate's) revenue stream."[70]

The resulting customization of television viewing, advertising, and audiences has direct implications for advocacy. As John Caldwell notes, "Conglomerate profitability works in part by critically theorizing the responsiveness and value of fragmenting (and thus individuated) tastes."[71] When expanding viewers' choice and control over what programming they watch and when they watch it, the television and marketing industries made use of social identities and lifestyle categories as the basis for the fragmentation and individualization Caldwell discusses. Joseph Turow argues that in the process of creating niche markets for smaller demographics, marketers and media makers exploited what he describes as "splits in the social fabric [of the nation]," in order to construct viable audience segments.[72]

Because of the continuing and increasing belief in the power of television visibility, these changes intensified calls for the crafting of television programming that could serve as both a mirror, reflecting US culture, and a window onto a part of the world that a viewer might not experience in their own lived reality, but one that might influence their perspectives about people and cultures different from their own. The personalization that accompanies television content, characters, and commercials arguably increases viewers' identification with their choices (even if, as Turow says, consumers are not in fact captains of their own ships, but rather marketers are, creating a misleading "rhetoric of consumer power").[73] In short, the proliferation of channels means that television audiences have more chances than ever to see themselves on the screen, and as a result, I contend, there is more pressure, not less, to increase visibility of sexual minorities, especially "realistic" LGBT characters.

The Identity Paradox in Advocacy

Television advocates' effort to increase the number of "realistic" images of LGBT people, especially within scripted programming, underscores a paradox about identity. On one hand, politics and popular culture promote a vision of a post-gay—even a post-identitarian—society; the parameters of "realistic"—gender-conforming, often white and middle-class, already out, marriage-seeking characters—align fully with post-gay language. I witnessed this over the two years I served on GLAAD's Television Jury in Los Angeles. Jury members regularly gave high marks to characters whose LGBT identity was unremarkable. Jurors, many of whom worked in the television industry themselves, praised stories that didn't revolve around a character's coming out or that did not make the narrative in any way about that character's sexual orientation, reflecting the ideal vision of a post-gay world where one's sexuality is not necessarily salient to the storyline.

These observations reflected the recognition that television representations were diverging from a well-established pattern; over the previous several decades, when sexual minorities appeared in television programs, the storylines tended to focus exclusively on their sexuality, as described earlier in this chapter.[74] From this historical perspective, GLAAD TV jurors understood that a shift was afoot, one worthy of acknowledgment. However, my fellow jurors overlooked the disconnection between post-gay representations and the real-life experiences of LGBT Americans. Things have clearly improved for many people who identify as LGBT, as both anecdotal and statistical evidence attests. And yet, even though such individuals have secured the legal rights to marry and enter the military, their sexual identity remains relevant to their ability to secure employment, housing, and public accommodations; to feel physically safe in the United States; and even simply to not be stared at when walking down the street.

Among criticisms of the idealization of post-gay culture is that when identity no longer plays a role in someone's sense of self or others' knowledge about that person, differences can be flattened out and become meaningless. As I discuss in the next chapter, about diversity, difference has played a central role in the American national imaginary since the country's founding and has also been at the core of debates about rights for social minorities.

One the other hand, the HRC's and the ACLU's uses of *Modern Family* focus precisely on the gay identity of the characters and their televised wedding in order to fight for political engagement (pun intended) and even literal political change. It is the sexual orientation of both characters that forms the foundation for the campaign and its political battle. In this context, it is not surprising that *Modern Family* has been mobilized as a mechanism of marriage advocacy efforts;[75] after all, the show has been credited with reviving the American sitcom, proving broadcast television still has life in it, and helping to change public opinion in favor of marriage rights through its homonormative narratives. Much like *Ellen* in the 1990s and *Brothers and Sisters* (ABC, 2006–2011) in the 2000s, *Modern Family* possesses a tenderhearted sensibility that makes it an ideal vehicle for starting conversations.

However, use of this show as a vehicle of advocacy work is inconsistent with a post-gay stance on social progress. Put another way, media advocacy organizations proactively promote an agenda that potentially renders those organizations irrelevant and unnecessary. In turn, this agenda challenges the basis of the contemporary rights movement for sexual minorities; if sexual identity is a nonissue then there is no need for identity-based organizations. I raise this paradox because it demonstrates that both marriage campaigns discussed in this chapter embody a constitutive and ongoing conflict between how we understand and experience sexual identity and the role it plays in cultural politics.

Conclusion

The blending of politics and scripted television is driven by demands for younger members and a willingness to experiment with strategies of social change. While I understand both sides of the debate about assimilation and liberation, I also believe it is precisely this polarity that limits the conversation. In order to move the conversation forward—past pragmatism and idealism—and think about what is at stake in living in a global neoliberal culture, it is critical to examine influential structures and institutions. As sexual politics shift so do LGBT advocacy philosophies and tactics. Looking behind the scenes, pulling back the curtain, reveals a set of intersecting, opposing, and overlapping needs, goals, and outcomes.

Mainstream LGBT advocacy understands television as a meaningful—even essential—tool to effect change. This is especially true for modern broadcast programming because of its normative representations and because it provides a way to connect with numerous voter demographics. In the fragmented and segmented media marketplace, where audience attention is a prized possession, organizations like the HRC and the ACLU use television shows—rather, for example, than films—to secure their place in the changing sociopolitical landscape. Although there is much debate about the definition and role of television in everyday life as technologies and media platforms change, advocacy leaders see it as a promising way to engage new voters and rebrand organizations' identities.[76]

I continue to explore these themes in the next chapter, within the context of "diversity." Whether in television production, representation, or promotion, it is a term that is bandied about as if it's going out of style. As with my study of "advocacy" and "visibility" before it, the next chapter proposes a way of looking at mainstream circuits of production that refuses an impasse between true equality and "virtual equality."[77] Rather, looking at how "diversity" operates in the contemporary television industry acknowledges the tenuousness of these oppositions. In particular, the work of television consultants — public relations executives, marketers, and leaders from GLAAD — introduces forces of variance and ambivalence that shape industrial diversity on a daily basis. Like advocacy, the borders of diversity are malleable and uneven.

CHAPTER 3

Diversity: Under-the-Radar Activism and the Crafting of Sexual Identities

Dev: They just don't want two Indians starring in a sitcom.

Ravi: But why?

Dev: Look man, Indians just aren't at that level yet! Yeah, there's more Indians popping up every now and then but we're just set decoration, we're not doin' the main stuff. We're not fucking girls and all that stuff. We're just not there yet. There can be one but there can't be two. Black people just got the "there could be two status." Even then though, there can't be three 'cause then it's like a black show or a black movie. Indians, Asians, gays, there can be one but there can't be two.

Ravi: But, there's two gay dudes in *Will & Grace*.

Dev: No, just Sean Hayes. Jack.

Ravi: No, there's two gay dudes in that show.

Dev: Who?

Ravi: Will! The lead dude. The show's about him, he's gay!

Dev: Really? Guess I never saw the show. Wow, that was in the '90s, props to the *Will & Grace* team.

Ravi: Two gay dudes on *Modern Family*.

Dev: Alright, I get it, there can be two gays. All right. Progress exists, shout out to gays.

Watching this scene in Netflix's original series *Master of None* (2015–), I laughed out loud, appreciative of the show's moment of self-reflection. In one rare and beautifully succinct exchange between two friends who are also aspiring Indian American actors in New York City, the show cuts to the heart of how much identity still matters on TV. Aware of how their Indian heritage affects their ability to land roles on US television, Dev (Aziz Ansari) and Ravi (Ravi Patel) critique television's version of diversity: its embrace of racial and sexual minorities in ways that keep those identities separate and constrained, if not tokenized, noting that the most "progress" has been made in incorporating LGBT characters, although mostly in incorporating "respectable" (read: normative) gay characters.[1]

A prized aesthetic and business ideal, "diversity" has become the watchword of the day among corporations and nonprofit advocacy organizations. As Peter Wood puts it, "*Diversity* is big. It's everywhere."[2] It is deeply embedded in systems of evaluation, especially when it comes to television programming, which generates, measures, and leverages LGBT diversity in various ways, presenting it as both an aspirational and an admirable quality. Numerous annual reports evaluate the medium for its diversity in programmatic representation. "Diverse" television representations are often heralded by LGBT advocacy organizations and by LGBT social movement leaders, and sometimes used as mechanisms for political change (as I discuss in the previous chapter). In turn, media companies use these reports as positive publicity for their content and work culture, banking on a return on their investment through attracting more diverse audiences. Finally, the popular press celebrates television's showcasing of sexual and gender minorities as a mark of social progress.

This industry-wide engagement with diversity offers a moment to assess how openly lesbian and gay industry workers conceive of diversity and how those conceptions are embedded in their daily work.[3] Rather than reviewing or critiquing the nature of representational diversity (what is seen on television), or debating the role of diversity in LGBT social movements, this chapter shows that diversity has both public and private definitions, depending on the stakeholder, the activist, and the cause. A behind-the-scenes view of television diversity creates a cross-sectional map that reveals a variety of hybrid, personal, and even subversive practices within the television industry. Notably, these practices are strategically and purposefully hidden from public view, constituting what I call "under-the-radar activism." As a result, this chapter reveals the need for a more robust definition of diversity when it comes to both LGBT activism and cultural workers.

Each interviewee in this chapter offers a different perspective on the production of LGBT television diversity. None of them works directly in television production or is listed on the credits of television programs. Rather, they are workers who influence programming choices and industry policies via a variety of roles, including advocacy, public relations, and corporate social responsibility (CSR). With this broad view, I address why it is important to investigate the notion of diversity, given fraught relations and how the term is variously deployed across issues of representation, industry policy, employment practices, corporate values, and brand identity in ways that do not necessarily follow clear patterns.

By showing how different cultural workers conceive of diversity and how they deploy it in their work, this chapter reveals how opportunities for intervention emerge and how activism and corporate media come together in unexpected ways. In this chapter I argue for "diversity as craft"—labor that is instrumental to production but that is not acknowledged as such by the industry because the work goes uncredited and there is no guild to which industry "diversifiers" can belong. This brings attention to nontraditional industry professionals; demonstrates how the interventions of these cultural workers produce forms of diversity different from those evident on the level of representational content (especially because their work is not immediately or necessarily ever visible to the viewing public); and broadens the meaning of "diversity" itself, a "diversifying of diversity" of sorts, to include work that is politically, culturally, and economically sophisticated.

The Public Face of Diversity

When comedian and late-night talk show host Jimmy Kimmel hosted the 2016 Emmy Awards, he used his opening monologue to boast: "There is more diversity than ever before. This year's nominees are the most diverse ever." Mocking the Hollywood self-promotion machine, Kimmel continued, "Here in Hollywood, the only thing we value more than diversity is congratulating ourselves on how much we value diversity." There is truth to Kimmel's joke; the industry seems to take every opportunity to flaunt its diverse representations and corporate policies in what I would describe as the "public" face of television diversity.

The purported need for visible diversity is a concern of scholars and activists who fear the implications of a culture that aspires to a narrow set of norms: white, male, middle-class, gender-conforming, marriage-seeking, etc. Put another way, rather than "diversity" implying respect for true *difference*, critics describe it as akin to window dressing that time and again reinforces the ways that sexual minorities are the *same* as their normative, heterosexual counterparts on television. Consider, for example, Lucas Hilderbrand's critique of *Glee* (Fox, 2009–2015), which was hailed as one of the most diverse shows in broadcast television history: "One of the recurring problems with the show's 'progress' toward tolerance . . . is that in making reductive equivalences between different kinds of marginalized experiences, it flattens out the complexity of difference."[4] In this and numerous other critiques, diversity amounts to what might be called "enlightened diversity." Here I am drawing on Susan Douglas's concept of "enlightened sexism" and Sut Jhally and Justin Lewis's term "enlightened racism."[5] In both definitions, "enlightened" refers to the notion that US culture, television included, presents an outward appearance of overcoming bias and discrimination—achieving equality—but underneath that superficial coating lie ever-present and pernicious systems of inequality.[6]

Television "diversity" also bears "little resemblance to the facts of American life," as Wood writes.[7] Both documentation and anecdotes about workplace and housing discrimination and statistics about youth bullying, sexual assault, suicide, and transgender murder rates prove that true LGBT diversity is hardly supported, accepted, or encouraged. "Enlightened diversity" largely overlooks these inequalities in favor of proclaiming a post-identitarian society, including one that is post-gay, wherein the category of sexuality is no longer central to a person's self-definition or relevant to one's experiences or opportunities for upward mobility in the United States. This "flattened" diversity, to borrow from Hilderbrand, is intimately bound up with post-gay ideologies because both reject the differences inherent in individual identity categories. "Rather than forging collective identity on the basis of 'us versus them,'" write Mary Bernstein and Verta Taylor, "postgay politics emphasizes perceived similarities to the majority, framed as 'us and them,' muting differences and suppressing what is distinctive about gay identity."[8]

As I describe in the previous two chapters, I regularly encountered the push for and the privileging of a post-gay US culture in my research for this project. Whether featured in news reports or political rhetoric, on television shows, in my university classrooms, or in the GLAAD jury room in Los Angeles, the notion that categories of sexual identity no longer matter permeates popular culture and politics. As a nation, the United States rhetorically inhabits a post-gay moment.

In the run-up to the 2016 elections, a newspaper in the staunchly conservative state of Kentucky ran a story titled, "Kentucky Has a Gay Senate Candidate—Does Anybody Care?" The article's lede makes no bones about its central argument: "America may be closer to a post-gay state of politics than most realize."[9] This report echoed earlier political news reports including one from the 2014 midterm elections, in which reporters discussed the potential election of Maine's Mike Michaud, who at the time would have "become the country's first openly gay governor" (ultimately, he lost to Republican Paul LePage).[10] The headline "America's First Post-Gay Governor" focuses on the fact that Michaud was indeed openly gay but was "someone whose sexual orientation is truly a non-issue in the campaign."[11]

A year earlier, the fall television season had seen the debut of a new broadcast sitcom, *Sean Saves the World* (NBC, 2013–2014), starring Sean Hayes, who played the effeminate gay character Jack on *Will & Grace*, and who himself came out as gay in 2010 after years of refusing to discuss his sexuality publicly. During a promotional interview for *Sean Saves the World* with the Television Critics Association (TCA), creator Victor Fresco told the audience, "Without *Will & Grace*, we would not be here right now, . . . but I think of this as a post-gay show where there is a gay man at the center but it's not about his being gay." [12] According to one reporter who attended the TCA event, "Indeed, for his part, Hayes is proud of the fact that primetime has now progressed to the point where a gay character's 'gayness' can be incidental. 'It's an afterthought just like any other character or minority now,' he emphasized, 'which is how it should be. It's even sad that it's a question, really.'" [13]

The supposed irrelevance of sexual identity to political candidates and lesbian and gay television characters—this post-gay rhetoric—is part of the push for assimilation, for arguing that lesbians and gays are more similar to than different from heterosexuals. [14] Although this strategy is not recent and has been successful in securing legal rights for sexual minorities, it has come under fire for promoting what Amin Ghaziani describes as "the acceptance of a segment of gays and lesbians who are gender conforming, middle class, upwardly mobile—in other words, those best able to take advantage of the benefits of assimilation and the valorization of a particular type of diversity." [15] This is a fair critique to level at those advocates, educators, journalists, politicians, and media makers who continually and unproblematically celebrate the limited diversity that comes with post-gay life. However, such criticisms account only for the parameters of diversity provided by promotions, representations, and news reports.

In contrast, the view from inside the television industry reveals a drastically different form of diversity, one that does understand the impetus for a post-gay culture but is simultaneously based on a conscious understanding of the politics of identity. What emerged from the interviews I conducted was a sense of the intentionality behind diversity-oriented work. I witnessed a pattern of strategic essentialism that challenges both the ubiquity of "enlightened diversity" and the notion that those working in television seek to produce, make visible, and reinforce post-gay representations.

Don't Come Out! The Uses of Identity Politics in a Post-Gay Era

When black comic Wanda Sykes came out as lesbian in 2008, fans, critics, and others celebrities claimed that she had changed for the better. On an episode of the *Oprah Winfrey Show*, Oprah told Sykes that since coming out she is "prettier and funnier. . . . I think that's what freedom does." Sykes agrees: in an interview with *TV Guide Magazine*, writer Lisa Bernhard asks her, "How has your career changed since you announced you married a woman?" Sykes responds, "If anything, it has helped my career, because creatively I don't have anything to dance around or be not so forthcoming with. Now it's just out there. I'm pretty much free to say whatever I want to say, and act the way I want to act. It's totally been liberating."[16] Sykes and Winfrey echo the language of coming out that has been used for decades and is familiar to those who realize they are not heterosexual. It echoes the prevailing logic about LGBT celebrities—that coming out is personally liberating—and also does the powerful work of changing public opinions of sexuality, a necessary element for social and political progress to occur. Kevin G. Barnhurst notes, "For individuals, coming out moves the self from self-consciousness to self-lessness, from duplicity to candor, and from isolation to inclusion."[17] Popular culture reflects these shifts whenever celebrities come out, especially after years in the closet, emphasizing the enormity of the differences of living "in the closet" versus being "out." As Lynne Joyrich writes, "Within our culture's construction of knowledge, sexuality is considered something 'inside' of each subject—permanent yet invisible unless brought to light, and thus calls to make it visible have been central in LGBTQ politics."[18]

In the twenty-first century, lesbian and gay (and increasingly transgender) celebrities, by coming out, have garnered power, respect, and loyalty from fans, cultural critics, and the popular press. National organizations like the HRC and GLAAD feature famous LGBT personalities during fundraisers and in promotional materials. LGBT publications such as the *Advocate*, the oldest and largest LGBT publication in the country, and the gay men's entertainment magazine *Out* annually assess the cultural significance of public figures, ranking them on the basis of wealth, political clout, and pop-culture resonance. Of *Out*'s annual "Power 50" list of the "most powerful gay men and women in America," its editors write, "Whether they're raking in millions, advancing the gay rights movement, entertaining us with snarky celebrity gossip, or selling us $2,000 cashmere sweaters, we're confident that these VIPs have exerted considerable sway over how we think, look, and act."[19] Conflating the work of activists, politicians, comedians, and advertisers, such publications reveal that whether or not celebrities are politically engaged, being out and famous allows them to be held up as icons and role models.

Ellen DeGeneres commented pointedly on this idea in her 2003 stand-up comedy special *Here and Now* (HBO). She opens the show with a rather post-gay joke about the fact that the audience all has one thing in common: "We're all gay." After teasing the audience for likely having "tendencies" even if they aren't gay, she says, "No, that's my one obligatory gay reference. I have to say something gay otherwise some people might leave here tonight going, 'She didn't do anything gay, she's not our leader. What happened to our leader?'" DeGeneres's observation reflects the many ways in which modern popular media—especially the overexposed social media culture—unconditionally celebrate extreme publicity, which ultimately is an inadequate metric on which to assess LGBT political gains, either representationally or otherwise.

The impetus for LGBT celebrities to come out, or to be outed, stems from associations with the closet as a place of shame and with individualism's stress on being "honest" with oneself and others about "who you are," as well as the premise of identity politics, which is that civil rights for LGBT people will come only from being out and proud about one's identity. It also comes from the binaries created between homosexual and heterosexual, which Eve Kosofsky Sedgwick describes as having "predictably varied and acute implications and consequences."[20] The closet remains a central metaphor for identity development among LGBT people, and it has been taken on by other stigmatized groups, such as the Mormon fundamentalists who are featured in shows such as *Sister Wives* (TLC, 2010-) and *My Five Wives* (TLC, 2013-) as well as undocumented immigrant youth in the United States.

For celebrities, the history of coming out in Hollywood is not particularly glamorous or appealing; careers have been ruined, and reputations smeared. Yet the push to be one's "authentic self" (or the threat of being outed as inauthentic) has been profoundly compelling for celebrities, especially since DeGeneres's 1997 coming out and subsequent career rise via her daytime talk show.

Celebrities rarely come out on their own, however. For decades, publicists have worked behind the scenes honing the craft of helping celebrities come out in ways that are genuine to who they are but also benefit their careers. My interview with veteran celebrity publicist Howard Bragman challenged the received wisdom about the nature of sexuality and gender in US culture, especially with respect to the limitations of the closet/coming-out paradigm as well as popular culture's insistence on creating a "post-identity" world.

Over a career that spans more than thirty years, Bragman has carved out a space for himself as an expert in the public coming out process. He calls it "taking someone out" because of the ways he designs each client's story for maximum positive public response and financial benefit. The stories Bragman told me in my interview with him painted sexuality as a deeply contested terrain. He detailed specific clients and the strategic moves he and his firm, Fifteen Minutes, make to guide a famous person through the mediated coming out experience. Some of these tactics — like asking someone to write a memoir to be promoted in concert with the pronouncement of their sexual orientation — reinforced my cynicism about the supposed "authenticity" of celebrity coming out stories, although most of what Bragman told me did not.

The examples from my interview with Bragman cannot be considered television celebrities per se, but are rather athletes, singers, and public personalities. I chose to use them as case studies, however, for several reasons. First, they highlight the multiplatform nature of twenty-first-century media, which requires celebrities to engage across as many media forms as possible for maximum exposure, brand building, and profit potential. Within media convergence, celebrity culture meets demands for the type of synergy required in the consolidated landscape of the digital age. In other words, because "synergy is the promotion and sale of a product (and all its versions) throughout the various subsidiaries of a media conglomerate, e.g., films, soundtracks or video games," celebrities coming out — and their publicists — can make use of this cross-platform environment to increase visibility and speak to targeted audiences.[21] As a result, the production of celebrity has become more visible to the public, evolving into an aspect of that culture itself and undermining the notion of a clear divide between public and private. In addition, regardless of a celebrity's chosen medium, television is integral to the public coming out process. Whether a publicist like Bragman facilitates an exclusive interview with a television journalist or an entertainment television news show reports on a celebrity's coming out, the medium, in large part, mediates and constructs this event.

Meeting Bragman, I immediately understood why he is "PR's gay guru."[22] He welcomed me into his office with warmth, charm, and humor. Given that celebrities call him when they are publicly coming out (sometimes by choice, and sometimes under the threat of being outed), this was the ideal mix of qualities to put someone at ease.[23] Much like the set of a daytime talk show, built for warmth and intimacy to maximize the confessions and admissions that often take place, Bragman's office is comfortable and large but not ostentatious, seemingly designed to create the feeling that clients, who pay large sums of money for his public relations expertise, are in professional but comforting hands. During our conversation, Bragman described himself as "publicist, rabbi, shrink," a list of roles that his office matched.

Bragman's work has become increasingly important with the commodification of celebrity culture, in which celebrities are seen as objects for fans, publicists, and producers to sell as a public investment. In this environment, publicists carefully and strategically manage the public presentation of celebrities' careers and personal lives, endeavoring to sustain their carefully crafted personas. This work includes deciding how much of a celebrity's personal life to reveal to the public. As scholars such as Richard Dyer and Christine Gledhill have argued, the allure of celebrity is that a person is elevated above the everyday and yet is made to seem, despite being rich and famous, "normal," which renders their celebrity status achievable.[24] Like the duality between the banal and the glamorous, almost every celebrity narrative traces troughs and peaks in a continuous cycle of failure and redemption that fulfills that person's cultural role of both fantasy figure and attainable reality.

Experts like Bragman, who had a regular segment called "The Spin Doctor Is In" on *Showbiz Tonight* (HLN, 2005–2014), reveal the artifice of celebrity, in which the private self no longer represents pure truth. "Instead," as Joshua Gamson says, "what is most true, most real, most trustworthy, is precisely the relentlessly performing public self."[25] The creation of celebrity no longer relies only on demands for personal revelation; rather, celebrity culture requires that celebrities perform as products themselves. In this way, Gamson says, "Celebrity personas are in a practical sense constructed such that distinctions between fact and fiction break down, the blend of truths and fictions settling dilemmas in the production setting."[26] Celebrities then exist in a "middle-range reality" where they appear both genuine and manufactured, offering audiences bits and pieces of their constructed "private" selves.

Sexual orientation, however, arguably demands an authenticity that other aspects of a celebrity's life do not. At the same time that popular discourse appears to call for and claim a post-identitarian culture, there is an insistence that LGBT celebrities publicly come out. There is some evidence that the terms of coming out are shifting; in October 2016, *Grey's Anatomy* (ABC, 2005–) star Sara Ramirez announced, speaking at the True Colors Fund's "40 to None Summit," that she identifies as "bisexual and queer."[27] In her speech, she says she identifies as a "woman, multi-racial woman, woman of color, queer, bisexual, Mexican-Irish American, immigrant, and raised by families heavily rooted in Catholicism on both my Mexican and Irish sides," embracing an intersectionality rarely seen in declarations by public figures. In addition to the rarity of claiming intersectional identities, few celebrities use the word "queer," given its status as a pejorative word and because it resists categorization and challenges the idea of an unchangeable sexual identity.

Surprisingly, instead of sharing with me a magic formula for how he helps celebrities come out in ways that maintain (if not enhance) their careers, Bragman detailed a range of methods and experiences, all of which have led him to conclude that "gender identity and sexuality are a lot more complex than we thought."[28] Bragman talked about many celebrities in the course of our conversation, but two cases in particular illustrate how—sometimes knowingly, sometimes unknowingly—he uses his role as a PR expert to complicate simplistic ideas that culture has somehow reached a post-gay moment. One of these involved his work with the country music singer Chely Wright, who publicly came out as lesbian in 2010. Her coming out was a big deal in the country music world, an industry notorious for homophobia, and its politically conservative and Christian audience base.

Our conversation about Wright arose from a 2012 cover article in *Entertainment Weekly* that discusses the increasing numbers of celebrities coming out in recent years. The title of the article summed up a perceived shift in how celebrities are coming out: "By the Way, We're Gay. The New Art of Coming Out" and included television actors like Jane Lynch, Andy Cohen, Neil Patrick Harris, and Jesse Tyler Ferguson.[29] "New Art" refers to the casual references to their sexual identities celebrities now make as opposed to the kind of highly publicized fanfare that accompanied previous coming out stories (think of DeGeneres in 1997). When I brought up the article, Bragman responded:

> They [*Entertainment Weekly*] never called me and . . . I found it a little offensive and I took it personal and maybe I shouldn't have. . . . Well, the new coming out is the way Jim Parsons is doing it, very matter-of-factly, and I think everybody has their own journey and their own reasons. If Chely Wright had come out matter-of-factly, she wouldn't have hit the *New York Times*. . . . Chely Wright wasn't on the number one TV show in America. Chely Wright was a country star who hadn't been relevant for a while and needed to tell her story a lot because the country community still is not where they need to be on this clearly and we needed to sell books [she was writing a memoir]. . . . We had to replace the audience and get out there as aggressively as we could. . . . So I think you have to look at each person and what they're trying to do and how they're trying to do it before you judge because there's not one way to come out.

Although Bragman's comment underscores the "management" of sexuality, especially in how LGBT celebrities engage with audiences, it also demonstrates that much of what goes on behind the scenes in the PR industry has very little to do with a post-gay agenda. Instead, it reveals that coming out narratives have never been neatly wrapped packages, churned out on an assembly line of gayness. Although Bragman acknowledged seeing a lot of change over his years in the business of helping people come out—the first two actors he worked with in this capacity were Dick Sargent and Sheila Kuehl, both 1960s television stars—his stories about a variety of clients did not describe the trajectory of his work as a steady path forward with constant improvement. With Wright, and others, he did not reinforce the teleological story of LGBT progress, wherein the United States is on the fast track to guaranteed full equality.

As with Wright, Bragman's work is often guided by the status and career needs of a specific LGBT celebrity rather than the need to formulate a universal coming out narrative applicable to all LGBT celebrities. Although one might argue that his career as a publicist depends on celebrities *needing* his expertise in order to come out (such that a truly post-gay society would mean the end to his career), I would say that his understanding of sexuality and identity formation do not lend themselves to such an easy explanation. First, Bragman explained that clients who are coming out make up about one percent of his time and income: "It's a huge percentage of my awareness [i.e., his own fame] but, God, I'm glad I don't have to depend on that." Second, his work with clients whose cases have not been straightforward coming-out stories offer insight into the operations of complex behind-the-scenes elements of Hollywood.

Bragman's work with professional basketball star Sheryl Swoopes provides a useful illustration of his differentiated approaches. Often referred to as the "female Michael Jordan," she was the first player to be signed by the WNBA when it was founded in 1997 and frequently appeared on television. In 2005, Swoopes hired Bragman to help her come out as lesbian. When she came out, she was one of the highest profile athletes to have done so. Six years later, though, in 2011, Swoopes announced she was leaving her female partner, was straight, and was engaged to a man. This announcement shocked many of her fans. But even more shocking to many LGBT-identified people was Swoopes's claim that her sexuality was a matter of "choice."

As discussed earlier in this chapter, because of a long history of oppression and discrimination, in which sexual minorities were subjected to heinous medical treatments and religious exorcisms, committed to mental institutions, and made criminals and social outcasts because of their sexual identities and sexual acts, the issue of "choice" has become a central battleground in the fight for recognition, validation, and equal rights. When Swoopes made this announcement, Bragman said, "Boy, I took a lot of grief from the community for that . . . [they said] 'how dare you say that, you've set us back.'" He

Figure 3.1. This 2012 cover story in *Entertainment Weekly* describes Hollywood as a place where celebrities can now casually come out and offers examples of various stars who came out quietly, without fanfare or repercussions.

explained that he understood the implications and ripple effect the comment set off. However, he said, "when I coach people, it's to be their best selves, not to put words in their mouth." In fact, Swoopes did not make this claim without consulting Bragman. When she came to him with news of her engagement to a man and her belief that she was simply choosing one identity over another at this point in her life, she asked him what to say. He said, as he would tell any other client, "You have to tell your truth." Despite claims about the "new art" of coming out, Bragman's approach with Swoopes, and with others, demonstrates a philosophy of sexual identity that doesn't adhere to strict binaries or to the notion that sexual identity is permanent and stable. Significantly, though, his approach also does not reject identity or suggest that it has become irrelevant. In fact, in some ways his approach strategically embraces fixed identities through the language of "telling the truth."

Bragman brought up Swoopes as he described how he works with LGBT clients, a process intricately connected to identity and to coming out. He said, "I can tell you that everybody's got a different reason, a different motivation, a different inspiration for telling the truth and the timing of what it is. I have a process, but I have never had a blueprint." He went on to talk about a procedure that resembled the work of both a therapist and a lawyer. First, he said, his job is about listening: "Where are you at? Why do you want to come out?" Learning the answers to these questions is vital for Bragman, because, he said, some celebrities who come to him simply are not ready for this undertaking. Usually, they have not come out to their families and close friends.

As many of our personal stories reflect, coming out as LGBT to those you are close to can be some of the most challenging, heartbreaking, and heartening moments of our lives. Bragman's concern is that closeted celebrities who have not yet taken those steps are not ready for the onslaught of personal questions and probing into their lives that such a public declaration usually involves. In and of itself, this first step places the coming out narrative squarely at the center of LGBT identity and not at the periphery, as those who argue for a post-gay culture would have it. The impact this announcement will have on an individual's life is uncertain, and remains powerful afterward. In his capacity as a "shrink," to use his words, Bragman often counsels celebrities, "Have your ducks in a row. Do the work that's required." The strongest evidence, Bragman explained, for the necessity of doing this personal work before publicly coming out is that the United States does not yet have a major gay male movie star who is out. He laughed as he finished that sentence, shaking his head about the endless tabloid headlines that have speculated about Tom Cruise and his sexual orientation.

Once he has made these initial determinations, Bragman explained, he prepares the LGBT celebrity for the media interviews and potential career impact, such as backlashes. Here he resembles a defense lawyer preparing his client for a brutal cross-examination by the prosecutor. He said, "My job is to sit down for as long as it takes and ask heinous questions so that there's nothing that will shock or surprise them."

I asked Bragman if he considered himself an activist—it seemed to me he was facilitating important conversations about the nature of sexuality, offering potential spaces to intervene in the assimilationist narrative of "born this way" now lodged in the public consciousness. He replied, "I identify as an activist in the same way that an out actor is an activist." I interpret this to mean that he feels that the nature of his work—helping celebrities to come out and be visible in their sexuality—serves a larger purpose than just earning income as a public relations expert. But I also observed what I would describe as a form of activism in some of Bragman's choices, for example about which media outlets celebrities use to come out. In most cases, a magazine or television news program gets an "exclusive" or first interview with the celebrity. These interviews are highly publicized and Bragman negotiates them, working with the client to assess the most effective outlet (maximum positive exposure to the right audience). In many cases, he uses his own values and judgments about whether a media outlet *deserves the story* based on their history of respect for LGBT people. He said, "I know who's earned it and who hasn't." For example when Jason Collins, the pro basketball player who came out in 2013, becoming the first male athlete from one of the four major North American team sports to come out while still playing, Bragman was frustrated. Collins chose to come out on his own and made a deal with *Sports Illustrated*, one of the biggest sports magazines in the country. This choice, Bragman said, disappointed him because he felt the magazine had a poor record supporting LGBT athletes.

In my analysis, Bragman's activism went beyond these kinds of choices. When he told me that "gender identity and sexuality are a lot more complex than we thought," he crucially added that he realizes this fact while also understanding that many "smart people don't get that." While not dismissing the intelligence of US media consumers, Bragman underscored that simplistic ideas about sexuality and gender are deeply engrained and naturalized in US culture. What is noteworthy here is that he says he keeps this in mind and works with that knowledge. Although his work with LGBT celebrities may not always seem explicitly progressive, I argue that at different moments, in different contexts, and in different ways Bragman's work expresses subtle and diverse articulations of sexual and gender identity as well as the complex meanings of coming out today. His responses to my questions show the limitations of the coming out narrative within the media industries, which simultaneously rely on such a narrative representationally while challenging it in their production practices.

Come Out! Transgender Visibility as Difference

One of the most captivating elements of my interviews for this chapter was discussing identity and coming out at the very moment that transgender television visibility gained unprecedented attention in the popular press. I say "captivating" because while calls for transgender coming out have never been stronger, post-gay television characters and celebrities have never been more praised. The clear contradiction in these patterns speaks to the question of how stable (or unstable) identity categories are in this age of twenty-first-century television production. In this section I explore how this contradiction plays out behind the scenes in the world of nonprofit television advocacy. I focus on the specific tactics and strategies that this group of cultural workers employ to redefine diversity.

In 2007, making the case for what he calls "post-closet television," Ron Becker says, "In recent years . . . gay men (and to a much lesser extent lesbians) have been seemingly (and at times seamlessly) integrated into the landscape of US television . . . with little to no fanfare."[30] As television features fewer coming out stories for lesbians and gays, audiences are introduced to more transgender characters and actors than ever before, and in more multidimensional roles. Bound up in the political and social culture of their time, these representations become symbols of progress, titillating or empowering tales of human variation, both as sources of debate over whether gender is a matter of "nature" or "nurture" and as exploitative, voyeuristic looks into the lives of "freaks."[31]

In his study of sexual minorities and television talk shows, Joshua Gamson reminds us that identity politics requires stable, identifiable, and binary categories—gay versus straight. He writes, "If there is a difference (between gay and straight), we want to be able to see it, and if we see a difference (a man in women's clothes), we want to be able to *interpret* it. In both cases, the conflation is fueled by a desire to *tell the difference*, to guard against a difference that might otherwise put the identity of one's own position in question."[32] The binaries between gay and straight tend to be more established and simpler for audiences to detect. Gamson says, "It is especially on programs focused on bisexuality and transsexualism that categorization gets troubled."[33] In the case of bisexuals, the immediate "problem" is that they do not fit the mold of identifying as one of two fixed and recognizable categories.[34] Transgender people on television talk shows, and I would argue on television more broadly, not only challenge notions of clearly defined sexuality but also blur the lines between male and female and between masculinity and femininity, posing the ultimate threat to a viewer's ability to *"tell the difference,"* challenging what constitutes a "man" and a "woman."[35]

As an aside, I would note that the television personalities, celebrities, and characters—whether child or adult (e.g., Jazz Jennings, Caitlyn Jenner, Laverne Cox [as Sophia Burset])—featured on reality and scripted series and held up as icons and role models are almost exclusively transgender *women.* Transgender *men* do not receive the same visibility or accolades. The potential meanings and implications of these trends, meaningful as they are to consider, are outside the scope of this analysis. This section examines the practices of advocates working with transgender visibility at a time when it is of enormous public interest and therefore at a precarious state of evolution in public consciousness.

GLAAD, as *the* national media LGBT advocacy organization, sets the standard for what news outlets, television networks, and audiences perceive as the LGBT community's political agenda. In its estimation, transgender visibility is so important and relevant that "in 2015 [GLAAD President Sarah Kate] Ellis added a full-time position for . . . director of the transgender media program."[36] The same year, I interviewed Matt Kane, who at the time was GLAAD's director of entertainment media. He monitored LGBT content online and on social media and worked directly with television networks, show creators, writers, and diversity departments, advising them how to represent LGBT people and stories using what he calls "quality" images: "We've seen representation on television really blossom in the last five years or so. We've seen the number of LGBT characters, and LGB specifically I should say, really multiply on television to the point where it's no longer about quantity, it's about specific quality and the diversity of those representations."[37] As a result, he told me, 75 percent of his work addresses transgender visibility and representation.

At the time of this interview in 2015, the biggest celebrity story was Bruce Jenner coming out as transgender. Jenner, a beloved American athlete famous for a record-setting gold medal win in the decathlon in the 1976 Olympics, was the kind of "all-American" athlete that Wheaties had put on its cereal boxes (in one of the earliest cases of celebrity branding).[38] Jenner's coming out was plastered all over national media. As Caitlyn, she was featured on the cover of *Vanity Fair* and made an impassioned speech about her gender identity upon receiving the Arthur Ashe Courage Award at the 2015 Excellence in Sports Performance Yearly Award (known as the ESPYS), an accolade pre-

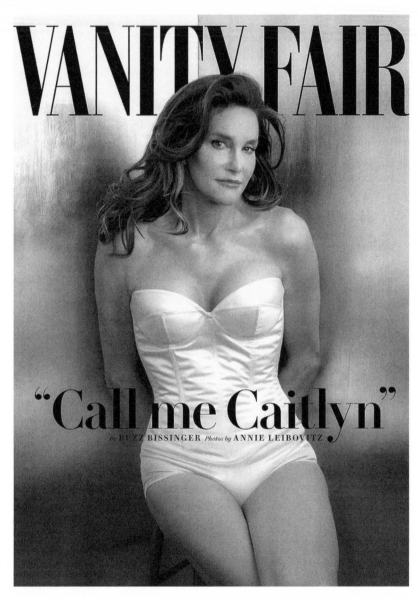

Figure 3.2. When Jenner announced her transition from male to female, she gave *Vanity Fair* an exclusive interview in which she revealed her name, Caitlyn, publicly.

sented by ABC recognizing sports-related achievements for the previous calendar year. She also did an exclusive two-hour interview with *20/20*'s Diane Sawyer, which was publicized weeks ahead of time, before the debut of her own reality series, *I Am Cait* (E!, 2015–) and participated in a two-part special episode of *Keeping Up with the Kardashians* (E!, 2007–) entitled "About Bruce."

The media frenzy over Jenner's transition was predated by several transgender television characters, which had taken many critics, audiences, and LGBT community leaders by storm. In 2014, for example, Amazon debuted *Transparent*, a story about a culturally sophisticated and well-to-do Los Angeles family's dysfunctional and dramatic lives following the discovery that the family patriarch (played by cisgender and straight actor Jeffrey Tambor) is transgender.[39] With a critically acclaimed cast, including a number of transgender actresses, the show received glowing reviews from even the harshest of critics, and found its place as an equally popular show among Amazon Prime members.[40]

A year after its debut, Tambor won an Emmy Award, television's highest honor, for his portrayal of Maura Pfefferman. In his acceptance speech he said, "I've been given the opportunity to act because people's lives depend on it," referring to the tragic numbers of transgender people who lose their lives, especially transgender women of color. He goes on to say that playing Maura is a role that is both a "responsibility" and a "privilege." With great sincerity, he closes by saying, "Not to repeat myself but to specifically repeat myself: I'd like to dedicate my performance and this award to the transgender community. Thank you for your patience, thank you for your courage, thank you for your stories, thank you for your inspiration. Thank you for letting us be part of the change. God bless you." Tambor's speech, televised in front of 11.9 million viewers, offers a mixture of recognition and respect for transgender Americans and the need to tell their stories; he, like many others quoted in this book, believes characters like Maura Pfefferman have an effect on public perceptions about social minorities. His comments also reflect an awareness that many critics believe transgender actors should play transgender roles. As a cisgender man playing a transgender woman, Tambor gives a subtle nod to this issue as if offering reassurance that he takes the responsibility of playing Maura all the more seriously.

In 2013, Netflix, one of the most successful online media distributors to produce original content, premiered *Orange Is the New Black*. The show, adapted from a memoir, is the story of Piper Chapman (played by Taylor Schilling), a woman sentenced to fifteen months in prison after being convicted of the decade-old crime of transporting money to her drug-dealing girlfriend.[41] One of the show's breakout stars, Laverne Cox, is a black transgender actress who portrays an out transgender character. The cover of a 2014 issue of *Time* magazine featured Cox with a tag line that read: "The Transgender Tipping Point: America's Next Civil Rights Frontier."[42] Reporter Katy Steinmetz writes that with the popularity of *Orange Is the New Black*, "she has emerged as a public leader of the trans movement, using her increasingly prominent perch to make the case for equal rights and touring the country giving a stump speech titled 'Ain't I A Woman?' When Cox says it, that refrain is not a question."[43]

Broadcast television, desperate to compete with the edgy content cable and online shows have used to brand themselves, has included regular transgender characters in both primetime and daytime soap operas, including *Glee* (Fox, 2009–2015) and *The Bold and the Beautiful* (CBS, 1987–). Among cable networks, transgender characters have appeared in the critically acclaimed shows *American Horror Story: Hotel* (FX, 2015–2016), *It's Always Sunny in Philadelphia* (FX and FXX, 2005–), and *The Fosters* (ABC Family, 2013–2015; Free Form, 2016–). Reality TV, one of the first genres to depict lesbian and gay people has incorporated or focused on transgender personalities in *I Am Jazz* (TLC, 2015–), *Becoming Us* (ABC Family, 2015), *Dancing with the Stars* (ABC, 2005–), and *Strut* (Oxygen, 2016–). In 2015 PBS's critically acclaimed series *Frontline* (1983–) aired a documentary entitled *Growing Up Trans* about transgender youth. Unlike many other television news reports and documentaries about childhood and gender identity, *Growing Up Trans* neither othered, tokenized, nor dismissed the lives of these children, their parents, or medical providers, offering instead a rare portrait of disparate transgender lives. In February 2017, National Geographic aired *Gender Revolution: A Journey with Katie Couric* and simultaneously launched a website also called Gender Revolution, which is dedicated to stories of transgender Americans and includes resources and information about gender identity. National Geographic promoted the documentary months ahead of its airdate and followed it with reflections from Couric on what she learned from the project.

Referring to shows with transgender characters, Kane said, "We're definitely in the updraft of it now. We're finally seeing a lot of projects get the green light that have transgender characters." He described what he called an "evolution" in television, one moving away from shows like *Ugly Betty* in which transgender characters were played by actors who were not transgender themselves. The change, Kane argued, is especially notable in the sheer numbers of transgender actors getting work as transgender characters beyond stock roles as the murder victim in a crime drama (as so many had before). Instead, they are regular cast members, part of the fully fleshed out characters that audiences invest in throughout a series.

The increase in his attention to transgender issues, he believes, is worth that level of effort for a specific reason: the numbers of people who actually know a transgender person are extremely low: "Therefore, TV is the place most people are getting those images and learning who they are. . . . They are not meeting transgender [people] in their lived experiences, but rather in the media they consume." He added, "So there's an added responsibility to that media that depictions of lesbian, gay, bisexual characters don't have to that degree."[44] As transgender visibility increases, the idea that television representations can operate in the service of introducing social minorities to broader culture remains strong.

Given GLAAD's mission—to rewrite "the script for LGBT acceptance"—and Kane's position within the organization, his impression of the significance of television's visibility is logical and to be expected. However, the way he goes about consulting with television shows on transgender characters presents an insightful portrait of how industrial diversity works in practice. Kane described a specific strategy he uses in working with shows that want to incorporate a transgender character but whose writers and producers are "uneducated," as he put it, about this identity. I quote him at length to detail the approaches he takes to strategically work with different shows.

> We created this trans representation study, [in] which we looked at all of the single-episode representation of trans characters over the last ten years and sort of broke them down not just by their identity but by what was their profession, what was their place in the story, were there anti-trans slurs used against them by the protagonist or antagonist, were they positioned as the antagonist themselves, were they the victim in the story, because it's usually police procedurals where we see trans characters popping up, and to figure out what the trends were and then since then, when we have meetings with the networks, we take this data directly to them. It's usually rather eye opening for them. We talk about the resources we can provide and basically try to form relationships where they're going to start coming to us with material on an ongoing basis; and we have that relationship with a number of different networks now, where I'll get an email asking me to read over a story treatment and give my thoughts or do some line editing on a script. A lot of that is not stuff we talk about publicly because it's a relationship that we want to continue with these networks; we don't make a big deal out of their mistakes when they're trying to fix them proactively.

Kane said it took him a long time to develop the ability to speak the language of each show creator and to find a persuasive means of connecting with producers and writers. Honing this skill over time, Kane learned to adjust his approach based on what he has identified as the goal of each show's creative team. The variety of goals he encountered points to how many different circumstances and for how many different reasons television produces transgender diversity.

Diversifying Activism

Several months before I interviewed Kane, GLAAD released its 2014 annual Network Responsibility Index (NRI). In response, media outlets across the country reported the depths to which "TV is tuned in to LGBT diversity."[45] The NRI, launched in 2006, looks backward at the previous television season and rates fifteen networks on LGBT-inclusive content, analyzing a total of 2,832 hours of national primetime programming (GLAAD does not track primetime broadcast hours programmed by local affiliate stations).[46] The index awards grades "based on the quality, diversity, and relative quantity of LGBT representations in each network's original programming."[47] Going forward, GLAAD announced, future reports will assign the top score only to networks that include "significant transgender content."[48] This particular requirement, the 2014 NRI report explains, arises from the notable transgender representations in online original content—specifically characters in the aforementioned *Orange Is the New Black* and *Transparent*. In light of the fact that these "new online content creators . . . feature some of the most groundbreaking and fully realized depictions of transgender characters," GLAAD challenges traditional television networks to push the boundaries of their representational diversity.[49]

This report and other types of diversity initiatives are increasingly visible in commercial businesses, both within and outside the media industries. The focus on maintaining diversity (be it real or imagined) in a deregulated media industry has fed a corporate culture equally invested in policies that publicly demonstrate LGBT value in hiring, human resources, and employee support. "Diversity Rhetoric and the Managerialization of Law," a foundational sociology article on the topic of diversity, explains the extent to which "talk of diversity pervades management periodicals, human resource networks, and business education. In each of these settings, diversity rhetoric extols the virtues of a diverse workforce and advocates 'managing diversity' and 'valuing diversity.'"[50] In fact, the term often stands in for other less "desirable" words. Writing about geographically dense gay communities called "gayborhoods," Ghaziani argues, "Diverse is a more palatable term than 'gay' for many heterosexuals who live in a gayborhood."[51] I contend the same metaphor holds true for corporate media spaces such as television studios, network offices, and the like. However, in contrast to representational diversity, which tends to be almost exclusively produced under the radar in the space of corporate culture, in matters of employee diversity and commitments to LGBT-friendly policies, diversity is produced and promoted both in public view and outside it.

For example, when the FCC and the US Department of Justice approved Comcast's acquisition of NBCUniversal from General Electric in early 2011, they made several demands of the company. These requirements were intended to help the new, massive company avoid the potential harms posed by the combination of Comcast, the nation's largest cable operator and Internet service provider, and NBCUniversal, which owns and develops a large portion of television and film content. Among these was a list of "diversity"-based requirements that targeted social class, geography, age, and language, but there was no mention of LGBT- or other identity-based categories of difference.

However, in response to harsh criticisms about mergers and acquisitions, the major media conglomerates that dominate the global marketplace have designed a host of "diversity" initiatives to reassure regulators, consumers, employees, and advertisers that their varied interests are at the heart of operating procedures. Comcast's publicity handbook, for example, opens with a single sentence typed in a large font that takes up half the page: "At Comcast-NBCUniversal, we believe that every individual within our ranks—from service technicians and call center associates to producers and movie stars—brings something unique and valuable to the table.... Diversity and inclusion are at the core of our operations."[52] The other half of the page features employees' varying faces—men, women, young, old, and racially diverse. The employees wear T-shirts that list their occupation at the corporation (tech ops, strategist, television director, engineer, etc.), which literally puts faces on this behemoth merger.

Such assertions of diversity function as pure and unabashed positive promotion for the corporation. In many respects, they amount to a commodified identity working in the service of brand development and capital expansion. Comcast and other media conglomerates feature "pride" days when employees wear lavender shirts in support of LGBT equality, offering workers the opportunity to either come out within the corporation or proclaim themselves as an ally. Through social media outlets like Facebook and Twitter, Comcast publicly reinforces its goals of connecting with a broad audience about initiatives like these. According to its diversity website, "We don't think it's enough to reflect the diverse cultures and backgrounds of our audiences. We want to celebrate them. By presenting positive role models, telling diverse stories, commemorating heritage, and fostering dialogue on a variety of platforms, we are creating powerfully engaging content that makes a real difference in people's lives."[53]

Statements like this use language that hearkens back to early FCC rhetoric about serving the public good as well as to the utopian ideals of early cable television, which promised a space for independent and minority voices who could offer views different from the mainstream.[54] Cable was seen as a remedy to many social ills, such as racism, sexism, and homophobia, because it would literally make room for more accurate representations to appear before its audiences. Moreover, much along the lines of Comcast's claims to "fostering dialogue," cable was also seen as a means of empowering citizens and creating stronger communities, and therefore as a potential inspiration for civic activism.

Operating under the Radar: Diversity Activism in the Twenty-First Century

In many of the interviews I conducted, industry workers appear to conceive of themselves as activists who work in corporate spaces, and therefore often strategically keep their socially progressive efforts out of public view. I came to see this theme as a defining aspect of how industry workers conceive of their own LGBT activism.

In 2009, I met with J. Michael Durnil, then the interim president of GLAAD. The organization was undergoing an internal restructuring based on what nonprofits call "strategic plans," which are primarily rebranding efforts. As I found out during our interview, Durnil has a doctorate in education and had spent many years of his professional life in the academy. He provided a unique viewpoint, one that I rarely encountered in my research for this project—he could compare activist-oriented work in both academic and non-profit advocacy institutions, speaking both languages and embodying both identities.

In my conversation with him, Durnil described a range of projects not disclosed to the public, providing a glimpse of the under-the-radar work an advocacy group like this does on a regular basis; such activities challenge the public image of the organization as an instrument of assimilation that is too cozy with Hollywood and too comfortable with the industry's normative modes of representation. Durnil explained that the only times GLAAD associates its name with, or more precisely against, a representation is when it is defamatory or potentially harmful to LGBT people. Durnil gave me the example of when a radio station was airing a highly offensive ad. GLAAD called the station three times without receiving a response. As a result of the radio station's lack of response, GLAAD issued a public statement condemning the station and calling for public action. However, a public call to action was not the organization's first activist strategy.

Discussing GLAAD's "under-the-radar" work, Durnil mentioned a state-based marriage campaign (whose name he would not give) that asked for GLAAD's help in the media portion of their communications strategy. In most instances where two organizations partner to support an issue and create a campaign, both names appear on publicity materials. However, given GLAAD's usual role as an invisible advocate, its name does not appear in this instance. Talking about this and other examples, he categorized most of GLAAD's work as "clandestine," a word I found surprisingly strong given its associations with secretiveness and even illicitness—although I know the latter is not what he meant.

While the logic and convenience of Durnil's approach contradict the view of coming out as symbolic of political progress, I would argue that the "under-the-radar" activism Durnil practices is an aspect of the "craft" that cultural-diversity workers perfect. He and other advocates learn how to manage publicity and privacy skillfully, in turn challenging conventional LGBT wisdom about advocacy and visibility politics.

Durnil had to finesse the balance around publicity because at the time of our interview he was interim president of GLAAD. As a nonprofit organization, GLAAD needs to secure both funding and continued public recognition, precisely the jobs Durnil was hired to do as president. He made sense of this difficult negotiation by saying, "Part of our work is in a real 'business to business model' so sometimes it gets missed—because . . . we're like 'Intel inside,'" a reference to the computer chipmaker. He went on, "Intel [doesn't] make the products; [they] make them better."[55] In other words, GLAAD does not make television shows but does try to improve the quality of LGBT representations in them, even if audiences don't know the organization is involved. The comparison to Intel's role in computers highlights that GLAAD is an integral part of the television industry, institutionalized in its role as an LGBT advocate; by extension, advocates like Durnil are cultural workers who form a key part of the television industry and its construction of sexuality.

Matt Kane occupied a dramatically different role within the organization than Durnil and, as such, offered a different vantage point on his own "under-the-radar activism." My interview with Kane took place on the same day that I interviewed Howard Bragman. It was intriguing then when Kane told me that the organization has "always operated as sort of a PR wing of the

[LGBT] movement. You don't put the publicist out in front of things; the publicist sits behind and tells the person what the best way to craft a statement is and then you disappear into the shadows." Much like Bragman's work as a public relations expert, Kane's work revolved around guiding television programs and networks in ways that were both commodifying and subversive.

For example, there is not a simple divide between GLAAD's public work, such as its annual award ceremony and its NRI, and its "clandestine" projects—which involve the kinds of consulting Kane did regularly for the eight years he worked at GLAAD. I asked him whether his work ever feels subversive, because, as he told me, he prefers to stay in the shadows. I quote him here at length because his response addresses the ongoing tensions existing even in GLAAD, which is such a prominent advocacy organization:

> I can tell you our development department likes it when we do things that are public. Those of us in the programmatic side are most comfortable working behind the scenes. Partly based on our personalities, and then development has these goals that they have to reach so it's very helpful that we can point to these things that we have done to help them raise money. It does feel subversive sometimes but . . . compared to, I guess, other organizations in the movement for whom most of what they do is really out there and public because they're trying to get certain statements out . . . and perspectives out. We do the same thing, we just work through other people who are going to be the other ones [such as television networks, showrunners, characters] who are ultimately going to be credited with whatever is going to actually happen.

I saw through these interviews the complex negotiations that take place in behind-the-scenes diversity-oriented work. The view from the outside—from publicity and trade press reports, for example—does little to reveal the inner workings through which representations of sexual minorities are developed and influenced. Significantly, this "under-the-radar activism" is in fact strategic, a fact that became impossible to ignore during one of the interviews I conducted. The information I heard in this interview reflects the lengths to which some industry workers go in order to conceal their progressive efforts on behalf of marginalized LGBT communities.

Through the contact who arranged several of my interviews, I set up a meeting with the head of a corporate social responsibility department (CSR) for a television network. CSR departments have sprung up across media industries in response to claims that media conglomerates monopolize the industry by merging with or buying other firms. Federal deregulation efforts have lowered, if not removed, the restrictions on how many companies one media corporation can own, meaning that competition decreases. Instead of competing, a major corporation will simply buy up the competition. As a result, widespread concerns have arisen about the effects these groupings have on diversity. Large corporations have created CSR departments to assuage concerns about diversity in these corporate structures where so much power is concentrated at the top. Critics fear that these CSR divisions are purely superficial and express concerns that they will do little to support or initiate anything beyond the most basic forms of "enlightened diversity."

In this particular case, I spoke with a CSR executive who was openly gay and dedicated to helping poor and young (often homeless) LGBT communities. He had been able to do a great deal of "under-the-radar activism" on these issues because when his CSR division was formed, he recognized that no one at his corporation seemed to know how such a division should operate. As a result, he was given free rein to make the department whatever he wanted it to be—in this case, a CSR division highly dedicated to LGBT causes. He claims this is true for other CSR executives he knows across Hollywood.

I am forced to be vague in my discussion about the interview because this individual would not speak on the record and said he would deny any of our conversation should it become public. He told me he never would have taken the meeting had his colleague not asked him to do so (a symbol of the power of connections in getting in the door for an interview). Off the record, then, he spent a great deal of time talking about the various programs and events he had orchestrated in support of LGBT communities that were quietly financed and sustained by the company. These initiatives ranged from fundraising for LGBT homeless youth, to anti-bullying efforts, to same-sex adoption campaigns. In his capacity heading up the relatively new CSR division of the company, he had been given tremendous latitude, and found ways to support causes important to him and other employees personally.

This work was always cloaked in the language of profit—over and over again he talked about his projects and initiatives as first and foremost "good for business." By "good for business," he meant things that not only benefited the company's bottom line but also encouraged employee pride, cooperation, and community. Central to the "good for business motto" also was serving the network's audiences; he insisted that many of the LGBT efforts undertaken through the network could not be disclosed publicly because many of its audiences he told me were "people who vote for Mike Huckabee," a Republican politician and an ordained Southern Baptist minister known for his fundamentalist (and anti-LGBT) views. In this case, "good for business" was how this interviewee, in his particular role within the television industry, diversified activism occurring under a large corporate umbrella, successfully meeting demands that seemed at odds and incompatible. Although this kind of completely off-the-record meeting happened only once, it offered a view both of the complexities of conducting this kind of industry research and running a "diversity" department in a highly consolidated media environment.

This interview also underscores the ways that activism and capitalism come together on unconventional terms. As an openly gay executive, this person had navigated the corporate space of his company in a way that allowed him to create opportunities for LGBT activism. Exploiting resources available to him when the department was created, he was able to set a precedent for how activism and profit motives could coexist. Although the stakes are undeniably high—he would not allow me to use his name under threat of legal action—opportunities have emerged during times of organizational change when temporary gaps open up within corporate structures, lending individual workers a surprising amount of authority. I thus witnessed openly gay industry workers engaging in the active integration of LGBT workers' diverse concerns, values, and causes. At the very least, the interviews analyzed in this chapter suggest the potential is there for "progressive" LGBT activism within corporate cultures that epitomize the values of capitalism and neoliberal beliefs and policies.

Conclusion

This chapter set out to answer several questions: How does behind-the-scenes work construct LGBT diversity? How does this approach to studying diversity deepen and nuance the definitions of diversity? What are the implications of adding this unofficial information to the map of "diversity," which encompasses representation, regulation, production, and promotion? The most significant answer is that much of this work takes place strategically out of public view, behind the scenes at television studios, advocacy organizations, and public relations firms. This characteristic stands out in an industry obsessed with self-promotion and publicity. Instinctively, I wondered whether this discovery meant researchers should push them out of the shadows given that these discoveries seemed essential in order to widen the scope of our understanding of diversity in television.

However, I believe that calling for behind-the-scenes processes to be put into public view is not necessarily the appropriate response, for doing so would put those efforts at significant risk in an industry that has numerous and conflicting demands to meet. Simply put, much of what I have identified as progressive political acts on behalf of LGBT people are effective precisely *because* they are kept hidden.

I argue from the information and analysis presented in this chapter that transparency is potentially both powerful and destructive. In addition, scholars must accept that studies of representation or promotion do not tell us the full story. In this vein, the worrisome image conjured in so much popular culture—that LGBT equality is inevitable and even achieved—is not nearly as fully realized as some scholars, critics, and activists seem to think. There is still room for intervention, even if it is not on ideal or unproblematic terms. For example, the tensions this chapter explores between the popularity of post-gay rhetoric and the diversity work that strategically embraces identity politics illustrates spaces where problems of homophobia, that often go unaddressed and unacknowledged, are directly addressed by individuals whose work influences LGBT television representation.

In this chapter, I have tried to connect areas of television diversity that do not have logical or obvious connections to one another. In practice, sectors within the industry work within their own spheres of influence. I have juxtaposed them in order to examine parallels and overlapping interests, needs, and practices. By drawing out interlocking and overlapping characteristics, this chapter creates a larger picture of what diversity can mean and how it is produced both on and beyond the television screen.

The next chapter takes the core ideas of activism, influence, and nontraditional television producers to the world of politics. I do so through a study of California's controversial 2008 ballot initiative, Proposition 8, a statewide ballot initiative that limited marriage to the union of one man and one woman. I examine the people and research that helped to produce TV commercials about Prop 8 in 2008 as well as the 2014 HBO documentary *The Case against 8*—through an analysis of their content, production, and distribution, data from polling and focus groups, as well as interviews with consultants who designed the commercial campaigns. My attention then turns to the politics of messaging, constituent mobilization, and profit, revealing the conflicts arising from differences in strategies and beliefs about televised LGBT political campaigns. I discovered that these clashes define rather than undermine their effectiveness.

CHAPTER 4

Equality: Proposition 8 and the Politics of Marriage on Television

"Here they come, here they come!" shouts a man standing in the crowd. A moment later, the camera pans to a young woman sprinting down the steps of the US Supreme Court building in Washington, DC. Following tradition, press interns wait for a decision to be handed down from the Supreme Court. Once they receive the ruling, they dash from inside the building to the television broadcasters positioned outside the building.

The date is June 26, 2013, and the documentary crew of *The Case against 8* (HBO, 2014) awaits the Court's decision in the case of *Hollingsworth v. Perry*. This landmark case considered whether the official sponsors of Proposition 8 (Prop 8 from here on), a California ballot measure that took away same-sex couples' right to marry, had standing to defend the measure's constitutionality when the state itself refused to do so.[1] The film cuts between reporters outside the court building and NBC's *Today Show* anchors inside the studio. Standing with the Supreme Court building perfectly centered behind him, Pete Williams says, "Okay, the Supreme Court has decided that it cannot take up the challenge to California's Proposition 8.... What this means is that same-sex marriage is now once again legal in the state of California."

For the plaintiffs and attorneys in *Hollingsworth v. Perry*, and many Americans across the country, this moment represented the victorious culmination of years of hard-fought battles—in the courtroom and in the court of public opinion. One the one hand, it symbolized the politically and emotionally charged legal battles that took place over the course of five years as state and federal courts considered the constitutionality of Prop 8. On the other hand, this ruling was particularly important for marriage-equality advocates, attorneys, and plaintiffs who ardently and patiently fought for marriage rights in the United States beginning in the early 1970s, when couples in Minnesota and Kentucky were denied marriage licenses by country clerks.[2]

When Prop 8 passed, it was hard for many voters not to see the irony that California voted the measure into law on the same day that Barack Obama was elected America's first African American President. The next year, Wanda Sykes's standup comedy special *I'ma Be Me* (HBO, 2009) describes an election night that was, for many citizens, both a triumph and a failure; the United States elected its first black president while, as Sykes says, lesbians and gays in California were back to being "second-class citizens." Being both black and gay, Sykes says, "I was up here and now back I'm down here. Actually I'm lower, I dropped lower, you know 'cause as a black woman at least I could do whatever, marry whoever, but as a gay, black woman . . . even lower." Given California's reputation as one of the most liberal states in the country, and in conjunction with Obama's historic election, many commentators expressed surprise—even shock—at Prop 8's passage.[3]

Over the next five years, the national press watched closely as Prop 8 made its way through the court system. Prop 8 stayed in the news partly because in 2010 the appeal was taken up by David Boies and Theodore Olson, an unlikely duo; Boies, a Democratic trial lawyer, and Olson, the solicitor general under President George W. Bush and a prominent conservative, were staunch rivals when they vociferously fought on opposing sides of *Bush v. Gore* in 2000, which determined that year's historic US presidential election. Prop 8's passage also inspired a panoply of media activism. In addition to *The Case against 8*, which aired on HBO in 2014, throughout California and across the country there were fundraisers, merchandise for sale, and hundreds of thousands of videos posted online.[4] Each sought to generate support and funding to overturn Prop 8 while raising public awareness. One of the most recognized efforts was the NOH8 (No Hate) Campaign, which photographer Adam Bouska created with his partner, Jeff Parshley. The phrase "NOH8" refers to "H8," short for "Proposition H8," a name used by critics of the ballot initiative. Bouska and Parshley conceived of the campaign as a silent protest, photographing subjects close-up against a blown-out white background with duct tape over their mouths and "NOH8" painted on one cheek. The campaign featured celebrities and politicians, and circulated widely in social and print media.

As a legal case that garnered national press attention and widespread name recognition in popular culture, Prop 8 is emblematic of public discourse about marriage equality, thus offering an opportunity to examine the landscape of modern LGBT media politics. Rather than attempting to establish an "authentic" version of the story of Prop 8, this chapter seeks to explore the story behind the onscreen content of the "No on Prop 8" television commercials—both for and against—which ran from September 29 to November 4, 2008.

Supporters and opponents raised $39.9 million and $43.3 million, respectively, making it the highest-funded ballot initiative campaign in California history up to that point.[5] Post-election polling indicated that television commercials were far more influential than direct mailings, telephone calls, and official websites.[6] As Toby Miller boldly claims, "In terms of . . . political advertising, television matters and the Internet doesn't matter. This can be explained fairly straightforwardly via ratings, surveys, and expenditure packages."[7] In addition, the "Yes on Prop 8" campaign became the largest recorded anti-gay campaign to date (Stone 2013). Seeking to eliminate the rights of lesbians and gays to marry in California, the "Yes" campaign aired television commercials claiming that marriage for lesbians and gays constituted a direct threat to religion and children's education. By contrast, the "No on Prop 8" television commercials either rebutted claims made by "Yes" campaign commercials or appealed to voters to treat lesbians and gays "equally" and "fairly."

This chapter argues that a close examination of the "No on Prop 8" television commercials provides a new perspective on the contours of contemporary LGBT media politics. The campaign forced the liberal activist legacy to stand under a single political umbrella. Liberal activists, in other words, must believe in the power of visibility and representation (which happens to be a commonly accepted notion with an ambivalent commercial side); in media market research and thus media industries; and in the labor of political campaigns. Examining the "No on Prop 8" television commercials in conjunction with interviews from those involved in the campaign, this chapter moves away from the critique that the mainstream media operates solely in the service of normalizing—even commodifying—LGBT identities. It also refutes the critique that media offer up LGBT sameness as the only route to social and political equality. Scholarship in sociology supports this position, arguing that the "current debate among LGBT activists over whether marriage is assimilationist or transformative is far too simplistic."[8] These studies assess political battles for marriage rights in local, state, and federal cases, focusing on the ways that activist strategies have affected the nationwide campaign for marriage equality. To date, however, the topic has not been addressed in relation to television and the production of political campaign ads. Looking behind the scenes at the circuits of cultural production—a process often shrouded in mystery—reveals variation and tension in the theories and research driving LGBT media campaigns.

Campaign Labor: "I ain't going through a beauty contest"

In the following pages, I detail the television commercials and the research conducted by the official "No on Prop 8" campaign. I draw on press releases, newspaper reports, and a long phone interview I conducted with Steve Smith, lead consultant on the campaign. He was hired when it began in 2007. Like most career campaign workers, Smith has been involved with numerous California elections over the years, beginning in 1999 when he was the state's secretary of labor. At the time he joined the "No on Prop 8" campaign, he had already worked extensively with union and with women's rights organizations, notably Planned Parenthood, as well as on a range of progressive issues campaigns.

Following the vote, LGBT groups heavily criticized Smith for not better strategizing against the "Yes on Prop 8" campaign. The *Bay Area Reporter* ran a story in mid-November of that year titled, "No on Prop 8 Official Grilled over Campaign."[9] According to the reporter, Dan Aiello, "members of the Stonewall Democrats were skeptical and frustrated with the remarks made by Steve Smith."[10] I suspect their frustration had to do with Smith's tone and directness. From my conversation with him, it was clear he shoots straight from the hip. One of the first questions I asked him was how he came to work on the campaign. We had been talking for only a few minutes and had not necessarily established a connection or engaged in easy banter, and so I interpreted his response as part of his general demeanor—the way he might speak to anyone. He said,

> When early in '07 it looked like [Prop 8] was going to show up in '08, a couple of the community leaders called me . . . and said would you quietly do a campaign plan and I said yeah and did a . . . really generalized version and then when it got more serious I went back to them and said, "Now you guys really ought to commission a poll and then let me do you a real campaign." And that happened. Then after that they said, "It's time to hire a firm," I said, "I'll tell you right now, I ain't going through a beauty contest, you now know me, you either hire me or not, I don't give a shit but you know" and they said, "Yup, ok, go." So essentially I got hired a year or more out from the vote.[11]

I spoke with Smith six months after Prop 8's passage. In evaluating my conversation with him, I pay attention to what James Spradley describes as the interviewee's "own language or dialect."[12] As "native speakers," in Spradley's words, political campaign workers are deeply entrenched in the institutional structures and belief systems that reinforce the needs and goals of their work; in the case of Prop 8, media consultants are invested in the reliability of campaign research (polling and focus group data), the ideal of the autonomous voter-individual, the naturalness of sexual identity categories, and the power of costly television commercials to persuade voters undecided on the issue.

At the same time, however, they are well aware of the precariousness or contrivance of these investments. I argue that campaign workers have a keen understanding of the tensions involved in serving the interests of electoral politics. I attribute this awareness to the nature of political campaigns, which differ significantly from more permanent organizations and institutions. Political campaigns exist for relatively short periods of time—sometimes only months—and bring together a diverse group of people committed to a single issue or candidate. According to a Pew Research Center report, political campaigns "emerge like pop-up shops ahead of Election Day, and are hastily disassembled shortly thereafter." For campaign staff, this means uncertain employment and what the Pew report describes as "nomadic lives, given the on-the-job demands of the campaign trail."[13] Thus, the inflected nature of Smith's comments—what John Caldwell calls "overt practitioner explanations"—is most valuable when examined within a more systematic study of the campaign itself, including its research methods and data as well as the context of the commercials' distribution in the television market.

I focus my analysis on four aspects of the "No on Prop 8" campaign's research: the choice not to feature lesbians and gays in the ads; the reliance on data that showed voters did not find a parallel between gay civil rights and black civil rights convincing or effective; and also the choice to persuade voters not to treat lesbians and gays "differently" than others rather than use the language of discrimination common to civil rights discourse. Finally, I address a theme of the campaign's most controversial ad, which tried to use an approach based on inner dissonance—the idea that a voter can simultaneously disapprove of homosexuality but still not want to take away the rights of another person.

In detailing this research, I challenge the critique of political campaign methods and data as sheer manipulation that says little about citizens' lived experiences. As Justin Lewis writes about public opinion polls, "[They] may not produce objective, scientific knowledge, but they produce *something*—and we need to consider what that something might tell us."[14] While cultural studies scholars question the methods and operations of political campaigns over their problematic uses of quantitative and qualitative data as well as the ways they reinforce normative ideas about race, class, gender, and sexuality, this chapter follows from Lewis's point that the "something" produced by those methods and operations is worthy of investigation because it can influence cultural constructions of identity and identity politics. In fact, I would go a step further and argue that the data and findings produced by the "No on Prop 8" campaign are cultural forms that construct knowledge about sexuality and its relationship to US politics.

While the public "No on Prop 8" campaign got underway immediately after the initiative qualified for the November 2008 ballot, polling had begun on the issue eighteen months earlier. The campaign was run by a group of prominent leaders from a number of civil rights organizations, including the Human Rights Campaign (HRC), the American Civil Liberties Union (ACLU), the National Center for Lesbian Rights (NCLR), and Equality California. Public polling indicated that 80 percent of California voters had already "decided" on Prop 8, meaning 20 percent were "undecided." The significance of these percentages, Smith said, is that pollsters make the assumption that nothing will change the minds of that 80 percent of voters. Consequently, the campaign's challenge becomes ignoring that 80 percent and somehow directing campaign messages only to the "undecided" 20 percent of voters. Smith added that while the official percentage of undecided voters was 20, he believed that the actual number was closer to only 10–15 percent.[15]

Smith, along with two pollsters, David Binder and Celinda Lake, designed and led the polling and focus groups that were used to create the "No on Prop 8" TV commercials. Binder and Lake are prominent Democratic pollsters and political strategists and founders of their own national political consulting firms. Binder runs David Binder Research and is a self-described "guru of all things research" who promotes his firm's "long-term ongoing partnership with President Barack Obama's White House, providing award-winning messaging work and conducting research on a number of different initiatives."[16] Lake Research Partners is based in Washington, DC, and Berkeley, California, and boasts among its list of clients former president Bill Clinton, former vice president Joe Biden, the AFL-CIO, the National Council of La Raza, and the Bill and Melinda Gates Foundation. By employing these consultants, the "No on Prop 8" campaign was taking advantage of tried and true political practices used across issues, individuals, and organizations, making it particularly useful as a case study of LGBT politics more broadly.

During our discussion, Smith took his time explaining the process of gathering data for the television ads. As a researcher unfamiliar with the procedures for designing political ads, I found myself intrigued by the information while also scrutinizing the process. For example, I was greatly concerned that the campaign was built on normative ideas about identity categories, especially the insistence on separate identities, as if multiple identities couldn't productively intersect and overlap in the ways trenchantly described by scholars such as Kimberlé Crenshaw, Patricia Hill Collins, and Chandra Talpade Mohanty. Initially I found this political research naïve, because it seemed to overlook the phenomenon in which cultural norms are both influenced and reproduced by the systems used to gather data. However, as I learned more about the process and about the behind-the-scenes conflicts that dominated the "No on Prop 8" campaign, I came to see a much less straightforward version of culture and politics than I expected.

Who Gets to Speak: "Neutral figures"

In 2007, the "No on Prop 8" campaign screened potential focus group participants in cities across California three times before accepting them into the final groups. Campaign staff asked a range of questions related to religious beliefs, political affiliation, and views on marriage. Because Smith and his colleagues assumed that 85–90 percent of lesbians and gays would vote "no" on Prop 8, participants who self-identified as lesbian or gay in the screening process were eliminated from the focus group. Once campaign staff selected the final focus groups, they asked participants more specific questions about what would persuade them to vote "no."

The first helpful piece of data the campaign isolated was that "undecided" voters felt there was no good public spokesperson for the "no" position. Because Prop 8 threatened to take away same-sex couples' right to marry, focus group participants reported that they did not want to see lesbian and gay couples in the commercials because of the feeling that on this issue same-sex individuals were inevitably self-serving. Instead, "undecided" voters said they wanted to see TV commercials that featured "neutral figures," but they could not determine who exactly those figures might be. Smith and his colleagues decided that a relatively "neutral figure" would be a family member of a lesbian or gay person. As a result, the campaign initially chose to feature straight citizens talking about their lesbian and gay family members.

The first television commercial aired by the "No on Prop 8" campaign was called "Thorons." It featured Julia and Sam Thoron, a real-life gray-haired, white, heterosexual couple, explaining that the law should treat their lesbian daughter and their straight daughters in the same way. Seated next to each other on their living room couch, Sam says, "Julia and I have been married for forty-six years." As they smile and turn to look at each other, Julia continues, "Together we've raised three children who are now adults." The camera moves to a close-up of Sam as he says, "My wife and I never treated our children differently, we never loved them any differently, and the law shouldn't treat them any differently either." As the camera pans across several family photos, the Thorons point out that the passage of Prop 8 will mean that their "gay daughter and thousands of . . . [other] Californians will lose the right to marry." The ad features the parents of a gay woman but incorporates only a photo of her, which the viewer glimpses among the family pictures.

Picking up on this theme, newspaper articles published during the campaign called attention to the fact that the ads did not feature lesbians and gays; the *Los Angeles Times* ran headlines such as: "Prop 8 Commercials' Invisible Gays." After its passage, Prop 8 opponents argued that leaving lesbians and gays out of television commercials had been tantamount to putting them back in the closet. On February 26, 2009, more than four hundred people gathered in San Francisco to vent their frustrations to "No on Prop 8" leaders. Echoing newspaper articles that criticized the campaign in the months leading up to election day, many citizens at the town hall–style meeting felt that the "No on Prop 8" campaign had made a fatal error by excluding lesbians and gays from the television campaign. This point was especially relevant to a lesbian and gay political campaign because sexuality is invisible to the eye; despite the notion that "you can tell just by looking," sexual orientation is not an externally visible trait. This is precisely why coming out and making oneself visible to others has been a battle cry of many activists and social movement organizations.

Responding to this reaction, John Ireland, a white, openly gay filmmaker and journalist based in Los Angeles, founded the "Get to Know Us First" campaign, a series of seven thirty-second public service announcements (PSAs) that aired throughout the state during January and February 2009. When I interviewed Ireland by email, he emphasized how important it was for voters to see images of lesbian and gay couples and families as the legal appeals process got underway.[17] Ireland wrote to me, "Our goal is to reach as many of these folks . . . as we can, so we have actively run cable and broadcast in English and Spanish in 42 of CA's 58 counties, where Proposition 8 garnered the majority of votes." The PSAs feature lesbian and gay couples and families describing their love for each other, their lifelong commitment to one another, and the myriad ways in which they resemble heterosexuals. In each one, lesbian and gay couples break the "fourth wall," looking directly into the camera, as if speaking to the viewer. This method of address reflects a strong belief in the power of individual stories, a belief that not just seeing but also "getting to know" lesbian and gay couples and families can influence voters' choices.

In contrast to the "No on Prop 8" commercials, the "Get to Know Us First" PSAs operated according to the strategy that lesbians and gays need to be the

Figure 4.1. In this television commercial produced by the "Get to Know Us First" campaign, Gina and Sonia are featured celebrating Christmas with their two young children and talking about their ordinary family life.

messengers of their own stories; at a 2008 press conference for "Get to Know Us First," participants were reminded that they were there to speak their own truth: "tell your story, that's the strength of it. We are all the experts of our families." The PSAs in particular reflect an intentional effort to reach Spanish-speaking voters; unlike the overwhelming whiteness of the "No on Prop 8" commercials, the "Get to Know Us First" PSAs feature black, Latino, white, and interracial families. According to Ireland, "many minds will change when culturally-held beliefs about the 'stereotypical gay' begin to break down . . . as the negative images are replaced with authentic ones."

These PSAs directly address the criticisms that the "No on Prop 8" television commercials rendered lesbians and gays invisible. Surprisingly though, according to Smith, "there was a hypersensitivity to staying in the closet" throughout the campaign. In part, this is surprising given the extensive amount of research done to determine the campaign's strategy and the patent critique of the commercials' representational politics. What is arguably more significant though is that political campaign success relies heavily on what is known as a "disciplined message." Among the committee formed to fight Prop 8, however, Smith observed an unusually high amount of internal disagreement about what the campaign's message should be. Smith described the campaign as more "contentious internally" than other campaigns he had worked on.

By his assessment, the LGBT civil rights leaders and organizations involved in the "No on Prop 8" campaign lacked the internal coherence and unified leadership that have helped other campaigns defeat similar ballot initiatives.[18] Smith told me about California's 2005 campaign for "No on Proposition 73," which was an attempt to amend the California Constitution to bar abortion for an unemancipated minor until forty-eight hours after the physician has notified the minor's parent or legal guardian, except in a medical emergency or with a parental waiver. Smith, who also worked on that campaign, explained that the leadership for "No on Prop 73" was concentrated in the Planned Parenthood organization. The campaign did not use the word "choice" in any of its advertising until six days before the election because polling data and focus groups indicated that not mentioning it would allow them to get the "no" votes needed. The campaign's strategy was successful, he insisted, because Planned Parenthood leaders understood the message required to defeat the initiative and were able to convey that message to their pro-choice base. Although Planned Parenthood leaders ideologically disagreed with the approach of the campaign, they understood its necessity in defeating Prop 73, the goal at the time.

Smith, however, was an outsider to the long history of LGBT rights struggles. He did not perceive that the inability (or refusal) of the "No on Prop 8" campaign, or the critics of the campaign, to recognize the need for pragmatism, or to convincingly communicate that message to its voter base, was the direct result of the dominance of the liberal activist legacy. Smith was, of course, speaking as a political campaign consultant, as someone dedicated to progressive issues but not immersed in the communities and people on whose behalf he works. His frustration about the contentiousness of the "No on Prop 8" campaign was rooted in his understanding of and experience in running campaigns, which operate under a strict set of rules. These rules demand in-depth, sophisticated research and creativity, and, I contend, all this is removed from the specific histories of social minorities. What Smith could not put his finger on during our conversation was that the campaign's approach to reaching "undecided" voters ran counter to the approach of the marriage equality movement.

Here I am referring to a uniquely US-based approach to fighting for access to the institution of marriage, which has taken a specific form based on the nation's social and political culture. In his discussion of the 1996 Defense of Marriage Act (DOMA), Barry D. Adam examines the strength of anti-gay public sentiment and state and federal legislation about marriage in relation to other advanced industrialized nations. He writes:

> At a time when the legal recognition of gay and lesbian relationships has
> been proceeding apace in advanced industrial nations around the world

(most notably, in Scandinavia, the Netherlands, Belgium, France, Canada, Germany, and Hungary and partially or locally in Australia, Austria, Brazil, Colombia, Czech Republic, New Zealand, Portugal, South Africa, Spain, Switzerland, and the United Kingdom), the efforts of US legislators to prohibit legal recognition demand explanation.[19]

His explanation, based on close study of ideas around "American exceptionalism," moral panics about marriage rights, labor and social citizenship, racial hierarchies, and gender and national identity, suggests that all of these constructs come together to produce a culture strongly opposed to marriage rights for same-sex couples. Summarizing the way these ideas work in conjunction with one another he writes, "Nation-building rhetoric employing analogies of the nation to the family (and thus marriage) inevitably manufactures a series of 'others' thrown out of the national family and uses marriage laws as a tool to mark that exclusion."[20] Lesbians and gays in the United States are the "others" who become a social minority excluded from the same rights built into the human rights frameworks of other industrialized nations.

Adam's article was published in 2003, only one year before Massachusetts became the first state to grant marriage rights to same-sex couples. His closing remarks provide a useful description of changes that were long under way but had finally gained mainstream traction: "National hierarchies and hegemonies . . . may be fully derailed only through the de(con)struction of the social mechanisms that generate the range of 'others' in opposition to which Anglo-Protestant, white, nativist identities and moralities manufacture themselves."[21] This indeed occurred with great momentum beginning in the early 2000s, through a particular set of strategic choices.

For example, in landmark state and federal court cases about marriage rights such as *Goodridge v. Department of Public Health* (Massachusetts, 2004), *United States v. Windsor* (2013), and *Obergefell v. Hodges* (2015), advocates framed their arguments in terms of individual identity categories and protections. Arguing that defining marriage as the union of one man and one woman was unconstitutional, attorneys pointed to tax, property, and healthcare benefits denied to each lesbian and gay person because they could not marry, to the rights denied to the children of lesbian and gay parents, and to the symbolic power of marriage to validate committed relationships. In each of these cases, attorneys made use of images of lesbians and gays to make their arguments.

It is important to note here that the strategies used to achieve state and federal marriage equality have come under harsh attack for privileging a narrow, homonormative culture that is generally white, male, educated, and middle class. Yet, as Jane Ward notes in her study of diversity in LGBT activist organizations, there are conditions under which the deployment of "normative logics" ends up achieving positive results for far more complex forms of activism.[22] She writes, "Viewing such efforts as 'strategic' focuses our attention on how activists, drawing on their own agency, define their local and contextual successes (i.e., Did they in fact produce more resources for legitimacy for LGBT people in their area? If so: strategic success)."[23] With this analysis, Ward offers a view of social movements that shows they are not simply assimilationist or radical, but rather often exist in various configurations of normativity and non-normativity.

From this view of social movements emerge compelling ideas about visibility and the different ways and ends to which it has been put in LGBT political battles. In particular, comparing the choices of the "No on Prop 8" campaign with patterns of LGBT television visibility provides a useful parallel for creating a dialogue between political campaign commercials and television more broadly. For example, the "No on Prop 8" campaign drew on fictional television's use of straight characters to speak for sexual minorities. Historically, coming out has been one of the primary storytelling strategies of media makers. However, because coming out stories involve a self-identified LGBT person "outing" him- or herself to others, they often become about the LGBT person asking for acceptance and love from family and friends. Suzanna Walters argues that a narrative that features a coming out story "almost always involves heterosexual unease, fear, and rejection, and therefore still [centers on] heterosexuality." They turn into stories about heterosexual struggles to come to terms with LGBT identities, preventing the story from moving beyond this "single cataclysmic moment."[24] Heterosexuality thus remains central to the narrative while LGBT sexualities are peripheral. Candace Moore proposes that this narrative structure is less about tending to the comfort of heterosexual audiences—an approach seen as assimilationist, even homophobic—and more about a bifurcated view of sexuality, a dual address, for straight and LGBT audiences.[25]

In Moore's analysis of Showtime's lesbian drama *The L Word* (2004–2009), she argues that the notion of the "tourist," as theorized by the media scholar Ellen Strain, offers a way to understand the show's use of Jenny Schechter, a character who identified as straight at the start of the series and whom lesbian audiences almost universally detested. In Moore's view, Jenny functions as a "tourist" guiding straight viewers into the show's upscale, urban Los Angeles lesbian culture. For Showtime, a premium cable network with a distinctly socially liberal brand seeking to draw a variety of subscribers, this argument is compelling and in many ways parallels the "No on Prop 8" campaign's focus group research. The campaign was trying to reach "undecided" voters, who were presumably predominantly straight, and the "Thorons" commercial offered an entrée into a family with a lesbian daughter. Julia and Sam Thoron act as real-life tourists, inviting voters into their home, showing them family photos, and guiding them to the understanding that their lesbian daughter is equal to their straight daughters.

Difference, Not Discrimination

The "No on Prop 8" campaign strategically scripted the "Thorons" commercial to emphasize that Julia and Sam treat their gay daughter no differently than their straight daughters. The word "differently" appears three times in the 39-second ad. As discussed earlier, the choice to couch the campaign in terms of differential treatment rather than discrimination emerged from two findings in the campaign's focus groups.

First—and contrary to the traditions of LGBT politics—focus group participants revealed that they did not find the parallel between black civil rights and LGBT civil rights convincing; they felt that racial discrimination operates differently from discrimination against lesbian and gay couples. John D'Emilio articulates this distinction: "The context of civil rights struggles has looked very different around matters of race and sexual identity. . . . For sexual minorities, while the immorality and injustice of invidious discrimination remain the same, its specific manifestations, and therefore the most effective means of resistance, are different."[26] From this perspective, although they are often compared to ethnic and racial minority groups such as African Americans, sexual minorities are not necessarily or inevitably visible; this difference is not marked on the body.[27] Visibility for gays and lesbians requires an active, public articulation of the self. Setting aside the range of visible practices LGBT communities have adopted—codes of dress, voice inflections, haircuts, physical mannerisms—to externally signify sexual identity, visibility has been touted as *the* vehicle for cultural inclusion and political equality. In Wanda Sykes's 2009 HBO special, the comedian echoes these differences in a segment about her own experience being both black and gay. She says, "you know what? It is harder. It's harder being gay than it is being black." As the audience applauds, she adds, "There are things that I had to do as gay that I didn't have to do as black." By "things," Sykes means coming out to her family and to the public: "I didn't have to come out black, . . . didn't have to sit my parents down and tell them about my blackness." Using language common to narratives of coming out, Sykes says, "Mom, Dad, I gotta tell you something.

I hope you still love me, I'm just gonna say it. Mom, Dad, I'm black." Imitating her mother's response, Sykes explodes into a hysterical rant, familiar to lesbians and gays who have received less than supportive responses from family members. She imagines her mother screaming frantically, "Oh lord, did she say that? Anything but black, Jesus. Give her cancer Lord, give her cancer. Anything but black Lord. . . . What did I do? What did I do? I knew I shouldn't have let you watch *Soul Train*. Was it *Soul Train*?"

While the notion of having to come out as gay but not as black has been used as a rhetorical strategy to distinguish the experiences of sexual minorities from those of racial minorities, Sykes uses it unconventionally; instead of focusing on how difficult it is to come out to family, friends, and coworkers as lesbian, Sykes plays out the scenario as if she was telling her parents that she is black.

The belief that the black civil rights struggle does not offer a narrative parallel to that of LGBT civil rights is in opposition to the legal arguments made by LGBT rights attorneys. In addition to *Hollingsworth v. Perry*, other legal decisions about marriage rights, including *Goodridge v. the Department of Public Health* (2003) in Massachusetts and Iowa's *Varnum v. Brien* (2009), drew parallels between black and LGBT civil rights, finding bans on marriage between blacks and whites (overturned federally in the 1967 Supreme Court case *Loving v. Virginia* and overturned in California in 1948 in *Perez v. Sharp*) to be discriminatory. Drawing parallels to *Perez* and *Loving*, attorneys in these later cases argued that lesbians and gays endure discrimination based on sexual orientation, biological sex, or both.[28] From this understanding of oppression, LGBT rights activists have argued that sexual orientation is either purely accidental or is a nonessential element of human nature.

The "No on Prop 8" campaign's focus group data, however, suggested that using the black civil rights framework of discrimination would be less effective than arguing that lesbians and gays should not be "treated differently" than heterosexual citizens. Based on these findings, "treated differently" became the semantic choice of the "No on Prop 8" campaign. Understood in legal terms as prejudice in action, discrimination functions as an exclusionary discourse. As a discursive construct, discrimination is a system of exclusions actively imposed on one population by another and based on individual categories of identity. Associated with stigma and premised on a set of constructed norms and deviance from those norms, discrimination produces a boundary between inclusion and exclusion. The notion of difference, on the other hand, denotes variation rather than the rigid binaries created by discourses of discrimination. "Difference" implies degrees of distinction, a progression rather than a distinct boundary. "Difference" is also structured in a more positivist and passive way, seen as the "natural" state of human variation. By positioning Prop 8 as a matter of treating lesbian and gay couples differently, the "No on Prop 8" campaign appealed to voters' perceived desire to treat people fairly.

Despite this finding, the internal dynamics of the campaign shifted its focus away from the concept of difference. In fact, two of the campaign's most significant commercials used the language of discrimination and made a direct comparison to black civil rights. The first commercial featured Senator Dianne Feinstein. Identified by the campaign as a prominent government official with a long history of support from mainstream feminist organizations such as the League of Women Voters and the National Organization for Women (NOW), Feinstein has a resolutely Democratic voting record, but one that is less progressive than California's junior senator, Barbara Boxer, making her the ideal politician to speak to "undecided" voters. By having Feinstein in the commercial, the "No on Prop 8" campaign aimed to appeal to politically moderate women swayed by allegiance to and respect for her causes.[29]

In the commercial, Feinstein, speaking directly to the voters, tells of the discrimination she's experienced in her time as a California senator: "I see it again in Proposition 8. Eight would be a terrible mistake for California. It changes our Constitution, eliminates fundamental rights, and treats people differently under the law." Rebuffing provocative claims made in the "Yes on Prop 8" commercials, Feinstein adds that Prop 8 is not about children or education; "it's about discrimination, and we must always say no to that." Revisiting the campaign's message that personal feelings about marriage are irrelevant, Feinstein says, "Voting 'no' is about being fair and treating people equally under the law."

The Feinstein commercial aired for four days, October 28–31; it was the only "No on Prop 8" commercial running during that time. After that, the campaign shifted, airing the commercial 30 percent of the total time given to the campaign's television ads. Despite the reduced circulation of the Feinstein commercial, postelection surveys indicated that it was the one voters most recalled.[30] Replacing the Feinstein commercial, the campaign aired an ad titled "Internment," which was narrated by the African American actor Samuel L. Jackson.

In "Internment" Jackson says, "It wasn't that long ago that discrimination was legal in California." As he speaks of the United States' Japanese internment camps, of how Armenians weren't able to buy a home in the Central Valley, and of how blacks and Latinos were told who they could and couldn't marry, black-and-white images from this past flash across the screen. He says, "It was a sorry time in our history." Jackson goes on to say that the supporters of Prop 8 want to eliminate fundamental rights. Without using the word "marriage" or "gay," Jackson closes by saying that "we have an obligation to pass along to our children a more tolerant, more decent society. Vote no on Prop 8. It's unfair, and it's wrong."

It was at this juncture that Smith describes the trajectory of the campaign as "going off message." Straying from the campaign's message not to treat lesbians and gays "differently," "Internment" focused on discrimination. According to Smith, "Internment" was supposed to be used only if the campaign got "desperate" and Proposition 8 appeared sure to pass. As election day neared, the campaign was underfunded, especially compared to the "Yes on Prop 8" campaign, creating a sense of panic among members of the campaign committee, and the decision was made to put the "Internment" ad on the air. At the last minute, though, money poured into the "No on Prop 8" campaign, and independent consultants produced several other commercials. Smith says in the week before the election, four different commercials, made by four different consultants, aired on television, and three of them, he says, were "off message." They strayed from the "don't treat differently" campaign mantra that focus groups said would be more effective in swaying undecided voters than a message purely about discrimination.

Who Sets the Agenda? "Whether you like it or not"

The "No on Prop 8" campaign's efforts to produce commercials based solely on its own research were greatly undermined by the "Yes on Prop 8" campaign's relentless focus on religion and children's education. As is not uncommon in homophobic campaigns, the rhetoric of "family values," Judith Stacey writes, "provides an infinitely malleable symbolic resource that is understandably irresistible to politicians from both major parties in the age of corporate-sponsored, mass-media politics."[31]

The first "Yes on Prop 8" commercial, titled "Whether You Like It or Not," opens with footage of San Francisco mayor Gavin Newsom giving a speech in response to the California Supreme Court's May 2008 decision that allowed same-sex couples to wed. Standing in front of a cheering audience, Newsom declares, "It's going to happen now, whether you like it or not." The commercial twists Newsom's words to criticize the Court's decision for "ignoring four million voters and imposing same-sex marriage on California." Adopting the view that lesbian and gay marriage rights are a matter of "personal belief" rather than a fundamental right, the commercial suggests that this decision opened a Pandora's box of problems: citizens will now sue over any personal belief; churches will lose their tax-exempt status; and so-called gay marriage will be taught in schools.

The "Yes on Prop 8" campaign followed this commercial with one called "Princes." With "Princes," the "Yes on Prop 8" campaign invoked the image of the innocent child living in a world where Prop 8 has been defeated. The commercial features a young girl excitedly telling her mother what she has learned in school that day: "A prince can marry a prince and I can marry a princess." Richard Peterson, who teaches law at Pepperdine University, a politically conservative school affiliated with the Churches of Christ, steps into the frame and says that education about marriage for lesbians and gays will become part of the public school curriculum in California. He claims that after Massachusetts's 2003 decision that allowed lesbians and gays to marry, second graders began learning "that a boy can marry a boy." He adds, "The courts had no right to object." The commercial closes with the warning that California's education code includes teaching marriage and that if marriage for lesbians and gays remains legal in the state, it will have to be taught in schools. The television commercial created so much public controversy that the "No" campaign immediately pulled its newest commercial from the air in order to work to rebut the claims made in "Princes."

Pierre Bourdieu argues that "the greater the *interest* one has in a problem, the more opinions one has on it." [32] "Interest" is determined, he says, by one's proximity to the issue at hand. These two "Yes on Prop 8" commercials create an urgency about the issue of marriage by exaggerating links between marriage and the institutions of religion and education, which hold treasured places in the national imaginary and in people's personal lives. The "Yes on Prop 8" campaign's commercials generated a relationship among these institutions in order to appeal to a broad range of voters who already considered themselves aligned with religious and/or education-based concerns. Lee Edelman argues that politics rely on a future-oriented logic that is intertwined with heterosexuality and with what he terms "reproductive futurism." [33] Heteronormativity builds itself around the future, which is always and powerfully represented by the child. Edelman says, "That Child, immured in an innocence . . . condenses a fantasy of vulnerability . . . in its form of sublimation: [it is] an insistence on sameness that intends to restore an Imaginary past." [34] This image of the child, just as the more general rhetoric of "family values," has been invoked to alter public policy, to discipline "deviant" citizens (such as sexual minorities), and to stigmatize unconventional family structures that "fail" to achieve the ideal of the heterosexual nuclear family.

The figure of the "Child" played a prominent role in the Prop 8 television commercials, and it has framed numerous social and political debates over time. When I began this research in 2007 I attended a legal forum on marriage rights in California. Although not surprised, I was nonetheless taken aback by how invested both sides were in the "Child." Kenneth Starr and John Eastman, speaking for the conservative side, offered statistics from social science research that they said shows children raised by both biological parents to be more likely to lead stable adult lives. Shannon Minter from the NCLR refuted the findings with studies that compare single-parent homes, (heterosexual) divorced homes, and (heterosexual) nuclear families, demonstrating that they have no relation to gay families. However, Minter fixated on the circumstances of the "Child"; at the time, he saw an undeniable "reality" that gay families exist and that within dominant paradigms, they weren't able to participate in heteronormative practices of their peers (e.g., children can't say their parents are married) and were vulnerable to legal circumstances (which might constrain, e.g., hospital visits or financial benefits) that are the privilege of heterosexual families.

By the time the "Princes" ad aired, "No on Prop 8" campaign leaders had made internal changes, and six consultants were now involved in the ad process. They all provided their own advice to the campaign manager, who made the final decisions. Smith articulated a key challenge in working within this structure: because of the sheer number of people involved in the campaign, moving from concept to air was slower than would be ideal, especially when trying to refute an ad that resonated as strongly with voters as "Princes" did. It took the "No on Prop 8" campaign nine days to get a response ad on the air. The commercial featured Jack O'Connell, California's state superintendent of public instruction at the time. In the ad, O'Connell says, "Prop 8 has nothing to do with schools or kids. Our schools are not required to teach anything about marriage and using kids to lie about that is shameful." The commercial concludes by saying that California teachers are against Prop 8 because "no matter how you feel about marriage, it's wrong to eliminate fundamental rights."

By using O'Connell for the response ad, Smith feels, the campaign moved away from targeting undecided women voters, who research showed were more movable than undecided male voters. This was a topic I brought up in my email interview with the "Get to Know Us First" campaign's John Ireland. Like Smith, he told me that campaign staff assumed that straight women, as Ireland put it, "are more likely than men to convert to support of marriage equality due to their likelihood to have social friendships with gay men."

Neither campaigns had empirical data to support the idea that women would be more easily persuaded to vote "no" or were likely to do so because of their assumed friendships with gay men.

A symbiotic relationship between straight women and gay men is a theme in my research about Prop 8 as well as in my research about marketing and branding, detailed in the first chapter. The association between straight women and gay men is a consumer-driven relationship, premised on shared interests in style, aesthetics, and consumption. Katherine Sender attributes this symbiosis to gay men's "historical association with taste and fashion, their status as straight women's best friends, and their availability as objects of desire."[35] This purported pairing sustains a belief that straight women are the ideal consumers for themselves and for the home. Gay men, moreover, are assumed to be the promoters of female consumption. In this coupling, gay men are also shown as asexual—in an effort to break long-standing associations with gay men as hypersexual. This image has come to be a prevalent stereotype, which carves out a cultural space for gay men premised on an intrinsic relationship to heteronormative femininity.

Both of the campaigns under discussion here relied on this consumer-driven relationship, drawing on social stereotypes that are culturally constructed. In this way, market-driven decisions dominated aspects of political decision making, especially at the level of voter data and research. In the case of Prop 8, the word "market" is not used in describing polling or focus group data, yet the political campaign process relied not only on identities constructed in the consumer marketplace but also on the actual integration of consumer experts and market researchers into the production of media campaigns.

Rather than interpret this information as representative of the all-encompassing influence of the market in politics, I argue it is actually representative of an active—even productive—integration of politics and consumer culture. David Skover and Kelly Testy argue that identity constructed in the marketplace must be a starting point for the legal framework of LGBT civil rights—both because they support the idea and because they believe it is an inevitable necessity. In an article for the *California Law Review* entitled "LesBiGay Identity as Commodity," they write, "America's commercial culture moves far too fast for America's legal and political systems to control it." Exploring the dissonance between the validation of gays as a viable commercial market and their simultaneous devaluation in the political and legal arenas, Skover and Testy continue, "As long as the structures of advanced capitalism remain in place, those structures that drive the modern commercial culture past the law, the emerging LesBiGay consumer identity is likely to overtake and define LesBiGay political and legal identity."[36] As a result, they call for gays to negotiate their law and politics through the image that is projected of them in the marketplace, a call that "No on Prop 8" takes up in a way that doesn't limit political work to consumer ideologies.

However, opponents of Prop 8 felt that these commercials were purely reactionary, and that by funneling precious funds into them, the "No on Prop 8" campaign was denying itself the opportunity to produce and disseminate informative, positive ads. In part, this was a by-product of the campaign's structure, where major decisions were handed over to political "experts" who were often quite removed from the histories of social minorities. While campaign officials felt they had no choice but to redress the misinformation of the "Yes" television ads, critiques of this tactic speak to the larger problem of letting opponents determine the strategies of LGBT politics.

In D'Emilio's essay "Born Gay?," he reminds scholars and activists to be wary of making decisions reactively. In discussing why claiming lesbians and gays are born gay is problematic, he says that "we cannot allow our opponents to shape our agenda, our self-conception, or how we choose to represent ourselves to the larger society."[37] A long pattern of this kind of reactionary politics in the United States exists, borne out of the medicalization and criminalization of homosexual acts and identity.[38] Historically, the experiences of LGBT people—including being arrested, institutionalized, and treated with electro-shock therapy—have produced a culture in which sexual minorities value coming out as a strategy to combat medical and popular beliefs about gayness as mental illness, disease, hormone deficiency or surplus, and what Jeffrey Escoffier describes as "accidents of birth."[39]

The "No on Prop 8" campaign fell into this trap, operating defensively against the claims of the "Yes" campaign. This response runs the risk of letting anti-gay forces set the agenda for our rights. The problem here, D'Emilio says, is that "this is not a secure foundation . . . on which to build a freedom movement."[40] The broader context of the campaign, however, complicates this critique and adds a surprisingly progressive element to the "No on Prop 8" strategy. In the final section, I look at this part of the campaign and how it offers a provocative challenge to normative LGBT politics.

Paradox and the "Tolerance Trap"

The "No" campaign commercial that was entirely "on message" was also its most publicly and internally controversial. "Conversation" was the second commercial produced by the campaign, and it aired following "Thorons."

With "Conversation," the campaign decided to try a tactic they hoped would sway undecided voters who might not change their opinion on marriage rights for lesbians and gays but who also might not be willing to take away rights from another group of citizens. In "Conversation" two female friends sit at the kitchen counter going through a stack of photos. With each photo, one woman identifies the person in the picture for her friend. She turns to a new photo and happily points to her niece and her niece's partner, a picture taken at their wedding ceremony. Her friend immediately clams up and says that she feels uncomfortable with the idea of marriage rights for lesbians and gays. Her friend calmly reassures her that it's okay to be "uncomfortable." But, she asks, "are you willing to eliminate rights and have our laws treat people differently?" Her friend immediately and emphatically replies, "No."

According to Smith, the "LGBT community hated 'Conversation'" and future commercials did not return to its theme, which hoped to convey the message that inner dissonance was okay. In other words, the commercial's theme suggested that a voter could be at once uncomfortable with lesbian and gay marriage rights or with homosexuality while also supporting the belief that all people should have access to the same legal rights. Smith said he hoped voters could "rise to their better nature" and say "'just because I'm uncomfortable with it, doesn't mean they shouldn't be able to do it.'" In our phone conversation, Smith expressed disappointment that such inner dissonance wasn't accepted or even fully understood by LGBT activists involved in the campaign. The concept of inner dissonance is difficult for lesbians and gays, as for any social minority, because we must accept others being uncomfortable with same-sex desire, and unwilling to change those views. That is, lesbians and gays would have to accept that others may disapprove of them but still vote in favor of legal equality.

The paradox of "Conversation" signals a progressive move toward a more nuanced identity politics, creating a space built on the negotiation of pragmatism and radical opposition. This perspective recognizes the need for access to the rights and privileges tied to marriage but does not base that need on the demand for social acceptance of homosexuality. As a political practice, this negotiation holds onto the queer stance against assimilation and homonormativity, refusing the need for approval from heterosexist society. Yet it also understands the practical protections required for economic, social, and political stability and viability in the United States. Marriage in the United States is a critical nexus for the distribution of public and private rights and benefits. George Chauncey's research on marriage details the extent to which the allocation of benefits is "a distinctly American approach" rooted in twentieth-century legal changes that made deviating from heteronormativity more and more costly.[41] Unlike other industrialized countries, the United States has built a system in which a host of benefits, including healthcare and social security, are linked to the institution of marriage, particularly to federally recognized marriage.[42]

However, the inner dissonance acknowledged by "Conversation" underscores that discourses of "tolerance" are both visible in the political campaign and also opposed to it. Here I am drawing on Walters's concept of the "tolerance trap." For Walters, "tolerance" has become the central approach of mainstream LGBT rights—in popular culture and politics. As Nikki Sullivan writes, "In short . . . the assumption was/is that tolerance can be achieved by making differences invisible, or at least secondary, in and through an essentalising, normalising emphasis on sameness."[43] The word "tolerance" itself, Walters notes, is something used to refer to experiences that we must endure. In a radio interview for *The Writer's Voice*, Walters describes how LGBT Americans have asked for tolerance, even though the word carries a negative connotation: "We speak of tolerating a bad movie whereas we don't speak of tolerating great sex."[44] "Because 'tolerance' allows broader anti-gay animus to go unaddressed," Walters points out, "single issues can emerge that straight allies can be 'tolerant' about without altering their more general beliefs about sex and gender."[45] To ask for tolerance is to ask for acceptance and inclusion within society as it already is and not to demand change at a society's most basic levels.

I suggest that, rather than see the response to "Conversation" only as a sign of the unstoppable push for assimilation or the limited version of equality offered by "tolerance," we understand it to reveal this paradox and its active negotiation within the political process. The "tolerance trap" has not, in fact, confined political work to a narrow set of homonormative tropes. Although the paradox was never fully realized, it was nonetheless a contradiction that surfaced in the campaign in powerful ways. "Conversation" ignited conflict and revealed the active tensions within a political campaign so seemingly normative from the outside. I see this commercial and the issues it raised as the most exciting moment in the campaign; it embodied a vitally progressive and paradoxical politics. Although neither the commercial nor the paradox ended up defining the campaign, "Conversation" reveals a rupture in the notion that LGBT politics has become synonymous with assimilationist politics. Simply put, this commercial and many of the campaign's strategies reveal careful and difficult negotiations of sexual politics.

This look at Prop 8 offers a view from the ground, presenting a perspective of LGBT politics significantly different from what is aired in television representations. Rather than assuming from representation that mainstream

LGBT politics operates methodically to normalize lesbians and gays, media campaigns are filled with conflicts and disputes that both shore up and destabilize assimilationist politics. The stories behind the "No on Prop 8" campaign demonstrate that representation alone is far too simplistic a mode of analysis for ascertaining the state of cultural politics. The nature of political campaigns produces numerous clashes of strategies and beliefs. These clashes, however, do not necessarily weaken the campaign or its legacy in LGBT political history. Rather, as Amin Ghaziani's research shows, conflict is a primary way that political workers and activists make decisions about goals and strategies.[46] That LGBT rights has focused on visibility in its quest for equality—often putting forward white, classy, gender-conforming images—does not mean that this particular visibility has been the movement's only focus or that this focus has rendered invisible and devalued a host of other important issues. Rather, LGBT political campaigns like Prop 8 are defined by competing demands, conflicting strategies, and controversial decisions.

As we enter a new landscape of LGBT equality, we need to keep this complex view of visibility in mind. With the US Supreme Court's June 2015 ruling in *Obergefell v. Hodges*, lesbians and gays can marry in any US state, and those marriages are fully recognized by the federal government. Commentators ask what's next for LGBT rights. Is the battle over? Are transgender rights the new frontier of visibility politics? What will battles for equality look like in the future, especially under the administration of a Republican president, Donald Trump, and a Republican-led Congress? What role will television play as Hollywood becomes increasingly vocal in its opposition to the administration's emerging policies on race, ethnicity, nationality, immigration, gender, sexuality, and reproductive rights? In the next chapter, I address these questions with an eye to the early conversations taking place within LGBT television programming since the Supreme Court's 2015 ruling.

Conclusion: The Personal Is
Still Political (and Profitable)

At the historical moment I came to the end of this project, it became more difficult to conclude it. Since the presidential campaign and election of 2016, as a result of which Donald Trump became the forty-fifth US president—having defeated Democratic candidate Hillary Clinton in a historic upset—divisive and discriminatory rhetoric about anyone deemed "different" has increased on an unprecedented scale.[1] The Trump administration has arguably reignited battles and civil unrest about the hard truths of the nation's pervasive and ongoing systems of inequality, unleashed and intensified by anger generated by President Barack Obama's popularity. Obama's eight years in office (2009–2017) produced a strong current of progressive rhetoric about how much cultural change was occurring in the country during that period and about how many more minorities were visible in mainstream US society. Just below the surface, however, lay a deep resentment about the shifts in power represented by the election of a black president, and this resulted in the strong resurgence of attitudes of white supremacy.

The current sociopolitical climate is witnessing a surge in verbal, physical, and legal attacks on minority groups, including immigrants, Muslims, women, people of color, and LGBT people, to name a few. I am personally concerned about the direction in which the United States appears to be headed—we are moving backward, and this regression will re-entrench forms of discrimination long thought to be gone or almost gone. What is especially distressing about this cultural moment is that it exposes the persistence of hatred and injustice, making clear that significant and contentious differences continue to exist in the United States. In a strange irony, the attention given to categories of identity, to bigotry and prejudice, seems to be moving identity politics back to the center of public discourse and overriding many of the assimilationist arguments of past decades. By putting racism, sexism, homophobia, ethnocentrism, ableism, classism, and religious intolerance at the core of protests, walkouts, and pride parades, the public is re-embracing identity—even intersectionality—and acknowledging how elemental difference is in US culture.

The optimist in me wants to see communities come together across the nation and look at differences not only as the basis for oppression, but also as a potential route to liberation. The cynic in me worries that we will neglect to connect to one another, fail to see shared experiences across multiple and overlapping lines of difference. Whatever happens, though, I believe transgender visibility is positioned to chart our path.

We are witnessing history. I say this to college students at the large public university where I work when we talk about transgender representation on television. As the years go by, more heads nod and more hands go up, as increasing numbers of students want to talk about their own gender identity and expression. Although I have been studying and teaching about gender and sexuality since I started graduate school, the topic of transgender identity began to enter the mainstream lexicon only in the mid-2010s. In the first months of the Trump administration, transgender identities have been pushed to the center of public discussion amid heated debates about the safety of transgender children, regulations on the use of public restrooms, educational standards and policies, and state and federal protections.[2]

Observing this shift, I realized that what seemed to me like "old news"—for lack of a better term—was hardly common knowledge to the greater public. For many years, the "T" in LGBT has been elided, and the acronym has served primarily as an umbrella term for sexual minorities. This is a crucial moment, then, because my students, the majority of whom were born in the late 1990s—blissfully unaware of the struggles Ellen DeGeneres endured after coming out in 1997—are witnessing transgender visibility and civil rights gain mainstream attention in the press and become battle cries of LGBT advocates.

I stake a claim here for the potential of transgender identity politics because in and of themselves, people who identify as transgender inhabit multiple identities; some talk about "being born in the wrong body" and experiencing life as both men and women. Others identify across gender and racial lines, particularly because of the tragically high numbers of transgender women of color who are brutalized and murdered. Engaging with transgender identities, then, means engaging with intersectionality, something mainstream social movements have struggled to negotiate. This intersection of identities offers a rare opportunity for cultural and political intervention.

As those who write about contemporary subjects know all too well, it is a process that closely resembles reporting on the daily news. The landscape can change from day to day, and even from minute to minute, or from tweet to tweet. As Elizabeth Bernstein and Laurie Schaffner observe in their own work about sexuality, "By the time one's thoughts are formulated, they may seem hopelessly out of date—vis-à-vis the world at large or vis-à-vis one's own political convictions."[3] Writing about my two contemporary subjects— television and sexuality—proved doubly challenging. Thinking through the complexities and implications of each new event made me feel simultaneously cutting edge and endlessly behind. How do you do justice to issues that change right before your eyes, issues with consequences that may not be evident for years to come?

This question left me wondering: as the technologies and cultural norms of television continue to change with digitization, convergence, and consolidation, as sexuality and gender continue to become part of everyday discourse in deeper and perhaps more dynamic ways, and as the administration of Republican president Donald Trump and its supporters in Congress appear determined to roll back state and federal programs and protections for social minorities, what role might television programming play as an interlocutor between culture and politics? Coming to the close of this project in these circumstances brought me back to the reasons I started it in the first place and foregrounded the lessons I learned.

When I proposed to look at how television workers conceive of and produce commonsense ideas about sexuality and sexual politics, I had only an inkling of how much I would learn from this approach. My goal was to push past existing critiques to see what lay beyond them. "Studying up" enabled me to examine the parameters of the power these industry leaders wield. As part of what Barbara Ehrenreich and John Ehrenreich call the "professional managerial class" (PMC), these industry workers in their day-to-day working lives must be understood in order for us to gain a broader public insight into how the television industry operates practically and ideologically. With the emergence of the "professional queer," where one's job often becomes about sexual identity, there are more opportunities to analyze a large group of openly gay industry leaders.[4]

Through this approach, I have come to see the role human agents, day-to-day events, and institutional procedures play in the industry's production of sexual minority representations. Instead of conceiving of above-the-line workers only as extensions of institutional interests, I view them as paradoxical figures: network executives are both activists (trying to increase LGBT media visibility) and business people (concerned with profits, audiences shares, and the financial bottom line); marketers try to build niche outlets dedicated to underrepresented minorities and simultaneously to create homogeneous, segmented audiences; market researchers offer television networks methods of customization and inclusion for sexual minorities and also turn sexuality into an effective marketing tool to draw high-quality audiences.

The themes that emerge from the case studies in this book are both predictable and unexpected; for example, television workers' jobs depend on their belief that representation is important and necessary in the struggle for minority recognition and validation. Thus, proclamations about the power of television became a formulaic theme in my interviews. In the light of their work, especially the financial bottom line, the formulation of a television "effects" model is not a revelation. However, it is worth noting this refrain because it comes from personal ideologies and industrial practices, which are sometimes naïve, sometimes politically motivated, and at other times strategic. In other words, however predictable some of my interviewees' comments about television's "effects" seem, they coexist with a range of circumstances that reflect the agency and authority available to industry workers.

This agency is most apparent in the activist work that is strategically kept out of public view, and even out of the view of television's corporate leaders. Although insiders swim in public opinion and commonsense ideas about social identity, I encountered individuals whose perspectives on the four themes addressed in the preceding chapters were nuanced and complex. In some ways, they towed the line; in others, they held onto the notion that sexuality is in and of itself a political act. What I have described as "under-the-radar activism" proves to be progressive and in the service of marginalized LGBT communities. It is also work that in other ways meets the profit-based demands of business.

This finding was surprising given the compelling arguments about the lack of individual control that results from deregulation and consolidation. The changes that occurred in regulation over the past several decades have created a media landscape at once defined by convergence, coming together through ownership consolidation, and expansion, the spreading out and fragmentation of outlets and audiences. As a result, the media industries are dominated by six major conglomerates, which are vertically and horizontally integrated so that one company owns the means of production, distribution, and exhibition, in an arrangement that Jennifer Holt aptly calls "empires of entertainment."[5] Despite claims about the benefits that would come from deregulating the media industries, the negative consequences to consumers and media makers have been marked. Holt summarizes, "Prices went up, service went down, concentration increased and as a result, media markets were less competitive."[6]

In these critiques of deregulation, media corporations tend to be depicted as giant monoliths that leave little room for employees to operate in ways that meet demands for efficiency and profit while also achieving activist-oriented goals on behalf of minority communities. Contrary to this logic, I found that industry workers actively integrate their own diverse concerns, values, and causes with the needs of the business. As my case studies document, I witnessed subversive practices within the worlds of production, marketing, advocacy, and public relations, many of them deliberately kept out of public view.

Although media critics often talk of consolidation as a top-down power structure, power runs both ways. This potential influence is certainly not equal or guaranteed, but I found it in a range of areas, including production, advocacy, public relations, market research, and political consulting. Put another way, these industry employees are not free from industrial constraints or profit motives but nonetheless have the capacity and often the desire to work effectively and powerfully within the system. The recognition that this activism can take different shapes in turn reveals the production of a more heterogeneous and less homogeneous landscape of creative labor in television. It is a space that perhaps offers opportunities for intervention in ways that are not often attributed to this commercial industry.

Making this heterogeneity more visible also challenges the logic of the fait accompli narrative of LGBT politics that I have detailed in the preceding chapters. I remember being struck by how mainstream this narrative is when I saw a 2013 cover of *Time* magazine. On the heels of three days of US Supreme Court arguments about marriage equality in early 2013, *Time* magazine published a cover story entitled "Gay Marriage Already Won."[7] Against a black-and-white close-up of either two women or two men kissing—the magazine circulated both versions in different markets—the cover proclaims: "The Supreme Court hasn't made up its mind—but America has."[8] The article itself summarizes the trajectory of the "gay rights" movement since 1970, describing key moments in the fight for marriage rights along the way.

Mixed in with statistics about public opinion, state legislation, and judicial rulings is a series of media events—moments of breakthrough LGBT visibility—that symbolize the gains made in this political fight: *All in the Family*'s first gay character (1971), Tom Hanks's portrayal of a gay man with AIDS in *Philadelphia* (1993), Tony Kushner's Pulitzer Prize for *Angels in America* (1993), Ellen DeGeneres's coming out (1997), the box office success of *Broke-*

back Mountain (2005), and the revival of the American television sitcom with *Modern Family* (ABC, 2009–). Emphasizing the media's role in this "seismic social shift," David Von Drehle writes,

> Through 2008, no major presidential nominee favored same-sex marriage. But in 2012, the newly converted supporter Barack Obama sailed to an easy victory over Mitt Romney, himself an avowed fan of *Modern Family*—a hit TV show in which a devoted gay couple negotiates the perils of parenthood with deadpan hilarity. When even a conservative Mormon Republican can delight in a sympathetic portrayal of same-sex parenthood, a working consensus is likely at hand.[9]

Von Drehle's claim that "a working consensus is likely at hand" connects *Modern Family*'s weekly stories about the funny but ordinary life of a gay couple with an adopted daughter to the rapid shifts in public opinion that favored marriage rights for lesbians and gays in the lead-up to the 2013 and 2015 Supreme Court rulings.[10] GLAAD reinforced this idea in an infographic it published, entitled "Television Characters Paving the Way on the Road to Marriage," which charts the rise in LGBT representation and correlates those

Figure 5.1. *Time* magazine's cover, published several months before the US Supreme Court's June 2013 rulings on California's Proposition 8 and section 3 of the Defense of Marriage Act, decisions that paved the way for full marriage equality in 2015.

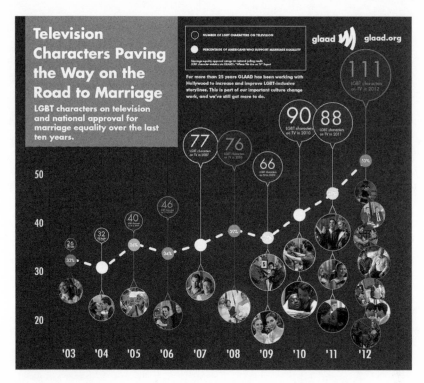

Figure 5.2. An infographic distributed by GLAAD that correlates fictional LGBT television representations to increasing public approval of marriage rights for same-sex couples.

increases to the shift in public opinion favoring marriage equality for lesbians and gays.

With discussions about social and political change came similar remarks about the lives of sexual minorities within this cultural climate, statements based on the idea that US society had reached a point beyond, or post-, homophobia. In such a post-gay era anyone differing from the white, straight, male norm would no longer have that difference be a factor in the ability to earn power, respect, or authority, and, in television, LGBT identity would not motivate the character or story. Routinely, television has been hailed for incorporating characters that just "happen to be [*fill in identity*]."

On one hand, there is both anecdotal and statistical evidence for progress. In 2015, cultural critic Michelangelo Signorile wrote:

> Imagine a group of people who have spent decades—generations, centuries—in fear, invisibility, struggle, and silence. Imagine they find their

voice, only to be decimated by an era of death and unthinkable loss made more bitter by crushing societal indifference to their predicament. Now imagine that, in a matter of a few short years, everything seems to change. At what feels like light speed, they make momentous gains. The world begins to open its arms to them in ways they had never thought possible. The experience is powerful, exhilarating, spellbinding even.[11]

"Momentous gains" refers to the changes in public opinion and in the law, most notably recognizing the rights of lesbians and gays to serve openly in the military and to marry in every state of the nation. "Light speed" refers to the sheer number of changes that took place between 2004, when Massachusetts became the first state to grant marriage rights to same-sex couples, and 2015, when the Supreme Court issued a ruling making marriage equality the law of the land and dismantling the 1996 Defense of Marriage Act (DOMA), which prohibited the federal government from recognizing same-sex marriages.[12] In an equally rapid change, the military's "Don't Ask, Don't Tell" policy, enacted in 1994, was reversed in 2011, bolstered by dozens of official reports and public opinion polls that deemed the policy ineffective and harmful.

On the other hand, despite the changes Signorile outlines, we do not live during a period in US history when one's sexual orientation or gender identity are irrelevant to securing employment, housing, or public accommodation or to guaranteed physical safety. In light of these conditions, Steven Seidman offers a concise—and, I would submit, accurate—assessment of life for many LGBT people in the early twenty-first-century United States: "Gay life today is very different than it was just a decade or two ago. . . . Gay life is defined by a contradiction: many individuals can choose to live beyond the closet but they must still live and participate in a world where most institutions maintain heterosexual domination."[13] His description, published in 2002, accurately summarizes the current situation—in which liberal reforms have been the driving force behind social change, to the extent that legal changes have been enacted, but underlying, heterosexist (and I would add racist, classist, and gendered) institutional structures remain intact.

A look at sociopolitical events indicates that post-gay claims are in many ways unfounded, overblown, or at the very least inaccurate. Accompanying great leaps forward are giant steps backward fueled by the interlocking relationship between the political right and the religious right. Across states, counties, and cities in the United States, anti-LGBT legislation (especially in the form of religious freedom bills) has proliferated, reproducing debates about the "will of the people," the relationship between church and state, and the consequences of judicial actions (i.e., "activist judges").[14]

Until Trump's election, the broader public seemed to accept the inevitable march toward progress. Even as we heard story after story of youth bullying and suicide, and were aware that in many states, at many companies, in many housing districts, LGBT people might be harmed, abused, killed, fired, evicted, and denied housing, post-gay discourses permeated popular culture. I should note that these discourses have not gone away; in February 2017, for example, ABC aired an eight-hour, four-part miniseries called *When We Rise*, which the network commissioned from the openly gay and politically active screenwriter Dustin Lance Bass. With a star-studded cast, the miniseries told the stories of twentieth-century LGBT activism, following figures such as HIV/AIDS and LGBT rights champion Cleve Jones, women's rights leader Roma Guy and her partner, Diane Jones, the black community organizer Ken Jones, and transgender activist Cecilia Chung. Creating a portrait focused on the struggles, but also the ultimate successes of these individuals, the story follows them from the Stonewall riots of 1969 through the AIDS epidemic of the 1980s, and into the new century. Thus, while post-gay rhetoric is still alive and well, it seems harder to support, and in some ways, appears to be receding in significance.

As chapter 3 documented, from broadcast networks to streaming content, television is also representing more transgender stories than ever before.[15] Whether these representations are interpreted as an exploitative marketing tool or as a symbol of social inclusion and cultural diversity (or a combination of both), they reflect the ways transgender stories—including intersectional identities and discourses of difference—are envisioned as part of the twenty-first-century cultural landscape.[16] There are questions to be asked about the quality and the social implications of these images, but, as I have argued throughout this book, whether or not television representations should have power and value is arguably less salient than the persistence of the belief that representation matters.

In closing, my hope is that television practitioners and LGBT advocates might find avenues for more cross-engagement with other sectors of activism and production. I also hope that researchers utilize an approach like this to look at the television industry and its relationship to identity politics in unconventional ways that can shed light on new systems of knowledge production. Finally, I hope that students interested in LGBT activism and/or in making television shows will see the potential power they can have and the ways in which their power might be operationalized in progressive ways.

Mary Bernstein writes, "What constitutes 'meaningful' change depends on whom one asks."[17] The varied interventions I have documented in the pages of this book might fall short of the kind of radical change some envision for those LGBT individuals and communities represented in television programming in the United States. The research here, however, reveals a distinct picture of what it means to work within the system. It is a picture that is motivated by radical and normalizing drives, simultaneously worrisome and aspirational. To me, these tensions point to fascinating conundrums and ambivalences that are symptomatic of larger contemporary cultural discourses. To repeat a well-worn feminist adage, I have learned that the personal is still political. It is also profitable. This is the "new gay for pay."

Notes

Introduction

1. In 2013, the ACLU published an infographic that began with the line "TV changes the way people think about the world." See "[Infographic] Remember That? TV Moments That Have Changed History," American Civil Liberties Union (accessed March 1, 2016), https://www.aclu.org/infographic/infographic-remember-tv-moments -have-changed-history.

2. Orangecountyfldems, "VP Joe Biden ENDORSES same-sex marriage" (filmed May 2012; posted May 2012; YouTube video, 02:48), https://www.youtube.com /watch?v=L8gWKzK1BBM.

3. Eliana Dockterman, "These Shows Helped Shape America's Attitudes about Gay Relationships," *Time*, June 26, 2015.

4. Andrew O'Hehir, "Did TV Change America's Mind on Gay Marriage?," Salon.com, March 30, 2013.

5. Jennifer Armstrong, "Gay Teens on TV," *Entertainment Weekly*, *EW.com*, http:// www.ew.com/article/2014/01/13/gay-teens-tv (accessed March 1, 2016).

6. Ibid.

7. James Bennett and Niki Strange, eds., *Television as Digital Media* (Durham, NC: Duke University Press, 2011), 5.

8. Amanda D. Lotz, *The Television Will Be Revolutionized* (New York: New York University Press, 2007).

9. Ibid., 29.

10. Henry Jenkins, *Convergence Culture: Where Old and New Media Collide*, rev. ed. (New York: New York University Press, 2008).

11. *The Out List*, dir. Timothy Sanders (Filmmakers Library, 2014).

12. Ellen Seiter describes media "effects" as "lay theories," or people's informal ideas about media effects, as influenced by polling data, advice literature, and popular discourse about media's role in society; see Seiter, *Television and New Media Audiences* (New York: Oxford University Press, 1999).

13. As an academic research method, the study of "media effects" was popular in the social sciences between the 1930s and 1970s, provoked by concerns about propa-

ganda, public opinion, and media saturation. The adage most commonly associated with this research model is that the more violence children are exposed to on television, the more likely they are to become violent themselves. Television studies, among other disciplines influenced by 1960s and 1970s British and American cultural studies, took up "effects" claims, complicating and debunking them through interpretive rather than scientific approaches, accounting for active audiences, daily experience, and the interactions of culture, economics, politics, industry, and social power. This scholarship made everyday culture the core of media studies, examining issues of race, gender, class, and sexuality, as well as society's unequal systems of power.

14. I'm invoking the Gramscian notion of "commonsense" ideas here.

15. See Richard Dyer, "Stereotyping," in *Gays and Film*, ed. Richard Dyer (London: British Film Institute, 1977), 27–39.

16. As I will mention throughout the book, I deliberately employ the term "LGBT" (as opposed to "queer" or other configurations used to identify sexual minorities). I do so because I believe that LGBT identities remain the primary way individuals navigate mainstream society, rendering our lives knowable to ourselves and making them definable to others. Simply put, they are "necessary fictions." As Ron Becker says, "Taxonomies of sexuality work to channel the infinite diversity of human sexual desires and behaviors into a limited set of options that people are expected to identify with and conform to" (*Gay TV and Straight America* [New Brunswick, NJ: Rutgers University Press], 7). While queer theorists argue for the impossibility of any natural sexuality—calling into question even terms such as "man" and "woman" and "masculine" and "feminine"—I contend that any study of television images and industrial practices calls upon the language of identity categories. In addition, most of my interviewees identified as openly lesbian or gay, which is significant because—as the book shows—their sexual orientation plays a role in their daily work, in their beliefs about media visibility, and in their perspectives on the landscape of contemporary LGBT television.

17. Timothy Havens, Amanda D. Lotz, and Serra Tinic, "Critical Media Industry Studies: A Research Approach," *Communication, Culture, and Critique* 2, no. 2 (June 2009): 234–253; Laura Nader, "Up the Anthropologist: Perspectives Gained from Studying Up" (1972), https://eric.ed.gov/?id=ED065375; Sherry B. Ortner, "Access: Reflections on Studying Up in Hollywood," *Ethnography* 11, no. 2 (June 1, 2010): 211–233, doi:10.1177/1466138110362006.

18. Anna Cristina Pertierra and Graeme Turner, *Locating Television: Zones of Consumption* (New York: Routledge, 2013).

19. *Production Studies: Cultural Studies of Media Industries*, ed. Vicki Mayer, Miranda J. Banks, and John Thornton Caldwell (New York: Routledge, 2009); Jennifer Holt and Alia Perren, eds., *Media Industries: History, Theory, and Method* (Malden, MA: Wiley-Blackwell, 2009); and Timothy Havens, Amanda D. Lotz, and Serra Tinic, "Critical Media Industry Studies: A Research Approach," *Communication, Culture, and Critique* 2 (June 2009): 234–253, provide in-depth examinations of the different approaches scholars utilize to study the media industries.

20. Cara Buckley, "ACLU, Citing Bias against Women, Wants Inquiry into Hollywood's Hiring Practices," *New York Times*, May 12, 2015.

21. Nader, "Up the Anthropologist," 284.

22. John Thornton Caldwell, *Production Culture: Industrial Reflexivity and Critical Practice in Film and Television* (Durham, NC: Duke University Press, 2008), 235.

23. During interviews, I used an audio recorder with the consent of the interviewees. Whenever possible, I met with interviewees in person; when interviewees were located in other cities the interviews took place by phone. I dreaded the moments when I had to ask to use the recorder. Although as "above-the-line" workers, they were accustomed to journalists recording their comments, I feared that mentioning the audio recorder would inhibit their responses and potentially limit our conversation.

24. Founded in 1985, in protest of the *New York Post*'s defamatory coverage of AIDS, GLAAD emerged in a time of intense conservatism, where right-wing backlash flourished in response to the gains of women's liberation, black civil rights, and the lesbian and gay civil rights movement.

25. See Jeffrey Weeks, *Sex, Politics, and Society: The Regulations of Sexuality since 1800*, 3rd ed. (New York: Routledge, 2012); Jeffrey Weeks, *Sexuality and Its Discontents: Meanings, Myths, and Modern Sexualities* (London: Routledge and Kegan Paul, 1985); Gayle Rubin, "Thinking Sex: Notes for a Radical Theory of the Politics of Sexuality" (1984), in *Social Perspectives in Lesbian and Gay Studies: A Reader*, ed. Peter Nardi and Beth Schneider (London: Routledge, 1998), 100–133; Judith Butler, *Gender Trouble: Feminism and the Subversion of Identity*, Thinking Gender series (New York: Routledge, 1990).

26. In the words of Gayle Rubin, "Sexuality is as much a human product as are diets, methods of transportation, systems of etiquette, forms of labor, types of entertainment, processes of production, and modes of oppression" (Rubin, "Thinking Sex," 106). Moreover, I understand modern categories of sexual identity in the United States as the product of raced, gendered, classed, and capitalist ideological structures. As John D'Emilio argues in his essay "Capitalism and Gay Identity" (in *Making Trouble: Essays on Gay History, Politics, and the University* [New York: Routledge, 1992], 3–16), the concept of sexual identity as we understand it did not exist before the rise of capitalism. The opportunities of industrial capitalism in late nineteenth-century Western societies, D'Emilio argues, "created the social conditions that made possible the emergence of a distinctive gay and lesbian identity" (3). Wage labor and commodity production specifically allowed individuals to move away from home and to work, often in urban centers where they could more easily act on same-sex desires and form communities. For the first time, D'Emilio says, "it was possible for homosexual desire to coalesce into a personal identity—an identity based on the ability to remain outside the heterosexual family and to construct a personal life based on attraction to one's own sex" (8). This construction of discrete sexual identity was far more possible for men than for women because women were limited by structures such as the "female wage scale" and the withholding of education.

I also work from scholarship that concludes that sexual identity in the United States has been constructed fundamentally around class and race-specific identities. Stephen Valocchi, for example, documents the conditions under which "the social construction of gay identity in the twentieth century took place in a structural context of state control of 'threatening' sexualities and middle class anxieties over gender non-conformity" ("The Class-Inflected Nature of Gay Identity," *Social Problems* 46, no. 2 [May 1999]: 208). Those who had access to political and economic resources, he explains, "defined the homosexual in terms of a middle class definition of same-sex desire. . . . Thus, these agents took the varieties of people with same-sex desires and practices and transformed this amorphous, heterogeneous set of populations into a somewhat coherent, unitary category of 'homosexuals'" (210) that had not existed before then.

Race has been equally important in the development of modern sexual identities, inflecting the nature of LGBT communities, politics, and economics. Scholars such as Roderick Ferguson, E. Patrick Johnson, Cheryl Clarke, and Cherríe Moraga, to name a few, articulate the powerful ways that whiteness has been a structuring element in LGBT sexualities. Addressing sociological research specifically, Ferguson writes, "sociology's understanding of social construction in general and of sexuality in particular arises in the midst of white racial formations" ("Race-ing Homonormativity: Citizenship, Sociologist, and Gay Identity," in *Black Queer Studies: A Critical Anthology*, ed. E. Patrick Johnson and Mae E. Henderson [Durham: Duke University Press, 2005], 53). Other disciplines' analyses of sexuality have equally asserted the dominance of white normativity. Such work builds bridges between studies of sexuality and race, delving into both scholarship about identity and the deployment of identity in contemporary US culture.

27. Amin Ghaziani, "Post-Gay Collective Identity Construction," *Social Problems* 58, no. 1 (February 2011): 99–125, doi:10.1525/sp.2011.58.1.99.

28. Nikki Sullivan, *A Critical Introduction to Queer Theory* (New York: New York University Press, 2003), 23.

29. Suzanna Danuta Walters, *All the Rage: The Story of Gay Visibility in America* (Chicago: University of Chicago Press, 2003), 117.

30. Suzanna Danuta Walters, *The Tolerance Trap: How God, Genes, and Good Intentions Are Sabotaging Gay Equality* (New York: New York University Press, 2014), 271.

31. George Chauncey explains that in post–World War II America, there was a "dramatic escalation in the policing of gay life," which included legal changes that banned gay businesses, "gay sex," and "homosexual conduct," and gay-themed publications as well as employment for gays in the federal government, the military, universities, hospitals, and grade schools. This "policing" also included the legalized confinement of gays to mental institutions and prisons. *Why Marriage: The History Shaping Today's Debate over Gay Equality* (New York: Basic Books, 2005), 24.

32. See Eve Kosofsky Sedgwick, *Epistemology of the Closet* (Berkeley: University of California Press, 1990); Ron Becker, "Post-Closet Television," *Flow* 7, no. 3 (November 2007).

33. For cultural histories centering on the function of television in the post–World War II period, see Lynn Spigel, *Make Room for TV: Television and the Family Ideal in Postwar America* (Chicago: University of Chicago Press, 2005); Spigel, *Welcome to the Dreamhouse: Popular Media and Postwar Suburbs* (Durham, NC: Duke University Press, 2001); William Boddy, *Fifties Television: The Industry and Its Critics* (Urbana: University of Illinois Press, 1993).

34. The problem with the idea that the proliferation of public images of LGBT people fosters greater freedom for all sexual and gender minorities is that it equates symbolic media representation with true political representation and social legitimation. Martha Gever says, "The causal relationship between visibility and power is not only difficult to demonstrate, it is also based on an unexamined faith in the unmediated

veracity of documentary evidence, including that produced by photographic media" (*Entertaining Lesbians: Celebrity, Sexuality, and Self-Invention* [New York: Routledge, 2003], 5).

35. Larry Gross, *Up from Invisibility: Lesbians, Gay Men, and the Media in America* (New York: Columbia University Press, 2002).

36. Heather Love, *Feeling Backward: Loss and the Politics of Queer History* (Cambridge, MA: Harvard University Press, 2009), 10.

37. Lisa Duggan, *The Twilight of Equality? Neoliberalism, Cultural Politics, and the Attack on Democracy* (Boston: Beacon, 2004).

38. Ghaziani, "Post-Gay Collective Identity Construction," 104.

39. The scope of this book does not allow for a comprehensive snapshot of either the LGBT political movement or the everyday lives of LGBT people in the United States. However, sociopolitical context matters greatly to the study of television. In describing some of the twenty-first century's most high-profile events, I do not in any way imply that this history matters more than events that did not make the national news or that do not fit the neat homonormative narrative prevalent in popular and political culture.

40. Frank Bruni, "The New Gay Orthodoxy," *New York Times*, April 5, 2014.

41. Michelangelo Signorile, *It's Not Over: Getting beyond Tolerance, Defeating Homophobia, and Winning True Equality* (Boston: Houghton Mifflin Harcourt, 2015); Walters, *The Tolerance Trap*.

42. Walters, *The Tolerance Trap*, 11 (emphasis in original).

43. Signorile, *It's Not Over*, 3.

44. Yasmin Nair, "Against Equality, against Marriage: An Introduction," in *Against Equality: Queer Revolution, Not Mere Inclusion*, ed. Ryan Conrad (Oakland, CA: AK Press, 2014), 17.

45. David Harvey, *A Brief History of Neoliberalism* (Oxford: Oxford University Press, 2007); Duggan, *The Twilight of Equality?*; Henry A. Giroux, *The Terror of Neoliberalism: Cultural Politics and the Promise of Democracy* (Boulder, CO: Paradigm, 2004); Jasbir Puar, *Terrorist Assemblages: Homonationalism in Queer Times* (Durham, NC: Duke University Press, 2007).

46. Laurie Ouellette has written extensively about the neoliberalism of television programming, especially reality television; see Ouellette, *Viewers Like You? How Public TV Failed the People* (New York: Columbia University Press, 2002); Ouellette and James Hay, *Better Living through Reality TV: Television and Post-Welfare Citizenship* (Malden, MA: Blackwell, 2008); Ouellette, *Lifestyle TV* (New York: Routledge, 2016).

47. That such a perspective is put forth by *Time* is not surprising. A subsidiary of media giant Time-Warner, which had a 2013 revenue of $22.1 billion, up 3.4 percent from the previous year, *Time* is part of the very system of mainstreaming and commodification to which I and many others react with such concern.

48. Walters, *The Tolerance Trap*, 270.

49. Vincent Mosco defines these three areas of research as "*institutional*, or research on the political economy of mass media; *organizational*, or research on the social constraints imposed by media bureaucracies; and *individual*, or research on the socialization of media workers." See Mosco, "Media Sociology and Media Workers," *Contemporary Sociology* 12, no. 2 (March 1983): 153.

Chapter 1: Visibility

1. Debbie Wells and Alison Zawack, "Lesbian Market Gains Strength with 2008 Consumer Survey," *Jane and Jane,* December 18, 2008, 3.

2. Community Marketing, Inc., "The Year of the Lesbian," press release, February 14, 2008.

3. This claim was noteworthy because of enduring stereotypical notions about lesbians as anti-feminine and anti-consumerist as well as the legacy of lesbian *invisibility* in mainstream media—gay, bisexual, and transgender also—but especially lesbian.

4. In the late 1980s, with the rise of cable television and the rapid deregulation of the media industries, Marguerite Moritz described what she called "the creation of prime time texts with lesbian characters" for the first time. In her analysis, she attributes this earlier (and smaller) rise in lesbian characters to "the relatively marginalized position of broadcast television brought on by increasing cable penetration and home video ownership, liberalized censorship guidelines on the part of the networks, the demonstrated commercial viability of gay-themed material in other mass media, the appeal of emerging social issues in general as a backdrop for broadcast productions, and an increased public awareness of Homosexuals triggered by the AIDS (Acquired Immune Deficiency Syndrome) epidemic" (Marguerite J. Moritz, "Coming Out Stories: The Creation of Lesbian Images on Prime Time TV," paper presented at the seventy-first annual meeting of the Association for Education in Journalism and Mass Communication [Portland, OR, July 2–5, 1988]). In 2001, Ann M. Ciasullo published an article looking at lesbian media representations from the 1990s across both visual and textual platforms. In "Making Her (In)visible: Cultural Representations of Lesbianism and the Lesbian Body in the 1990s," *Feminist Studies* 27, no. 3 (2001): 577–608, Ciasullo argues that although the decade saw a rise in the numbers of lesbian representations, these images primarily catered to straight male audiences by depicting only "femme" lesbians, completely erasing images of "butch" women. For more critiques of the ways mainstream media has traditionally represented lesbian characters see Louise Allen, *The Lesbian Idol: Martina, KD, and the Consumption of Lesbian Masculinity* (London: Cassell, 1997); Teresa de Lauretis, "Sexual Indifference and Lesbian Representation," *Theatre Journal* 40, no. 2 (1988): 155–177; Martha Gever, *Entertaining Lesbians: Celebrity, Sexuality, and Self-Invention* (New York: Routledge, 2003); Judith Halberstam, *Female Masculinity* (Durham, NC: Duke University Press, 1998); Judith Mayne, *Framed: Lesbians, Feminists, and Media Culture* (Minneapolis: University of Minnesota Press, 2000); Lisa Walker, "How to Recognize a Lesbian: The Cultural Politics of Looking Like What You Are," *Signs* 18 (Summer 1993): 878–879; Patricia White, *Uninvited: Classical Hollywood Cinema and Lesbian Representability* (Bloomington: Indiana University Press, 1999).

5. See Ron Becker's *Gay TV and Straight America* (New Brunswick, NJ: Rutgers University Press, 2006) for a detailed analysis of the economic, political, and social issues that explain why lesbian and gay characters became more prominent on broadcast television shows of the 1990s.

6. Ibid., 108.

7. Renee DeLong, "The Stylized Image of the White Lesbian: A Model Minority," in Kylo-Patrick R. Hart, ed., *Queer TV in the 21st Century: Essays on Broadcasting from Taboo to Acceptance* (Jefferson, NC: McFarland, 2016), 94.

8. Rosemary Hennessey, *Profit and Pleasure: Sexual Identities in Late Capitalism* (New York: Routledge, 2000), 177.

9. For descriptions and analyses of industry deregulation and consolidation see Amanda Lotz, *The Television Will Be Revolutionized* (New York: New York University Press, 2007); William M. Kunz, *Culture Conglomerates: Consolidation in the Motion Picture and Television Industries* (Lanham, MD: Rowman and Littlefield, 2007); Jennifer Holt, *Empires of Entertainment: Media Industries and the Politics of Deregulation, 1980–1996* (New Brunswick, NJ: Rutgers University Press, 2011); Philip Napoli, *Audience Evolution: New Technologies and the Transformation of Media Audiences* (New York: Columbia University Press, 2011); Thomas Streeter, *Selling the Air: A Critique of the Policy of Commercial Broadcasting in the United States* (Chicago: University of Chicago Press, 1996); Michele Hilmes, *Hollywood and Broadcasting: From Radio to Cable* (Urbana: University of Illinois Press, 1990); Benjamin Compaine and Douglas Gomery, *Who Owns the Media?* (London: Erlbaum, 2000).

10. Holt, *Empires of Entertainment*, 171.

11. Catherine Johnson, *Branding Television* (New York: Routledge, 2012), 1.

12. Raymond Williams, *Television: Technology and Cultural Form* (New York: Schocken Books, 1975).

13. Sarah Banet-Weiser, *Authentic™: The Politics of Ambivalence in a Brand Culture* (New York: New York University Press, 2012).

14. Melissa Aronczyk and Devon Powers, eds., *Blowing Up the Brand: Critical Perspectives on Promotional Culture* (New York: Peter Lang, 2010).

15. Jane Feuer, "Bravo! Stars: An Ode to Jeff, Bethenny, and Tabatha," *Flow* 8, no. 7 (September 4, 2008).

16. Marisa Guthrie, "Bravo Is Casting a Wider Net with Deal for Online Fan Site," *Daily News*, March 14, 2007, 83.

17. Jon Lafayette, "Bravo Making Digital Mandatory: All Projects to Be Designed with Broadband Components," *Television Week*, May 15, 2006, 5.

18. Andrew Hampp, "How Bravo's President Lures 'Affluencers' to Bravo Fold," *Advertising Age*, April 9, 2007, S:2.

19. Erin Copple-Smith, "'Affluencers' by Bravo: Defining an Audience through Cross-Promotion," *Popular Communication* 10 (2012): 299.

20. For more on HBO and its brand, see Gary R. Edgerton and Jeffrey P. Jones, eds., *The Essential HBO Reader* (Lexington: University Press of Kentucky, 2008).

21. See, for example, Rosalind Gill, *Gender and the Media* (Cambridge: Polity, 2006); Amanda Lotz, "Postfeminist Television Criticism: Rehabilitating Critical Terms and Identifying Postfeminist Attributes," *Feminist Media Studies* 1, no. 1 (2001): 105–121; A. McRobbie, "Post-Feminism and Popular Culture," *Feminist Media Studies* 4, no. 3 (2004): 255–264; Yvonne Tasker and Diane Negra, "'In Focus': Postfeminism and Contemporary Media Studies," *Cinema Journal* 44, no. 2 (2005): 107–110.

22. Although touted for their embrace of masculine lesbian characters and actors (including the comedian Lea DeLaria on *Orange Is the New Black*, who regularly integrates her tattoo that says "Butch" into the show's narrative), these shows have also come under heavy fire for their representations of race, the police, the criminal justice system, and the US prison system. I include several shows originally aired on the online outlets Netflix and Amazon because of their use of lesbian sexuality both as a symbol of progressive, quality television and as a marketing tool to demonstrate the ways these

content creators push the boundaries of traditional television. While they are technically not cable channels, they make use of similar niche marketing and branding techniques to attract viewers.

23. Business and Entertainment Editors, "Showtime Networks Launches Phase 2 of alt.SHO.com Targeting Viewers/Consumers," *Business Wire*, September 28, 2000.

24. For a more detailed discussion of multiplexing, see Amanda Lotz, "If It's Not TV, What Is It? The Case of US Subscription Television," in *Cable Visions: Television beyond Broadcasting*, ed. Sarah Banet-Weiser, Cynthia Chris, and Anthony Freitas (New York: New York University Press, 2007), 85–102.

25. Mike Hale, "Fishing Online for Cable Viewers," *New York Times*, February 18, 2011.

26. Julie Levin Russo, "Labor of Love: Charting *The L Word*," in *Wired TV: Laboring Over an Interactive Future*, ed. Denise Mann (New Brunswick, NJ: Rutgers University Press, 2014), 105.

27. Patricia White, *Uninvited: Classical Hollywood Cinema and Lesbian Representability* (Bloomington: Indiana University Press, 1999), 14.

28. Jonathan Gray, *Show Sold Separately: Promos, Spoilers, and Other Media Paratexts* (New York: New York University Press, 2010.)

29. Martha Gever, *Entertaining Lesbians: Celebrity, Sexuality, and Self-Invention* (New York: Routledge, 2003), 170.

30. Linda Williams, "*Personal Best*: Women in Love," *JumpCut*, no. 27 (July 1982): 11.

31. Quoted in *Elle* magazine, "About US," 2008.

32. Lya Carrera, "Style from the Streets: ATKM and DITC Reinvent Lesbian Fashion," *Curve* 18, no. 7 (September 2008): 52.

33. Katherine Sender, "Dualcasting: Bravo's Gay Programming and the Quest for Women Audiences," in *Cable Visions: Television beyond Broadcasting*, ed. Sarah Banet-Weiser, Cynthia Chris, and Anthony Freitas (New York: New York University Press, 2007), 311.

34. See Marguerite J. Moritz, "Lesbian Chic: Our Fifteen Minutes of Celebrity?," in *Feminism, Multiculturalism, and the Media: Global Diversities*, ed. Angharad Valdivia (Thousand Oaks, CA: SAGE, 1995), 127–145.

35. Danae Clark, "Commodity Lesbianism," in *The Gay and Lesbian Studies Reader*, ed. Henry Abelove, Michele A. Barale, and David M. Halperin (New York: Routledge, 1993), 186.

36. Clark, "Commodity Lesbianism," 190.

37. Katherine Sender, *Business, Not Politics: The Making of the Gay Market* (New York: Columbia University Press, 2005), 174.

38. Sender, *Business, Not Politics*, 189.

39. Sut Jhally and Justin Lewis, "Affirming Inaction: Television and the Politics of Television Representation," reprinted in Sut Jhally, *The Spectacle of Accumulation: Essays in Culture, Media, and Politics* (New York: Peter Lang, 2006), 206.

40. Philip Napoli, "Media Economics and the Study of Media Industries," in *Media Industries: History, Theory, and Method*, ed. Jennifer Holt and Alisa Perren (Malden, MA: Wiley-Blackwell, 2009), 1.

41. Eileen Meehan, *Why TV Is Not Our Fault: Television Programming, Viewers, and Who's Really in Control* (Lanham, MD: Rowman and Littlefield, 2005), 117.

42. Meehan, *Why TV Is Not Our Fault*, 23.

43. Federal Communications Commission, "Regulation of Cable TV Rates," *FCC Guide.*

44. Nielsen Media Research requires that a channel be available in 3.3 percent of US households for it to be included in the Nielsen Cable Activity Report, which provides cable networks with average and cumulative household-audience information for both cable and broadcast networks. A cable channel must also earn at least a 0.1 rating in those households to be included in the report (http://www.nielsenmedia .com/glossary/terms/C/).

45. Lotz, *The Television Will Be Revolutionized*, 126.

46. See Arlene M. Dávila, *Latino Spin: Public Image and the Whitewashing of Race* (New York: New York University Press, 2008); Esteban del Río, "The Fringe Benefits of Symbolic Annihilation," *Flow* 13, no. 3 (2010); Lisa Duggan, "The Anguished Cry of an 80's Fem: 'I Want to be a Drag Queen,'" *Out/Look* 1, no. 1 (1988): 62–65; Lisa Henderson, *Love and Money: Queers, Class, and Cultural Production* (New York: New York University Press, 2013); Rosemary Hennessey, *Profit and Pleasure: Sexual Identities in Late Capitalism* (New York: Routledge, 2000); José Esteban Muñoz, *Cruising Utopia: The Then and There of Queer Futurity* (New York: New York University Press, 2009).

47. Lynne Joyrich, "Epistemology of the Console," *Critical Inquiry* 27, no. 3 (Spring 2001): 36.

48. This advertisement circulated across a range of LGBT-dedicated websites during the casting of the show. I have quoted it from The Godfather, "The Real L Word," *Boxed Lunch: LA Lesbians*, September 23, 2009, http://boxedlunchlalesbians.blogspot .com/2009/09/real-l-word.html.

49. Lillian Fadermen and Stuart Timmons, *Gay LA: A History of Sexual Outlaws, Power Politics, and Lipstick Lesbians* (New York: Basic Books, 2006), 245.

50. Ibid., 250.

51. Amin Ghaziani, "Post-Gay Collective Identity Construction," *Social Problems* 58, no. 1 (February 2011): 99–125.

52. Martin Meeker, *Contacts Desired: Gay and Lesbian Communications and Community, 1940s–1970s* (Chicago: University of Chicago Press, 2006), 101.

53. Dana Heller, "Out for Life: Makeover Television and the Transformation of Fitness on Bravo's *Work Out*," *Continuum: Journal of Media and Cultural Studies* 22, no. 4 (August 2008): 533.

54. Ibid.

55. Fadermen and Timmons, *Gay LA*, 242.

56. As quoted in ibid., 243.

57. Ibid., 243.

58. For analyses of the different functions femme and butch identities can serve see texts such as Sue-Ellen Case, "Toward a Butch-Femme Aesthetic," *Discourse* 11, no. 1 (1988–1989): 55–73; Judith Butler, *Bodies That Matter* (New York: Routledge, 1993); Judith Butler, *Gender Trouble* (New York: Routledge, 1990); Teresa de Lauretis, "Sexual Indifference and Lesbian Representation," *Theatre Journal* 40, no. 2 (1988): 155–177; Biddy Martin, "Sexualities without Genders and Other Queer Utopias," *Diacritics* 24, no. 2/3 (1994): 104–121; Joan Nestle ed., *The Persistent Desire: A Femme-Butch Reader* (Boston: Alyson, 1991); Gayle Rubin, "Thinking Sex: Notes for a Radical Theory of the Politics of Sexuality" (1984), in *Social Perspectives in Lesbian and Gay Studies: A Reader*, ed. Peter Nardi and Beth Schneider, 100–133 (London: Routledge,

1998); Eve Kosofsky Sedgwick, *Epistemology of the Closet* (Berkeley: University of California Press, 1990).

59. My interview with Andy Cohen took place on May 2, 2008; all further quotations from him are drawn from this interview.

60. My interview with Robert Greenblatt took place on June 3, 2008; all further quotations from him are drawn from this interview.

61. Ilene Chaiken was interviewed by Howard Rosenberg at the University of Southern California on October 27, 2008.

62. Alessandra Stanley, "Women Having Sex, Hoping Men Tune In," *New York Times*, January 16, 2004, 2.

63. For decades, debates about pornography have raged among feminist media scholars. Michelle Citron, B. Ruby Rich, Chris Straayer, and Linda Williams, to name just a few, have debated the relationships between media, women, and pornography. Much of what is called lesbian "mainstreaming," where lesbianism is an accessory to heterosexuality, has its roots in girl-on-girl pictorials of the 1950s, in magazines like *Playboy*. These arguments continue today in response to television industry claims that "lesbian sex, girl-on-girl, is a whole cottage industry for heterosexual men" (Richard Huff, "The Final Frontier: Lesbians. Showtime teases *L-Word*," *New York Daily News*, October 24, 2003, 143).

64. This quotation is from season 2, episode 5 of *The L Word*, entitled "Labyrinth."

65. My interview with Amy Shpall took place on February 22, 2008; all further quotations from her are drawn from this interview.

66. See, for example, Alice E. Marwick and danah boyd, "I Tweet Honestly, I Tweet Passionately: Twitter Users, Context Collapse, and the Imagined Audience," *New Media and Society* 13, no. 1 (2010): 114–133; Meehan, *Why TV Is Not Our Fault*; Meehan, "Why We Don't Count: The Commodity Audience," in *Logics of Television: Essays in Cultural Criticism*, ed. Patricia Mellencamp (Bloomington: Indiana University Press, 1990), 117–137; Philip M. Napoli, "Audience Measurement and Media Policy: Audience Economics, the Diversity Principle, and the Local People Meter," *Communication Law and Policy* 10, no. 4 (2005): 349–382; Beretta Smith-Shomade, "Narrowcasting in the New World Information Order: A Space for the Audience?," *Television and New Media* 5, no. 1 (2004): 69–81; Joseph Turow, "Audience Construction and Culture Production: Marketing Surveillance in the Digital Age," *Annals of the American Academy of Political and Social Science* 597 (2005): 103–121.

67. Nielsen Media Research announced the launch of these ratings through their website's pressroom: http://www.nielsen.com/us/en/press-room/2013/nielsen -launches-nielsen-twitter-tv-ratings.html (accessed June 3, 2014).

68. Sender, *Business, Not Politics*, 142.

69. Meehan, *Why TV Is Not Our Fault*, 117.

70. Carly Litzenberger, personal communication, 2010.

71. M. V. Lee Badgett, "A Queer Marketplace: Books on Lesbian and Gay Consumers, Workers, and Investors" (review), *Feminist Studies* 23, no. 3 (1997): 608.

72. Sender, *Business, Not Politics*, 154.

73. Katherine Sender goes into detail about the definitions of each of these three in *Business, Not Politics*.

74. Although popular press articles have listed this last category as "Metro-Competitors" and sometimes included a fourth demographic, "Newborn Grownups,"

I am drawing on the categories defined in a publication by the Advertising Research Foundation, which honored Bravo for its successful business strategy in the "affluencer" campaign. The Advertising Research Foundation defined these audience segments as follows: "Wills and Graces": predominantly female and gay men, metropolitan, often single, professional, and trendy; "PTA Trendsetters": predominantly female, live in B and C counties (B counties have a population over 150,000 or are part of consolidated statistical areas with a population over 150,000, and C counties have a population over 40,000) yet have metropolitan aspirations, are more likely to have children, and are heavy television viewers; and "Metro-Climbers": more likely to be male, urban, and professional, with an overrepresentation of LGBT individuals. Source: "Bravo: Meet the Affluencers," 2009 press release from the Advertising Research Foundation (available from thearf.org/Ogilvy-09-CS-Bravo.pdf).

75. "Bravo: Meet the Affluencers," 2009 press release from the Advertising Research Foundation.

76. "Bravo Media and the Fiat Brand Team Up to Drive Viewer Engagement in First-Ever Watch What Happens Live Wedding Extravaganza," Bravo press release, September 9, 2013.

77. My interview with Thomas Roth took place on June 18, 2009; all further quotations from him are drawn from this interview.

78. Ien Ang, *Desperately Seeking the Audience* (London: Routledge, 1991), 8.

79. Sender, *Business, Not Politics*, 142.

80. Stuart Ewen, *Captains of Consciousness: Advertising and the Social Roots of Consumer Culture* (New York: McGraw Hill, 1979), 37.

81. Roth and Paisley were insistent that businesses should not target a singular "gay market," yet they consistently described a singular LGBT "community."

82. Jeffrey Escoffier, *American Homo: Community and Perversity* (Berkeley: University of California Press, 1998), 65.

83. Dan Baker, "A History in Ads: The Growth of the Gay and Lesbian Market," in *Homo Economics: Capitalism, Community, and Lesbian and Gay Life*, ed. Amy Gluckman and Betsy Reed (New York: Routledge, 1997), 12.

84. My interview with Meredith Kadlec took place on January 22, 2008; all further quotations from her are drawn from this interview.

85. Ron Becker, "Post-Closet Television," *Flow* 7, no. 3 (November 2007).

86. Suzanna Danuta Walters, *All the Rage: The Story of Gay Visibility in America* (Chicago: University of Chicago Press, 2003), 105.

87. Alessandra Stanley, "Sex and the Gym: 'Work Out' and the Gaying of Bravo," *New York Times*, July 19, 2006, section E.

88. Sender, "Dualcasting," 309.

89. Walters, *All the Rage*, 113.

90. See Banet-Weiser, *Authentic™*; Henry Jenkins, *Convergence Culture: Where Old and New Media Collide* (New York: New York University Press, 2008).

91. Sender, *Business, Not Politics*, 189.

92. Lotz, "If It's Not TV, What Is It?," 5.

93. Joseph Turow, *Breaking Up America: Advertisers and the New Media World* (Chicago: University of Chicago Press, 1997), 55.

94. Alisa Perren, "In Conversation: Creativity in the Contemporary Cable Industry," *Cinema Journal* 50, no. 2 (2011): 138.

Chapter 2: Advocacy

1. This announcement was timed to coincide with National Coming Out Day during LGBT History Month.

2. Laura Nader, "Up the Anthropologist: Perspectives Gained from Studying Up" (1972), http://www.eric.ed.gov/contentdelivery/servlet/ERICServlet?accno=ED065 375.

3. Roopali Mukherjee and Sarah Banet-Weiser, eds., *Commodity Activism: Cultural Resistance in Neoliberal Times* (New York: New York University Press, 2012), 3.

4. When we spoke, it had been three years since Solmonese left the HRC and started a corporate consulting firm based in Washington, DC. This distance helped make the conversation candid and not as laden with the public relations spin I was accustomed to hearing during research for this project.

5. Bruce Feiler, "What 'Modern Family' Says about Modern Families," "This Life," *New York Times*, January 21, 2011.

6. The show has received five Television Critic Awards, five Writers Guild of America Awards, two Directors Guild Awards, two Screen Actors Guild Awards, one Golden Globe Award, four AFI awards, and twenty-one Primetime Emmy Awards.

7. In September 2016, advocacy groups and news outlets recognized *Modern Family* as the first scripted series to feature an openly transgender child actor. Throughout its run, GLAAD, the nation's leading LGBT media advocacy organization, has given both the show and its home network, ABC, high marks for their gay representations. In its 2015 Network Responsibility Index (NRI), GLAAD reports, "ABC produced not only the highest total number of original programming hours (812) of any broadcast network, but also the highest number of hours that included some kind of LGBT impression (258.5)" (August 24). The report adds, "With [*Modern Family's*] seventh season premiering in the fall, Mitch and Cam remain one of television's most enduring and popular gay couples." Every year since its debut, the show has been nominated for GLAAD's award for "Outstanding Comedy Series." From GLAAD's perspective, *Modern Family* is a show that pretty much does everything right. In October 2010, only a year after its debut, *Modern Family* was presented with the Inspiration Award from the Gay, Lesbian, Straight Education Network (GLSEN), which recognizes both individuals and corporate leaders who have helped propel GLSEN's efforts to ensure safe schools for US students, regardless of sexual orientation or gender identity/expression.

8. *Modern Family* also displaces popular reality competition shows such as *The Voice* (NBC, 2011–) and *Dancing with the Stars* (ABC, 2005–), which regularly top the list of the ten most popular shows of the year.

9. The syndication rights to the show were also sold to USA and ten Fox affiliates. In the weeks leading up to *Modern Family's* premiere on USA, the channel aired a series of promotional spots focused on the show's new "home," trumpeting the program as "TV's best comedy." Industry reports attributed USA's increased ad prices at the annual up-front negotiations that year to the purchase.

10. Lacey Rose, "'Modern Family': USA Plans Unprecedented Syndication Rollout," *Hollywood Reporter*, September 18, 2013.

11. In today's globalized television culture, *Modern Family's* popularity is not limited to the United States. The business structure of the show—characterized by effi-

ciency, calculability, and predictability—allows it to be easily customized to other domestic cultures. For example, Chile's MEGA channel was the first to purchase the rights to the show, producing a version entitled *Familia Moderna*. However, as *Variety* reported in 2014, same-sex marriages and adoptions are illegal in Chile; to get around these national differences, the Chilean adaptation features a gay couple, one of whom has "a brief fling with a woman, who becomes pregnant. The couple takes over custody of the child when her mother goes on an extended trip" (Anna Marie de la Fuente, "Chile's Version of 'Modern Family' Facing Unique Set of Obstacles," *Variety*, June 13, 2014). The same year, Iran made a version of the show, *Haft Sang*, produced by the Islamic Republic of Iran Broadcasting. *Haft Sang* replaces the gay couple with a straight couple in addition to replacing the Dunphy's oldest daughter, Hailey, with a male character. Like earlier broadcast shows that feature sexual minorities, including *Ugly Betty* (ABC, 2006–2010) and *The Office* (NBC, 2005–2013), *Modern Family*'s adaptable format makes it an ideal vehicle for economic and cultural success around the globe.

12. Daniel D'Addario, "ACLU Pushes for 'Modern Family' Gay Wedding," Salon .com, May 15, 2013.

13. Rosenberg, television critic for the *Los Angeles Times* from 1978 until 2003, was joined by writer/producer David Milch, director/producer Michael Zinberg, and Horace Newcomb (emeritus director of the Peabody Awards) to discuss how television storytelling has shifted since the 1970s, to describe what kinds of creative opportunities are available for writers, producers, and directors that were not available in the past, and to address the television shows that have had the greatest influence on today's media professionals.

14. See http://flowtv.org/flowconference2014/core/.

15. Alexander Doty, "*Modern Family*, *Glee*, and the Limits of Television Liberalism," *Flow* 12, no. 9 (2011).

16. See, for example, Esteban del Río and Kasey Mitchell, "Modern Family's Indictment of Modern Families," *Flow* 12, no. 5 (2010).

17. Isabel Molina-Guzmán, "*Modern Family*'s Latina Spitfire in the Era of White Resentment," *Flow* 17, no. 1 (2013).

18. Lynn Spigel and Jan Olsson, eds., *Television after TV: Essays on a Medium in Transition* (Durham, NC: Duke University Press, 2004), 1.

19. Kelly Kessler offers an important counterargument to this claim. In her assessment of the lesbian characters on *Friends* and *Mad About You*, Kessler argues that "the formula of the situation comedy, especially the role identified for the secondary character, inhibits significant progressive representations of marginalized groups, and inversely, in the spirit of a liberal pluralist democracy, neutralizes the difference, rendering the representations ineffective and destructive" (Kessler, "Politics of the Sitcom Formula: *Friends, Mad About You*, and the Sapphic Second Banana," in *The New Queer Aesthetic on TV: Essays on Recent Programming*, ed. James R. Keller and Leslie Stratyner (North Carolina: McFarland, 2007), 131.

20. Bonnie Dow, *Prime-Time Feminism: Television, Media Culture, and the Women's Movement since 1970* (Philadelphia: University of Pennsylvania Press, 1996), 37.

21. Stephen Tropiano, "*Flow* Favorites: Gaycoms in a Progressive Age? Partners and *The New Normal*," *Flow* 17, no. 13 (2012).

22. Ibid.

23. Ibid.

24. John D'Emilio, "Introduction: Progress and Representation," in *Media/Queered: Visibility and Its Discontents*, ed. Kevin G. Barnhurst (New York: Peter Lang, 2007), 25.

25. For detailed descriptions of these programs and the specific character types they featured see Steven Capsuto, *Alternate Channels: The Uncensored Story of Gay and Lesbian Images on Radio and Television, 1930s to the Present* (New York: Ballantine Books, 2000).

26. Kathryn Montgomery, *Target: Prime Time: Advocacy Groups and the Struggle over Entertainment Television* (New York: Oxford University Press, 1990).

27. While television scholars have long considered fictional television to be politically powerful, Montgomery is one of the few media studies scholars to write extensively about the history of *television advocacy*, although there is now Allison Perlman's 2016 book *Public Interests: Media Advocacy and Struggles over US Television*. The focus in most scholarly writing about media advocacy is on news programming and its relationship to public opinion, agenda setting, and social and political change.

28. In 2013, GLAAD announced that it was formally dropping the words "Gay and Lesbian Alliance Against Defamation" from its name and would thereafter be known as GLAAD, the LGBT Media Advocacy Organization. The *Advocate* quoted GLAAD spokesperson Wilson Cruz: "It is a natural progression that reflects the work GLAAD's staff is already leading. . . . We respect and honor the full name that the organization was founded with, but GLAAD's work has expanded beyond fighting defamation to changing the culture. Our commitment to marriage equality, employment nondiscrimination, and other LGBT issues is stronger than ever, and now our name reflects our work on transgender issues as well as our work with allies" (http://www.advocate.com /politics/2013/03/24/glaad-affirms-commitment-trans-and-bi-people-alters-name).

29. I provide more detail about the history and contemporary operations of GLAAD in the next chapter, when I discuss LGBT television diversity.

30. Montgomery, *Target*, 78.

31. Ibid., 78–79.

32. John Ellis, *Visible Fictions: Cinema, Television, Video* (New York: Routledge, 2002), 107.

33. Larry Gross, *Up from Invisibility: Lesbians, Gay Men, and the Media in America* (New York: Columbia University Press, 2001), 48.

34. Suzanna Danuta Walters, *All the Rage: The Story of Gay Visibility in America* (Chicago: University of Chicago Press, 2003), 104.

35. Larry Gross, *Up from Invisibility*, 252.

36. Michael Bronski, *A Queer History of the United States* (Boston: Beacon, 2012), 212.

37. Montgomery, *Target*, 85.

38. Henry Jenkins, *Convergence Culture: Where Old and New Media Collide*, rev. ed. (New York: New York University Press, 2008).

39. Lesley Goldberg, "A 'Modern Family' Wedding? ACLU Wants One," *Hollywood Reporter*, May 15, 2013.

40. Ibid.

41. Amanda Terkel, "ACLU Pushes for Cam and Mitch to Get Hitched on 'Modern Family,'" *Huffington Post*, May 15, 2013.

42. Ibid.

43. The DOMA ruling meant that same-sex married couples living in a state that recognized their marriage would have access to the 1,138 federal rights and protections granted by marriage. The ruling on Prop 8—that its backers did not have standing to appeal lower court rulings given that the state of California had chosen not to defend the measure—upheld previous court rulings, which determined the measure to be unconstitutional because it violated the state's equal protection clause. This decision meant that same-sex couples could marry in the state of California whether residents or nonresidents.

44. Michael O'Connell, "'Modern Family' Considering a Gay Wedding after Supreme Court Rulings," *Hollywood Reporter*, June 27, 2013.

45. Walters, *All the Rage*, 192.

46. Charlie Joughin, "Sharon's 'Modern Family' Dinner Date," Human Rights Campaign press release, February 20, 2013, http://www.hrc.org/blog/entry/sharons -modern-family-dinner-date.

47. Ibid.

48. Michael Curtin, Jennifer Holt, and Kevin Sanson, *Distribution Revolution: Conversations about the Digital Future of Film and Television*, ed. Michael Curtin, Jennifer Holt, and Kevin Sanson (Berkeley: University of California Press, 2014), 3.

49. Despite multiple attempts to contact ACLU staff, I was unable to secure an interview to find out the details of the campaign.

50. Lisa Duggan, *The Twilight of Equality? Neoliberalism, Cultural Politics, and the Attack on Democracy* (Boston: Beacon, 2004), 15.

51. Urvashi Vaid, *Virtual Equality: The Mainstreaming of Gay and Lesbian Liberation*, 2nd ed. (New York: Anchor Books, 1996), 106.

52. The push for marriage rights has been at the heart of these critiques. Securing legal equality under US law has been centered on marriage rights to the extent that organizations have been established with the exclusive goal of seeking state and federal marriage rights for lesbians and gays. However, this is not to say this critical paradigm is new with marriage debates. As historian Vicki Eaklor notes, "as soon as there was a sustained GLBT movement there were arguments over assimilation. Even before that the issue was always lurking beneath the actions of publicly 'flamboyant men' and 'masculine women' on the one hand and the closeted people who sought distance from the public queers on the other. After World War II the twin impulses towards asserting rights and conforming were at a peak and affected the new homophile movement" (*Queer America: A People's GLBT History of the United States* repr. New York: New Press, 2011], 159). Yet, as Suzanna Walters writes, "Rarely have we seen social movements so identified with one single issue and that issue then become so all encompassing that it becomes synonymous with the struggle itself" (*The Tolerance Trap: How God, Genes, and Good Intentions Are Sabotaging Gay Equality* [New York: New York University Press, 2014], 181).

53. My interview with Joe Solmonese took place on May 11, 2015; all further quotations from him are drawn from this interview.

54. Among Ryan Murphy's many projects are *Popular* (WB, 1999-2001), *Nip/Tuck* (FX, 2003-2010), *Glee* (Fox, 2009-2015), *American Horror Story* (FX, 2011-), *The New Normal* (NBC, 2012-2013), *Scream Queens* (Fox, 2015-), and *Feud* (FX, 2017-).

55. Quoted in Lynnette Rice, "DOMA Reaction: 'Modern Family' Considering Gay Marriage," *Entertainment Weekly*, June 26, 2013.

56. Alan Ball quoted in Denise Martin, "TCA: Alan Ball: 'True Blood' Is Not a Metaphor for Gay People," *LA Times Blogs—Show Tracker*, July 10, 2008.

57. My interview with Anastasia Khoo took place on May 10 and 11, 2015; all further quotations from her are drawn from this interview.

58. Andrew Sullivan, "The Case against the Case against 8," *The Dish*, 2014, http://dish.andrewsullivan.com/2014/06/23/the-case-against-the-case-against-8/ (accessed July 3, 2015).

59. For a detailed history of television writers, see Miranda J. Banks, *The Writers: A History of American Screenwriters and Their Guild* (New Brunswick, NJ: Rutgers University Press, 2015).

60. See the previous chapter for a full description of "multicasting." For a full explanation of Curtin's concept of "matrix media" see Michael Curtin, "Matrix Media," in *Television Studies After TV: Understanding Television in the Post-Broadcast Era*, ed. Graeme Turner and Jinna Tay (New York: Routledge, 2009), 9–19.

61. Frank Bruni, "'I Do' and the ACLU" (Frank Bruni's Blog), *New York Times*, May 15, 2013.

62. Leigh Ann Wheeler, *How Sex Became a Civil Liberty* (New York: Oxford University Press, 2014), 44.

63. Ibid., 154.

64. "ACLU Action Launches Campaign to Get Cam and Mitch Hitched on 'Modern Family,'" American Civil Liberties Union press release, May 15, 2013.

65. Cecilia Kang and Matea Gold, "With Political Ads Expected to Hit a Record, News Stations Can Hardly Keep Up," *Washington Post*, October 31, 2014.

66. F. Hollis Griffin, *Feeling Normal: Sexuality and Media Criticism in the Digital Age* (Bloomington: Indiana University Press, 2016), 169.

67. Jennifer Holt, *Empires of Entertainment: Media Industries and the Politics of Deregulation, 1980–1996* (New Brunswick, NJ: Rutgers University Press, 2011), 165.

68. Ronald V. Bettig and Jeanne Hall, *Big Media, Big Money: Cultural Texts and Political Economy* (Lanham, MD: Rowman and Littlefield, 2003).

69. Holt, *Empires of Entertainment*, 166.

70. Jennifer Gillan, *Television and New Media: Must-Click TV* (New York: Routledge, 2010), 4.

71. John T. Caldwell, "Critical Industrial Practice: Branding, Repurposing, and the Migratory Patterns of Industrial Texts," *Television and New Media* 7, no. 2 (2006): 124.

72. Joseph Turow, *Breaking Up America: Advertisers and the New Media World* (Chicago: University of Chicago Press, 1997), 7.

73. Joseph Turow, *The Daily You: How the New Advertising Industry Is Defining Your Identity and Your Worth* (New Haven, CT: Yale University Press, 2012).

74. See Larry Gross, *Up from Invisibility*; Larry P. Gross and James D. Woods, eds., *The Columbia Reader on Lesbians and Gay Men in Media, Society, and Politics* (New York: Columbia University Press, 1999); Capsuto, *Alternate Channels*; Stephen Tropiano, *The Prime Time Closet: A History of Gays and Lesbians on TV* (New York: Applause Theatre and Cinema Books, 2002).

75. Between 2010 and 2011, several major newspapers, including the *Los Angeles Times* and the *Wall Street Journal*, credited *Modern Family* with the revival of the half-hour sitcom: http://www.wsj.com/articles/SB10001424052748704240004575508

5590627459182; http://articles.latimes.com/2011/oct/30/entertainment/la-ca-modern
-family-20111030 (accessed January 16, 2015).

76. Lisa Henderson practices this mode of analysis, calling it "queer relay," in *Love
and Money: Queers, Class, and Cultural Production* (New York: New York University
Press, 2013).

77. Vaid, *Virtual Equality*.

Chapter 3: Diversity

1. Dev's comment about *Will & Grace* addresses the stereotypes of gay men that
have dominated the medium over the course of its history. Because Will is conventionally masculine and "straight-acting," Dev assumes that he is heterosexual and that
Jack—flamboyant and effeminate—is the show's only gay character. For analyses of
the show's representations, see Kathleen Battles and Wendy Hilton-Morrow, "Gay
Characters in Conventional Spaces: *Will and Grace* and the Situation Comedy Genre,"
Critical Studies in Media Communication 19, no. 1 (2002): 87–105; Denis M. Proven-
cher, "Sealed with a Kiss: Heteronormative Narrative Strategies in NBC's *Will &
Grace*," in *The Sitcom Reader: America Viewed and Skewed*, ed. Mary M. Dalton and
Laura R. Linder (Albany: State University of New York Press, 2005), 177–190.

2. Peter Wood, *Diversity: The Invention of a Concept* (San Francisco: Encounter
Books, 2004), 8.

3. I say "lesbian and gay industry workers" as opposed to "LGBT" because none
of my interviewees openly identified as bisexual or transgender or embraced any other
category of sexual minority, such as queer.

4. Lucas Hilderbrand, "Stage Left: *Glee* and the Textual Politics of Difference,"
Flow 11, no. 3 (2009).

5. For Douglas, "enlightened sexism" refers to popular culture's embrace of being
feminist in its outward appearance but sexist in its intent. Jhally and Lewis use "enlightened racism" in their discussion of race, television, and *The Cosby Show* (NBC,
1984–1992). See Sut Jhally and Justin Lewis, *Enlightened Racism: The Cosby Show, Audiences, and the Myth of the American Dream* (Boulder, CO: Westview, 1992); Susan J.
Douglas, *The Rise of Enlightened Sexism: How Pop Culture Took Us from Girl Power to
Girls Gone Wild* (New York: St. Martin, 2010).

6. Fans and industry critics alike have celebrated television programs like *Glee*,
Modern Family (ABC, 2009–), *Grey's Anatomy* (ABC, 2005–), *Empire* (Fox, 2015–),
Game of Thrones (HBO, 2011–), and *The L Word* (Showtime, 2004–2009) for their representations of diverse LGBT characters. These same shows have been the subject of
academic criticism that argues that the so-called diversity in these shows reinforces
sexual and gender normativity (and non-normativity). Other scholars offer more opti-
mistic critiques of contemporary programming. Writing about racial diversity on television, for example, Mary Beltrán describes what she terms "meaningful diversity," in
which characters of color are, in Beltrán's words, "fully realized individuals" with in-
teriority and agency created by writers who seem to have an insight into the communities with which the characters are affiliated; Mary Beltrán, "Meaningful Diversity:
Exploring Questions of Equitable Representation on Diverse Ensemble Cast Shows,"
Flow 12, no. 7 (September 2010).

Moreover, the diversity of the cast connects purposively to the setting in which the program takes place. Melanie Kohnen extends Beltrán's argument to include race and sexuality in her analysis of *The Fosters* (ABC Family, 2013–2015; Freeform, 2016–), a show about an interracial lesbian couple and their multiracial children. Kohnen contends the show's representations carve out a hopeful space for what diversity on television could look like or what steps those inside the writers' room and casting office of a show could take to create more "meaningful diversity" that resonates with audiences' own identities and experiences; Melanie Kohnen, "Cultural Diversity as Brand Management in Cable Television," *Media Industries* 2, no. 2 (2015): 124.

Programs such as *Transparent* (Amazon, 2014–) and *Orange Is the New Black* (Netflix, 2013–) have generated analyses about the power of diverse representations to create powerfully "post-patriarchal" representations that challenge hierarchies of race, gender, and sexuality; Ariel Levy, "Dolls and Feelings," *New Yorker*, December 14, 2015. The most acclaim though, from both the popular press and academics, has been for black television creator Shonda Rhimes. With her series of successful shows—including *Grey's Anatomy*, *Private Practice* (ABC, 2007–2013), *How to Get Away with Murder* (ABC, 2014–), and *Scandal* (2012–), Rhimes has created an empire of fans and followers who celebrate her "meaningful" incorporations of racially and sexually diverse characters and storylines.

7. Wood, *Diversity*, 21.

8. Mary Bernstein and Verta Taylor, eds., *The Marrying Kind? Debating Same-Sex Marriage within the Lesbian and Gay Movement* (Minneapolis: University of Minnesota Press, 2013), 17.

9. Alex Roarty, "Kentucky Has a Gay Senate Candidate—Does Anybody Care?," *Roll Call*, August 24, 2016.

10. David Freedlander, "America's First Post-Gay Governor," *The Daily Beast*, October 24, 2014.

11. Ibid.

12. The Deadline Team, "TCA: Sean Hayes on 'Post-Gay' Sitcom 'Sean Saves the World,'" *Deadline*, July 27, 2013.

13. The Deadline Team, "TCA: Sean Hayes on 'Post-Gay' Sitcom 'Sean Saves the World.'"

14. I use "lesbian" and "gay" here rather than LGBT because it is almost exclusively these characters and celebrities who are included in post-gay rhetoric. Bisexual and transgender characters and celebrities, by contrast, are more often celebrated as "diverse" and as symbols of television's continued "progress" toward inclusive representations.

15. Amin Ghaziani, "Post-Gay Collective Identity Construction," *Social Problems* 58, no. 1 (February 2011): 104.

16. Lisa Bernhard, "Wanda Sykes Uncensored!" *TV Guide Magazine*, November 4, 2009.

17. Kevin G. Barnhurst, ed., *Media Q: Media/Queered: Visibility and Its Discontents* (New York: Peter Lang, 2007), 3.

18. Lynne Joyrich, "Epistemology of the Console," reprinted in *Queer TV: Theories, Histories, Politics*, ed. Glyn Davis and Gary Needham (New York: Routledge, 2008), 17.

19. Out.com editors, "The Power 50," *Out*, April 3, 2007.

20. Eve Kosofsky Sedgwick, *Epistemology of the Closet* (Berkeley: University of California Press, 1990), 7.

21. Richard Campbell, Christopher R. Martin, and Bettina Fabos, *Media and Culture: Mass Communication in a Digital Age*, 9th ed. (Boston: Bedford/St. Martin, 2013), 213.

22. Alex Cohen, "PR's 'Gay Guru' Helps Celebrities Come Out," NPR.org, April 28, 2011.

23. For an account of the politics of outing see Larry Gross, *Contested Closets: The Politics and Ethics of Outing* (Minneapolis: University of Minnesota Press, 1993).

24. See Christine Gledhill, ed., *Stardom: Industry of Desire* (London: Routledge, 1991); Richard Dyer, *Heavenly Bodies: Film Stars and Society*, 2nd ed. (London: Routledge, 2003).

25. Joshua Gamson, *Claims to Fame: Celebrity in Contemporary America* (Berkeley: University of California Press, 1994), 54.

26. Ibid., 172.

27. Erin Rook, "'Grey's Anatomy' Star Sara Ramirez Comes out as Bisexual and Queer," *LGBTQ Nation*, October 8, 2016.

28. My interview with Howard Bragman took place on May 7, 2015; all further quotations from him are drawn from this interview.

29. Mark Harris, "By the Way, We're Gay: The New Art of Coming Out," *Entertainment Weekly*, July 2, 2012.

30. Ron Becker, "Post-Closet Television," *Flow* 7, no. 3 (November 2007).

31. "Freaks" is a reference to Joshua Gamson's book *Freaks Talk Back: Tabloid Talk Shows and Sexual Nonconformity* (Chicago: University of Chicago Press, 1999), which provides a nuanced look at the role of tabloid talk shows, well known for exploiting those who are "different" or "freaks" for the sake of ratings and capitalizing on voyeurism. Unlike work that looks at the construction of gender and sexuality only at the level of discourse, Gamson's project examines LGBT "freaks" as they are produced in the specific institutional setting of the talk show. What Gamson's sociological approach thus brings to the table is an emphasis on analyzing both the cultural content and institutional contexts of television talk show production.

32. Ibid., 150 (emphasis in original).

33. Ibid., 152.

34. For an analysis of bisexuality in media, see Maria San Filippo, *The B Word: Bisexuality in Contemporary Film and Television* (Bloomington: Indiana University Press, 2013).

35. Gamson, *Freaks Talk Back*.

36. Ramin Setoodeh, "How Sarah Kate Ellis Brought GLAAD into the 21st Century, *Variety*, September 27, 2016.

37. My interview with Matt Kane took place on May 7, 2015; all further quotations from him are drawn from this interview.

38. By the time Jenner came out as a transgender woman, she was part of reality TV royalty. In 1991, Jenner (Bruce at the time), married Kris Kardashian, the former wife of Robert Kardashian, a lawyer who was infamous for defending football star O. J. Simpson in the 1994 murder of his ex-wife, Nicole, and her friend Ronald Goldman. Jenner, Kris, and their children became reality TV stars in 2007 when *Keeping Up with the Kardashians* (E!, 2007–) debuted.

39. The story did not just spring into being at that moment. Jill Soloway had worked on the show for years, shopping it around from network to network.

40. *Transparent* is available with the cost of the Prime membership.

41. *Orange Is the New Black* has come under criticism for a number of reasons: its representation of prison life, critics argue, grossly distorts reality; others point out that Piper Kerman, author of the best-selling memoir the show is based on, has sold rights to stories of women that aren't hers to sell (the show centers on Piper's character but is also significantly about the prison's other inmates, most of whom are poor, uneducated women of color). Critics also point to the ways the show seems to refuse to engage with broader critiques about the economic and social systems that unfairly and disproportionately target poor women and women of color, and especially poor women of color. Critiques of the prison industrial system remain limited in focus and when they do appear, it is Piper, the educated, middle-upper-class prisoner who points them out.

42. Katy Steinmetz, "Laverne Cox Talks to TIME about the Transgender Movement," *Time*, May 29, 2014.

43. It is important that a *black* transgender woman, who embraces her multiple identities, has come to be a voice for these markedly underserved and underrepresented communities.

44. Kane's comments echo the notion that LGB equality is a done deal, and that television producers, writers, and developers have a clear sense for how to create dynamic, complex, and quality characters who are lesbian, gay, or bisexual. This statement, one might argue, not only is inaccurate but even potentially puts LGB characters at risk of being marginalized. Suzanna Walters writes about this idea when she talks about the "new gay visibility" of the early 2000s. In this mode of representation, jokes about an LGBT character, for example, pretend that equality exists more fully than it actually does, ignoring and even reinforcing homophobic norms; see Suzanna Walters, *All the Rage: The Story of Gay Visibility in America* (Chicago: University of Chicago Press, 2003).

45. Kirthana Ramisetti, "GLAAD Report Shows TV Is Tuned In to LGBT Diversity," *New York Daily News*, October 1, 2014.

46. GLAAD differentiates the NRI from its annual "Where We Are On TV" report: "while the *NRI* looks backward at the previous season and rates networks on LGBT-inclusive content between June 2013 and May 2014, the *Where We Are on TV* report is a character count and analysis of scripted characters in the upcoming 2014–2015 season."

47. "GLAAD 2015 Network Responsibility Index," *GLAAD*, August 24, 2015, http://www.glaad.org/nri2015.

48. Matt Kane, "GLAAD Releases 2015 Network Responsibility Index | Benton Foundation," Benton Foundation press release, September 3, 2015.

49. One year later, when GLAAD released the 2015 index, the organization also announced that it would also be the last. In a press release, Matt Kane writes, "The organization will now turn its focus to increasing the diversity of LGBT images on TV through its annual 'Where We Are On TV Report.'" This report analyzes the overall diversity of primetime scripted series regulars on broadcast networks and looks at the number of LGBT characters on cable networks. GLAAD's website also says, "[The] annual TV report not only propels national conversations about LGBT representation,

but informs GLAAD's own advocacy within the television industry. GLAAD uses this yearly data to create a clearer picture of the stories and images being presented by television networks, and to encourage networks to include diverse LGBT representations within them."

In my interview with Kane, though, he gave a different explanation for the elimination of the NRI. He said it had come down to a matter of resources. "It's such a time commitment and can be done with other reports. It will also allow us to examine something new we might do that would allow us to examine areas that haven't been addressed before that would allow us to diversify the types of messages that we're trying to get across to the media industry. . . . When we first started it, it was a much different landscape than it is now. It's interesting because with the media awards nominees, there was a time when you had to pick from ten shows and finding five that were actually really high quality was sometimes difficult, we had 89 potential nominees for our TV categories this year, which is very different. With film we're still struggling."

50. Lauren B. Edelman, Sally Riggs Fuller, and Iona Mara Drita, "Diversity Rhetoric and the Managerialization of Law," *American Journal of Sociology* 106, no. 6 (May 2001): 1589–1641.

51. Amin Ghaziani, *There Goes the Gayborhood?* (Princeton, NJ: Princeton University Press, 2014).

52. Comcast Corporation, "Comcast Diversity Booklet 2013.pdf," 2013, http://corporate.comcast.com/images/Comcast-Diversity-Booklet-2013.pdf.

53. Ibid.

54. For histories and cultural analyses of these time periods and technologies, see Anna McCarthy, *The Citizen Machine: Governing by Television in 1950s America* (New York: New York University Press, 2013); Megan Mullen, "The Fall and Rise of Cable Narrowcasting," *Convergence: The International Journal of Research into New Media Technologies* 8, no. 1 (2002): 62–83; Thomas Streeter, *Selling the Air: A Critique of the Policy of Commercial Broadcasting in the United States* (Chicago: University of Chicago Press, 1996); Newton N. Minow, *Equal Time: The Private Broadcaster and the Public Interest* (New York: Atheneum, 1964).

55. My interview with J. Michael Durnil took place on March 17, 2009; all further quotations from him are drawn from this interview.

Chapter 4: Equality

1. On June 2, only weeks after the Supreme Court justices issued their decision, anti-gay activists qualified Prop 8 for the ballot. The official summary read: the measure "changes the California Constitution to eliminate the right of same-sex couples to marry in California." The justices had made the unprecedented ruling that lesbians and gays are a suspect class, giving them the protections afforded by minority group status. Being given the status of a suspect class legally acknowledges that lesbian and gay individuals are likely to be the subject of discrimination, and often have been historically. In the United States, other suspect classes include race, gender, religion, and national origin. As a result, these classes receive strict scrutiny by courts when a discriminatory claim is made. The Supreme Court's decision was part of a long and fiercely debated

battle over the status of marriage rights for lesbians and gays in California that began in 2000. That year, 61 percent of state voters passed an initiative, Proposition 22, which said that California would only recognize marriages between a man and woman. While Proposition 22 consists of only fourteen words ("Only marriage between a man and a woman is valid or recognized in California"), its intent and meaning prompted debate. By a vote of 61.4 percent to 38 percent, it passed and was added to section 308 as section 308.5 to the state's Family Code. Section 308 reads: "A marriage contracted outside this state that would be valid by the laws of the jurisdiction in which the marriage was contracted is valid in this state." LGBT activists and attorneys argued that because Proposition 22 had been added to a Family Code section that addressed only marriages performed outside the state of California, Proposition 22 could therefore only apply to marriages performed outside the state. In this argument, Proposition 22 did not deny California's lesbian and gay citizens the right to marry, it simply stated that California would recognize only marriages between a man and a woman when a married couple visited or moved to the state from outside California.

2. On May 18, 1970, a Minnesota couple, Richard Baker and James Michael McConnell, were denied a marriage license by the Hennepin County District Court's clerk. More than three years later, on November 9, 1973, the Kentucky Court of Appeals ruled in *Jones v. Hallahan* that same-sex couples could not marry. This ruling came after two women, Marjorie Jones and Tracy Knight, applied for and were denied a marriage license in Jefferson County, Kentucky.

3. See Julia Himberg, ed., *Race, Sexuality, and Television*, special issue of *Spectator: The University of Southern California Journal of Film and Television Criticism* 31, no. 2 (Fall 2011).

4. One month after Prop 8's passage, musical theater composer Marc Shaiman wrote a mini-musical (three minutes in length) called *Prop 8—The Musical*, which went viral on the website FunnyorDie.com. With an all-star comedy cast including Jack Black, Maya Rudolph, Allison Janney, Margaret Cho, Rashida Jones, Kathy Najimy, and Neil Patrick Harris, the video satirizes the anti-gay argument against marriage rights, especially Christian churches that selectively choose biblical doctrines to follow. *Prop 8—The Musical* received 1.2 million Internet hits in its first day and won the 2009 Webby Award in the category of "Comedy: Individual Short or Episode," as well as a GLAAD media award. The 2010 documentary *8: The Mormon Proposition*, written by journalist and filmmaker Reed Cowan and narrated by filmmaker and LGBT rights activist Dustin Lance Black, traces the involvement of the Mormon Church (both Cowan and Black were raised Mormon) in the passage of Prop 8. Although reviewers criticized the film for its heavy-handed treatment of the Mormon Church, it won GLAAD's 2011 award for "Outstanding Documentary."

5. Lisa Leff, "Donors Pumped $83M to Calif. Gay Marriage Campaign," February 2, 2009, http://www.foxnews.com/printer_friendly_wires/2009Feb02/0,4675,Gay MarriageMoney,00.html.

6. David Binder Research, "Proposition 8: Post-Election California Voter Survey," n.d., http://freemarry.3cdn.net/fae2a432c126ec47d8_brm6bzxix.pdf (accessed March 3, 2009).

7. Toby Miller, "The Hammer Museum Talk 2010," 2010, http://www.tobymiller .org/hammertalk2010.html.

8. Mary Bernstein and Verta Taylor, eds., *The Marrying Kind? Debating Same-Sex*

Marriage within the Lesbian and Gay Movement (Minneapolis: University of Minnesota Press, 2013), 2.

9. Dan Aiello, "The Bay Area Reporter Online | No on Prop 8 Official Grilled over Campaign," *Bay Area Reporter*, November 13, 2008, http://www.ebar.com/news/article.php?sec=news&article=3475.

10. Ibid.

11. My interview with Steve Smith took place on March 17, 2009; all further quotations from him are drawn from this interview.

12. James P. Spradley, *The Ethnographic Interview* (New York: Harcourt Brace Jovanovich, 1979).

13. George Gao, "The Up and Down Seasons of Political Campaign Work," Pew Research Center, November 17, 2014, http://www.pewresearch.org/fact-tank/2014/11/17/the-seasonal-nature-of-political-campaign-work/.

14. Justin Lewis, *Constructing Public Opinion* (New York: Columbia University Press, 2001), x.

15. According to Smith, at the beginning of most ballot initiative campaigns, one third of the voters are "undecided," a much larger percentage than Prop 8's.

16. David Binder Research, "Homepage," DB Research (accessed July 23, 2015), http://db-research.com/.

17. My interview/email exchange with John Ireland took place on March 21, 2009; all quotes from Ireland come from that correspondence. Ireland specifically wanted to target voters whom he called "the movable middle."

18. "No on Prop 8" was led by several LGBT rights organizations under an umbrella group, Equality for All, which was formed specifically to fight Proposition 8. The LGBT rights groups involved included Equality California, a nonprofit civil rights organization that advocates for the rights of LGBT Californians, NCLR (the National Center for Lesbian Rights), HRC (Human Rights Campaign), and the ACLU (American Civil Liberties Union). The campaign's executive committee included Geoff Kors, executive director of Equality California, Kate Kendall, attorney and executive director of the NCLR, Lorri Jean, executive chief officer of the Los Angeles Gay and Lesbian Center, Marty Rouse, national field director for the HRC, and Heather Carrigan and Maya Harris from the ACLU.

19. Barry D. Adam, "The Defense of Marriage Act and American Exceptionalism: The 'Gay Marriage' Panic in the United States," *Journal of the History of Sexuality* 12, no. 2 (2003): 259, https://muse.jhu.edu/article/48722/summary.

20. Ibid., 274.

21. Ibid., 276.

22. Jane Ward, *Respectably Queer: Diversity Culture in LGBT Activist Organizations* (Nashville, TN: Vanderbilt University Press, 2008).

23. Ward, *Respectably Queer*, 134.

24. Suzanna Danuta Walters, *All the Rage: The Story of Gay Visibility in America* (Chicago: University of Chicago Press, 2003), 105.

25. Candace Moore, "Having It All Ways: The Tourist, the Traveler, and the Local in *The L Word*," *Cinema Journal* 46, no. 4 (2007): 3–22.

26. John D'Emilio, William B. Turner, and Urvashi Vaid, eds., *Creating Change: Sexuality, Public Policy, and Civil Rights* (New York: St. Martin's, 2000), ix.

27. Despite the statement that sexual identity is not visible on the body in the

same way race is, there is a long history of coded behavior and dress to identify one's self as a sexual minority both a as way of challenging sex/gender binaries and as a way of forming community. Moreover, a 2015 documentary, "Do I Sound Gay?" (dir. David Thorpe, IFC Films), explores the cultural history of the "gay voice" in film and television.

28. Anti-gay activists, on the other hand, contended that there is no basis for a discrimination case. They argue that marriage is by definition between a man and a woman, that it is so engrained in law that it cannot be changed, and that because sexual orientation has not been ruled a suspect class at the federal level, like race and biological sex have, it is not eligible for the same kinds of legal protections. Religious conservatives add that marriage is for procreation, and that allowing same-sex couples to marry would demean and threaten the institution of marriage. Employing the rhetoric of "family values" to portray marriage rights for lesbians and gays as a threat to children and the social order, they claim that marriage is a sacred and preordained institution.

29. Feinstein has not always supported LGBT civil rights. After the death of Harvey Milk, Feinstein became San Francisco's acting mayor. In 1983, as mayor, Feinstein angered San Francisco's LGBT community by refusing to march in a pride parade as well as by vetoing domestic partner legislation. In a 2008 interview with Maureen Dowd for NBC's *Nightly News*, Feinstein said, "I think as more and more people have gay friends, gay associations, see gay heroism, that their views change. . . . I think people are beginning to look at it differently, I know it's happened for me. I started out not supporting it. The longer I've lived, the more I've seen the happiness of people, the stability that these commitments bring to a life. Many adopted children who would have ended up in foster care now have good solid homes and are brought up learning the difference between right and wrong. It's a very positive thing."

30. David Binder Research, "Proposition 8: Post-Election California Voter Survey."

31. Judith Stacey, *In the Name of the Family: Rethinking Family Values in the Postmodern Age* (Boston: Beacon, 1997), 100–101.

32. Pierre Bourdieu, *Sociology in Question* (Thousand Oaks, CA: SAGE, 1993), http://search.ebscohost.com/login.aspx?direct=true&scope=site&db=nlebk&db=nlabk&AN=47887.

33. Lee Edelman, *No Future: Queer Theory and the Death Drive* (Durham, NC: Duke University Press, 2004).

34. Ibid., 21.

35. Katherine Sender, "Dualcasting: Bravo's Gay Programming and the Quest for Women Audiences," in *Cable Visions: Television beyond Broadcasting*, ed. Sarah Banet-Weiser, Cynthia Chris, and Anthony Freitas (New York: New York University Press, 2007), 310.

36. David M. Skover and Kellye Y. Testy, "LesBiGay Identity as Commodity," *California Law Review* 90, no. 1 (January 2002): 223.

37. John D'Emilio, "Born Gay?," in *The World Turned: Essays on Gay History, Politics, and Culture* (Durham, NC: Duke University Press Books, 2002), 163.

38. Jeffrey Weeks, *Sex, Politics and Society: The Regulations of Sexuality since 1800*, 3rd ed. (New York: Routledge, 2012).

39. Jeffrey Escoffier, *American Homo: Community and Perversity* (Berkeley: University of California Press, 1998).

40. D'Emilio, *The World Turned*, 164.

41. George Chauncey, *Why Marriage: The History Shaping Today's Debate over Gay Equality* (New York: Basic Books, 2005).

42. For a discussion of the unique rights, responsibilities, and privileges tied to marriage in the United States, see Nancy D. Polikoff, *Beyond (Straight and Gay) Marriage: Valuing All Families under the Law* (Boston: Beacon, 2008).

43. Nikki Sullivan, *A Critical Introduction to Queer Theory* (New York: New York University Press, 2003), 23.

44. Suzanna Walters, interview by Francesca Rheannon, "The Writer's Voice," August 7, 2014, http://www.writersvoice.net/2014/08/suzanna-danuta-walters-the-toler ance-trap-alex-sinha-with-liberty-to-monitor-all/.

45. Suzanna Walters, *The Tolerance Trap: How God, Genes, and Good Intentions Are Sabotaging Gay Equality* (New York: New York University Press, 2014), 189.

46. Amin Ghaziani, "Post-Gay Collective Identity Construction," *Social Problems* 58, no. 1 (February 2011): 99–125.

Conclusion

1. On February 15, 2017, the Southern Poverty Law Center (SPLC) published a report detailing an increase in the number of hate groups across the country. According to the report, "The SPLC found that the number of hate groups operating in 2016 rose to 917—up from 892 in 2015. The number is 101 shy of the all-time record set in 2011, but high by historic standards" (SPLC, "Hate Groups Increase for Second Consecutive Year as Trump Electrifies Radical Right," February 15, 2017, https://www .splcenter.org/news/2017/02/15/hate-groups-increase-second-consecutive-year -trump-electrifies-radical-right).

2. For an account of transgender history, see Susan Stryker, *Transgender History* (Berkeley: Seal Press, 2009).

3. Elizabeth Bernstein and Laurie Schaffner, eds., *Regulating Sex: The Politics of Intimacy and Identity*, Perspectives on Gender (New York: Routledge, 2005), xi.

4. Barbara Ehrenreich and John Ehrenreich, "The Professional-Managerial Class," *Radical America* 11, no. 2 (March–April 1977): 12–17; Kevin G. Barnhurst, ed., *Media Q. Media/Queered: Visibility and Its Discontents* (New York: Peter Lang, 2007).

5. Jennifer Holt, *Empires of Entertainment: Media Industries and the Politics of Deregulation, 1980–1996* (New Brunswick, NJ: Rutgers University Press, 2011).

6. Holt, *Empires of Entertainment*, 166.

7. "Gay Marriage Already Won" (cover), *Time*, April 8, 2013; http://content.time .com/time/covers/0,16641,20130408,00.html (accessed March 1, 2016).

8. Ibid.

9. David Von Drehle, "How Gay Marriage Won," *Time*, April 8, 2013, 16.

10. I am not making a causal statement about the effect of public opinion on the Supreme Court's rulings. Rather, I mention them together because public opinion contributed to the vast numbers of what are called "amicus briefs" submitted to the Court in support of marriage equality. These are filed by individuals or groups that are not directly involved in the case, but who want to express an opinion on the issue at hand, often because they have a stake in the outcome.

11. Michelangelo Signorile, *It's Not Over: Getting beyond Tolerance, Defeating Homophobia, and Winning True Equality* (Boston: Houghton Mifflin Harcourt, 2015), 1.

12. I discuss the Supreme Court's rulings in detail in chapter 4.

13. Steven Seidman, *Beyond the Closet: The Transformation of Gay and Lesbian Life* (New York: Routledge, 2002), 6.

14. The scope of this book does not provide for a comprehensive snapshot of either the LGBT political movement or the everyday lives of LGBT people in the United States. However, sociopolitical context matters greatly to the study of television. In describing some of the twenty-first century's most high-profile events, I do not mean to imply that this history matters more than other events that did not make the national news or that do not fit the neat homonormative narrative prevalent in popular and political culture.

15. See chapter 3 for a detailed discussion of contemporary shows that feature transgender characters and personalities.

16. A rich tradition of scholarship exists on LGBT television and tends to focus on representation, looking at whether LGBT representations are socially and politically progressive; how they reinforce or challenge binary notions of sexuality, gender, and race; whether they engage with theories and practices of queer and feminist thought; and whether they reflect a change in public perceptions about sexuality. Consequently, LGBT representations in these analyses are treated as artifacts largely removed from industrial history and theory. Moving away from representational politics, a smaller set of texts has made a case for the transgressive potential of television programming, expanding notions of what constitutes queerness within the television apparatus and industry. See Glyn Davis and Gary Needham, eds., *Queer TV: Theories, Histories, Politics* (London: Routledge, 2009); Barnhurst, *Media Q*; Rebecca Beirne, ed., *Televising Queer Women: A Reader* (New York: Palgrave Macmillan, 2008); Beirne, *Lesbians in Television and Text after the Millennium* (New York: Palgrave Macmillan, 2008); James Penney, *After Queer Theory: The Limits of Sexual Politics* (London: Pluto, 2013); Samuel A. Chambers, *The Queer Politics of Television* (London: Tauris, 2009); Amy Villarejo, *Ethereal Queer: Television, Historicity, Desire* (Durham, NC: Duke University Press, 2014); Villarejo, *Lesbian Rule: Cultural Criticism and the Value of Desire* (Durham, NC: Duke University Press, 2003); Lynne Joyrich, "Queer Television Studies: Currents, Flows, and (Main)streams," *Cinema Journal* 53, no. 2 (Winter 2014): 133–139; Joyrich, "Epistemology of the Console," *Critical Inquiry* 27, no. 3 (2001): 439–467; Sean Griffin, *Tinker Belles and Evil Queens: The Walt Disney Company from the Inside Out* (New York: New York University Press, 2000).

17. Mary Bernstein, "Identities and Politics," *Social Science History* 26, no. 3 (2002): 531–581.

References

Interviews

Howard Bragman, May 7, 2015
Ilene Chaiken (interviewed by Howard Rosenberg, University of Southern California), October 27, 2008
Andy Cohen, May 2, 2008
J. Michael Durnil, March 17, 2009
Robert Greenblatt, June 3, 2008
John Ireland, March 21, 2009 (via email)
Meredith Kadlec, January 22, 2008
Matt Kane, May 7, 2015
Anastasia Khoo, May 10-11, 2015
David Paisley, January 16, 2009
Thomas Roth, June 18, 2009
Amy Shpall, February 22, 2008
Steve Smith, March 17, 2009
Joe Solmonese, May 11, 2015

Articles and Books

"About Us." *Elle* magazine, 2008.
Adam, Barry D. "The Defense of Marriage Act and American Exceptionalism: The 'Gay Marriage' Panic in the United States." *Journal of the History of Sexuality* 12, no. 2 (2003): 259–276.
Aiello, Dan. "The Bay Area Reporter Online | No on Prop 8 Official Grilled over Campaign." *Bay Area Reporter*, November 13, 2008.
Allen, Louise. *The Lesbian Idol: Martina, KD, and the Consumption of Lesbian Masculinity*. London: Cassell, 1997.
Ang, Ien. *Desperately Seeking the Audience*. London: Routledge, 1991.
Armstrong, Jennifer. "Gay Teens on TV." *Entertainment Weekly*, 2011. EW.com (accessed March 1, 2016).

Aronczyk, Melissa, and Devon Powers, eds. *Blowing Up the Brand: Critical Perspectives on Promotional Culture*. New York: Peter Lang, 2010.

Badgett, M. V. Lee. "A Queer Marketplace: Books on Lesbian and Gay Consumers, Workers, and Investors" (review). *Feminist Studies* 23, no. 3 (1997): 607–632.

Baker, Dan. "A History in Ads: The Growth of the Gay and Lesbian Market." In *Homo Economics: Capitalism, Community, and Lesbian and Gay Life*, ed. Amy Gluckman and Betsy Reed, 11–20. New York: Routledge, 1997.

Banet-Weiser, Sarah. *Authentic™: The Politics of Ambivalence in a Brand Culture*. New York: New York University Press, 2012.

Banet-Weiser, Sarah, and Charlotte Lapsansky. "RED Is the New Black: Brand Culture, Consumer Citizenship, and Political Possibility." *International Journal of Communication*, no. 2 (2008): 1248–1268.

Banks, Miranda J. *The Writers: A History of American Screenwriters and Their Guild*. New Brunswick, NJ: Rutgers University Press, 2015.

Banks, Miranda J., Bridget Conor, and Vicki Mayer. *Production Studies, the Sequel: Cultural Studies of Global Media Industries*. New York: Routledge, 2016.

Barnhurst, Kevin G., ed. *Media Q. Media/Queered: Visibility and Its Discontents*. New York: Peter Lang, 2007.

Battles, Kathleen, and Wendy Hilton-Morrow. "Gay Characters in Conventional Spaces: *Will and Grace* and the Situation Comedy Genre." *Critical Studies in Media Communication* 19, no. 1 (2002): 87–105.

Becker, Ron. *Gay TV and Straight America*. New Brunswick, NJ: Rutgers University Press, 2006.

———. "Post-Closet Television." *Flow* 7, no. 3 (November 2007).

Beirne, Rebecca. *Lesbians in Television and Text after the Millennium*. New York: Palgrave Macmillan, 2008.

———, ed. *Televising Queer Women: A Reader*. New York: Palgrave Macmillan, 2008.

Beltrán, Mary. "Meaningful Diversity: Exploring Questions of Equitable Representation on Diverse Ensemble Cast Shows." *Flow* 12, no. 7 (September 2010).

Bennett, James, and Niki Strange, eds. *Television as Digital Media*. Durham, NC: Duke University Press, 2011.

Berlant, Lauren, and Michael Warner. "Sex in Public." *Critical Inquiry* 24, no. 2 (1998): 547–566.

Bernstein, Elizabeth, and Laurie Schaffner, eds. *Regulating Sex: The Politics of Intimacy and Identity*. Perspectives on Gender. New York: Routledge, 2005.

Bernstein, Mary. "Identities and Politics." *Social Science History* 26, no. 3 (2002): 531–581.

Bernstein, Mary, and Verta Taylor, eds. *The Marrying Kind? Debating Same-Sex Marriage within the Lesbian and Gay Movement*. Minneapolis: University of Minnesota Press, 2013.

Bettig, Ronald V., and Jeanne Hall. *Big Media, Big Money: Cultural Texts and Political Economy*. Lanham, MD: Rowman and Littlefield, 2003.

Boddy, William. *Fifties Television: The Industry and Its Critics*. Urbana: University of Illinois Press, 1993.

Bourdieu, Pierre. *Sociology in Question*. Thousand Oaks, CA: SAGE, 1993.

Bronski, Michael. *A Queer History of the United States*. Boston: Beacon, 2012.

Bruni, Frank. "'I Do' and the ACLU" (Frank Bruni's Blog). *New York Times*, May 15, 2013.

———. "The New Gay Orthodoxy." *New York Times*, April 5, 2014.

Buckley, Cara. "ACLU, Citing Bias against Women, Wants Inquiry into Hollywood's Hiring Practices." *New York Times*, May 12, 2015.

Business and Entertainment Editors. "Showtime Networks Launches Phase 2 of alt .SHO.com Targeting Viewers/Consumers." *Business Wire*, September 28, 2000.

Butler, Judith. *Gender Trouble: Feminism and the Subversion of Identity*. Thinking Gender. New York: Routledge, 1990.

———. *Bodies That Matter*. New York: Routledge, 1993.

Caldwell, John Thornton. "Critical Industrial Practice: Branding, Repurposing, and the Migratory Patterns of Industrial Texts." *Television and New Media* 7, no. 2 (2006): 99–134.

———. "Cultures of Production: Studying Industry's Deep Texts, Reflexive Rituals, and Managed Self-Disclosures." In *Media Industries: History, Theory, and Method*, ed. Jennifer Holt and Alisa Perren, 199–213. Malden, MA: Wiley-Blackwell, 2009.

———. *Production Culture: Industrial Reflexivity and Critical Practice in Film and Television*. Durham, NC: Duke University Press, 2008.

Caldwell, John T., Richard Campbell, Christopher R. Martin, and Bettina Fabos. *Media and Culture: Mass Communication in a Digital Age*. 9th ed. Boston: Bedford/ St. Martin, 2013.

Capsuto, Steven. *Alternate Channels: The Uncensored Story of Gay and Lesbian Images on Radio and Television, 1930s to the Present*. New York: Ballantine Books, 2000.

Carrera, Lya. "Style from the Streets: ATKM and DITC Reinvent Lesbian Fashion." *Curve* 18, no. 7 (September 2008): 52–53.

Case, Sue-Ellen. "Toward a Butch-Femme Aesthetic." *Discourse* 11, no. 1 (1988–89): 55–73.

Chambers, Samuel A. *The Queer Politics of Television*. London: Tauris, 2009.

Chauncey, George. *Why Marriage: The History Shaping Today's Debate over Gay Equality*. New York: Basic Books, 2005.

Ciasullo, Ann M. "Making Her (In)visible: Cultural Representations of Lesbianism and the Lesbian Body in the 1990s." *Feminist Studies* 27, no. 3 (2001): 577–608.

Clark, Danae. "Commodity Lesbianism." In *The Gay and Lesbian Studies Reader*, ed. Henry Abelove, Michele A. Barale, and David M. Halperin, 186–201. New York: Routledge, 1993.

Compaine, Benjamin, and Douglas Gomery. *Who Owns the Media?* London: Erlbaum, 2000.

Conrad, Ryan, ed. *Against Equality: Queer Revolution, Not Mere Inclusion*. Oakland, CA: AK Press, 2014.

Copple-Smith, Erin. "'Affluencers' by Bravo: Defining an Audience through Cross-Promotion." *Popular Communication* 10 (2012): 286–301.

Curtin, Michael. "Matrix Media." In *Television Studies after TV: Understanding Television in the Post-Broadcast Era*, ed. Graeme Turner and Jinna Tay, 9–19. New York: Routledge, 2009.

Curtin, Michael, Jennifer Holt, and Kevin Sanson, eds. *Distribution Revolution: Conversations about the Digital Future of Film and Television*. Berkeley: University of California Press, 2014.

D'Acci, Julie. *Defining Women: Television and the Case of Cagney and Lacey*. Chapel Hill: University of North Carolina Press, 1994.

D'Addario, Daniel. "ACLU Pushes for 'Modern Family' Gay Wedding." Salon.com, May 15, 2013.

Dávila, Arlene M. *Latino Spin: Public Image and the Whitewashing of Race*. New York: New York University Press, 2008.

Davis, Glyn, and Gary Needham, eds. *Queer TV: Theories, Histories, Politics*. London: Routledge, 2009.

de la Fuente, Anna Marie. "Chile's Version of 'Modern Family' Facing Unique Set of Obstacles." *Variety*, June 13, 2014.

de Lauretis, Teresa. "Sexual Indifference and Lesbian Representation." *Theatre Journal* 40, no. 2 (1988): 155–177.

DeLong, Renee. "The Stylized Image of the White Lesbian: A Model Minority." In *Queer TV in the Twenty-First Century*, ed. Kylo-Patrick R. Hart, 93–110. Jefferson, NC: McFarland, 2016.

del Río, Esteban. "The Fringe Benefits of Symbolic Annihilation." *Flow* 13, no. 3 (2010).

del Río, Esteban, and Kasey Mitchell. "*Modern Family*'s Indictment of Modern Families." *Flow* 12, no. 5 (2010).

D'Emilio, John. "Introduction: Progress and Representation." In *Media/Queered: Visibility and Its Discontents*, ed. Kevin G. Barnhurst, 23–26. New York: Peter Lang, 2007.

——. *Making Trouble: Essays on Gay History, Politics, and the University*. New York: Routledge, 1992.

——. *The World Turned: Essays on Gay History, Politics, and Culture*. Durham, NC: Duke University Press, 2002.

D'Emilio, John, William B. Turner, and Urvashi Vaid, eds. *Creating Change: Sexuality, Public Policy, and Civil Rights*. New York: St. Martin, 2000.

Dockterman, Eliana. "These Shows Helped Shape America's Attitudes about Gay Relationships." *Time*, June 26, 2015.

Doty, Alexander. *Making Things Perfectly Queer: Interpreting Mass Culture*. Minneapolis: University of Minnesota Press, 1993.

——. "*Modern Family*, *Glee*, and the Limits of Television Liberalism." *Flow* 12, no. 9 (2011): 14.

Douglas, Susan J. *The Rise of Enlightened Sexism: How Pop Culture Took Us from Girl Power to Girls Gone Wild*. New York: St. Martin, 2010.

Dow, Bonnie. *Prime-Time Feminism: Television, Media Culture, and the Women's Movement since 1970*. Philadelphia: University of Pennsylvania Press, 1996.

Duggan, Lisa. "The Anguished Cry of an 80's Fem: 'I Want to be a Drag Queen.'" *Out/Look* 1, no. 1 (1988): 62–65.

——. *The Twilight of Equality? Neoliberalism, Cultural Politics, and the Attack on Democracy*. Boston: Beacon, 2004.

Dyer, Richard. "Stereotyping." In *Gays and Film*, ed. Richard Dyer, 27–39. London: British Film Institute, 1977.

——. *Heavenly Bodies: Film Stars and Society*. 2nd ed. London: Routledge, 2003.

Eaklor, Vicki L. *Queer America: A People's GLBT History of the United States*. Repr. New York: New Press, 2011.

Edelman, Lauren B., Sally Riggs Fuller, and Iona Mara-Drita. "Diversity Rhetoric and the Managerialization of Law." *American Journal of Sociology* 106, no. 6 (May 2001): 1589–1641.

Edelman, Lee. *No Future: Queer Theory and the Death Drive.* Durham, NC: Duke University Press, 2004.

Edgerton, Gary R., and Jeffrey P. Jones, eds. *The Essential HBO Reader.* Lexington: University Press of Kentucky, 2008.

Ehrenreich, Barbara, and John Ehrenreich. "The Professional-Managerial Class," *Radical America* 11, no. 2 (March–April 1977): 12–17.

Ellis, John. *Visible Fictions: Cinema, Television, Video.* New York: Routledge, 2002.

Erhart, Julia. "Gay Fathers in *Modern Family* and *The New Normal*: Class, Consumption, Sexuality, and Parenting." In *Queer TV in the 21st Century*, ed. Kylo-Patrick R. Hart, 128–141. Jefferson, NC: McFarland, 2016.

Escoffier, Jeffrey. *American Homo: Community and Perversity.* Berkeley: University of California Press, 1998.

Ewen, Stuart. *Captains of Consciousness: Advertising and the Social Roots of Consumer Culture.* New York: McGraw Hill, 1979.

Faderman, Lillian, and Stuart Timmons. *Gay LA: A History of Sexual Outlaws, Power Politics, and Lipstick Lesbians.* New York: Basic Books, 2006.

Federal Communications Commission. "Regulation of Cable TV Rates." *FCC Guide.* http://www.fcc.gov/guides/regulation-cable-tv-rates. Accessed June 2, 2014.

Feiler, Bruce. "What 'Modern Family' Says about Modern Families." "This Life," *New York Times*, January 21, 2011.

Ferguson, Roderick A. "Race-ing Homonormativity: Citizenship, Sociology, and Gay Identity." In *Black Queer Studies: A Critical Anthology*, ed. E. Patrick Johnson and Mae E. Henderson, 52–67. Durham: Duke University Press, 2005.

———. *Aberrations in Black: Toward a Queer of Color Critique.* Minneapolis: University of Minnesota Press, 2003.

Feuer, Jane. "Bravo! Stars: An Ode to Jeff, Bethenny, and Tabatha." *Flow* 8, no. 7 (September 4, 2008).

Foucault, Michel. *The History of Sexuality*, vol. 1: *An Introduction.* Trans. Robert Hurley. Reissue ed. New York: Vintage, 1990.

Freedlander, David. "America's First Post-Gay Governor." *Daily Beast*, October 24, 2014.

Gamson, Joshua. *Claims to Fame: Celebrity in Contemporary America.* Berkeley: University of California Press, 1994.

———. *Freaks Talk Back: Tabloid Talk Shows and Sexual Nonconformity.* Chicago: University of Chicago Press, 1999.

Gao, George. "The Up and Down Seasons of Political Campaign Work." Pew Research Center, November 17, 2014.

Gever, Martha. *Entertaining Lesbians: Celebrity, Sexuality, and Self-Invention.* New York: Routledge, 2003.

Ghaziani, Amin. "Post-Gay Collective Identity Construction." *Social Problems* 58, no. 1 (February 2011): 99–125.

Gill, Rosalind. *Gender and the Media.* Cambridge: Polity, 2006.

Gillan, Jennifer. *Television and New Media: Must-Click TV.* New York: Routledge, 2010.

Giroux, Henry A. *The Terror of Neoliberalism: Cultural Politics and the Promise of Democracy*. Boulder, CO: Paradigm, 2004.

Gitlin, Todd. *Inside Prime Time*. Berkeley: University of California Press, 2000.

Gledhill, Christine, ed. *Stardom: Industry of Desire*. London: Routledge, 1991.

Gluckman, Amy, and Betsy Reed, eds. *Homo Economics: Capitalism, Community, and Lesbian and Gay Life*. New York: Routledge, 1997.

Goldberg, Lesley. "A 'Modern Family' Wedding? ACLU Wants One." *Hollywood Reporter*, May 15, 2013.

Gray, Jonathan. *Show Sold Separately: Promos, Spoilers, and Other Media Paratexts*. New York: New York University Press, 2013.

Gray, Mary L. *Out in the Country: Youth, Media, and Queer Visibility in Rural America*. New York: New York University Press, 2009.

Griffin, F. Hollis. *Feeling Normal: Sexuality and Media Criticism in the Digital Age*. Bloomington: Indiana University Press, 2016.

Griffin, Sean. *Tinker Belles and Evil Queens: The Walt Disney Company from the Inside Out*. New York: New York University Press, 2000.

Gross, Larry. *Contested Closets: The Politics and Ethics of Outing*. Minneapolis: University of Minnesota Press, 1993.

———. "Gideon Who Will Be 25 in the Year 2012: Growing Up Gay Today." *International Journal of Communication* 1, no. 1 (2007): 18.

———. *Up From Invisibility: Lesbians, Gay Men, and the Media in America*. New York: Columbia University Press, 2001.

Gross, Larry P., and James D. Woods, eds. *The Columbia Reader on Lesbians and Gay Men in Media, Society, and Politics*. Between Men—Between Women. New York: Columbia University Press, 1999.

Guthrie, Marisa. "Bravo Is Casting a Wider Net with Deal for Online Fan Site." *Daily News*, March 14, 2007, 83.

Halberstam, Judith. *Female Masculinity*. Durham, NC: Duke University Press, 1998.

Hale, Mike. "Fishing Online for Cable Viewers." *New York Times*, February 18, 2011.

Hall, Donald E., and Annamarie Jagose, eds. *The Routledge Queer Studies Reader*. London: Routledge, 2012.

Halperin, David M. *Saint Foucault: Towards a Gay Hagiography*. New York: Oxford University Press, 1997.

Hampp, Andrew. "How Bravo's President Lures 'Affluencers' to Bravo Fold." *Advertising Age*, April 9, 2007, S:2.

Harris, Mark. "By the Way, We're Gay: The New Art of Coming Out." *Entertainment Weekly*, July 2, 2012.

Hart, Kylo-Patrick R., ed. *Queer TV in the 21st Century: Essays on Broadcasting from Taboo to Acceptance*. Jefferson, NC: McFarland, 2016.

Harvey, David. *A Brief History of Neoliberalism*. Oxford: Oxford University Press, 2007.

Havens, Timothy, Amanda D. Lotz, and Serra Tinic. "Critical Media Industry Studies: A Research Approach." *Communication, Culture, and Critique* 2, no. 2 (June 2009): 234–253.

Heller, Dana. "Out for Life: Makeover Television and the Transformation of Fitness on Bravo's *Work Out*." *Continuum: Journal of Media and Cultural Studies* 22, no. 4 (August 2008): 525–535.

————. *Cross Purposes: Lesbians, Feminists, and the Limits of Alliance*. Bloomington: Indiana University Press, 1997.

Henderson, Lisa. *Love and Money: Queers, Class, and Cultural Production*. New York: New York University Press, 2013.

Hennessy, Rosemary. *Profit and Pleasure: Sexual Identities in Late Capitalism*. New York: Routledge, 2000.

Hilderbrand, Lucas. "Stage Left: *Glee* and the Textual Politics of Difference." *Flow* 11, no. 3 (2009).

Hilmes, Michele. *Hollywood and Broadcasting: From Radio to Cable*. Urbana: University of Illinois Press, 1990.

Holt, Jennifer. *Empires of Entertainment: Media Industries and the Politics of Deregulation, 1980–1996*. New Brunswick, NJ: Rutgers University Press, 2011.

Holt, Jennifer, Michael Curtin, and Kevin Sanson, eds. *Distribution Revolution*. Berkeley: University of California Press, 2014.

Holt, Jennifer, and Alisa Perren, eds. *Media Industries: History, Theory, and Method*. Malden, MA: Wiley-Blackwell, 2009.

Huff, Richard. "The Final Frontier: Lesbians Showtime Teases 'L-Word.'" *New York Daily News*, October 24, 2003.

Irvine, Janice M. "From Difference to Sameness: Gender Ideology in Sexual Science." *Journal of Sex Research* 27, no. 1 (February 1990): 7–24.

Jenkins, Henry. *Convergence Culture: Where Old and New Media Collide*. Rev. ed. New York: New York University Press, 2008.

Jhally, Sut, and Justin Lewis. "Affirming Inaction: Television and the New Politics of Race." Reprinted in Sut Jhally, *The Spectacle of Accumulation: Essays in Culture, Media, and Politics*, 203–218. New York: Peter Lang, 2006.

————. *Enlightened Racism: The Cosby Show, Audiences, and the Myth of the American Dream*. Cultural Studies. Boulder: Westview, 1992.

Johnson, Catherine. *Branding Television*. New York: Routledge, 2012.

Joyrich, Lynne. "Epistemology of the Console." *Critical Inquiry* 27, no. 3 (Spring 2001): 439–467.

————. "Queer Television Studies: Currents, Flows, and (Main)streams." *Cinema Journal* 53, no. 2 (Winter 2014): 133–139.

Kang, Cecilia, and Matea Gold. "With Political Ads Expected to Hit a Record, News Stations Can Hardly Keep Up." *Washington Post*, October 31, 2014.

Kellner, Douglas. "Media Industries, Political Economy, and Media/Cultural Studies: An Articulation." In *Media Industries: History, Theory and Method*, ed. Jennifer Holt and Alisa Perren. Malden, MA: Wiley-Blackwell, 2009.

Kessler, Kelly. "Politics of the Sitcom Formula: Friends, Mad About You, and the Sapphic Second Banana." In *The New Queer Aesthetic on TV: Essays on Recent Programming*, ed. James R. Keller and Leslie Stratyner, 130–146. Jefferson, NC: McFarland, 2007.

Kirchick, James. "How GLAAD Won the Culture War and Lost Its Reason to Exist." *Atlantic*, May 3, 2013.

Klein, Naomi. *No Logo: 10th Anniversary Edition with a New Introduction by the Author*. New York: Picador, 2009.

Kohnen, Melanie. "Cultural Diversity as Brand Management in Cable Television." *Media Industries* 2, no. 2 (2015): 88–103.

Kolko, Beth E., Lisa Nakamura, and Gilbert B. Rodman, eds. *Race in Cyberspace*. New York: Routledge, 2000.

Kunz, William M. *Culture Conglomerates: Consolidation in the Motion Picture and Television Industries*. Lanham, MD: Rowman and Littlefield, 2006.

Lafayette, Jon. "Bravo Making Digital Mandatory: All Projects to Be Designed with Broadband Components." *Television Week*, May 15, 2006, 5.

Leff, Lisa. "Donors Pumped $83M to Calif. Gay Marriage Campaign." Fox News, February 2, 2009.

Levy, Ariel. "Dolls and Feelings." *New Yorker*, December 14, 2015.

Lewis, Justin. *Constructing Public Opinion*. New York: Columbia University Press, 2001.

Lotz, Amanda. "If It's Not TV, What Is It? The Case of US Subscription Television." In *Cable Visions: Television Beyond Broadcasting*, ed. Sarah Banet-Weiser, Cynthia Chris, and Anthony Freitas, 85–102. New York: New York University Press, 2007.

———. "Postfeminist Television Criticism: Rehabilitating Critical Terms and Identifying Postfeminist Attributes." *Feminist Media Studies* 1, no. 1 (2001): 105–121.

———. *The Television Will Be Revolutionized*. New York: New York University Press, 2007.

Love, Heather. *Feeling Backward: Loss and the Politics of Queer History*. Cambridge, MA: Harvard University Press, 2009.

Martin, Biddy. "Sexualities without Genders and Other Queer Utopias." *Diacritics* 24, no. 2/3 (1994): 104–121.

Martin, Denise. "TCA: Alan Ball: 'True Blood' Is Not a Metaphor for Gay People." *LA Times Blogs—Show Tracker*, July 10, 2008.

Marwick, Alice E., and danah boyd. "I Tweet Honestly, I Tweet Passionately: Twitter Users, Context Collapse, and the Imagined Audience." *New Media and Society* 13, no. 1 (2010): 114–133.

Mayer, Vicki. *Below the Line: Producers and Production Studies in the New Television Economy*. Durham, NC: Duke University Press, 2011.

Mayer, Vicki, Miranda J. Banks, and John T. Caldwell, eds. *Production Studies: Cultural Studies of Media Industries*. New York: Routledge, 2009.

Mayne, Judith. *Framed: Lesbians, Feminists, and Media Culture*. Minneapolis: University of Minnesota Press, 2000.

McCarthy, Anna. *The Citizen Machine: Governing by Television in 1950s America*. New York: New York University Press, 2013.

McChesney, Robert. *The Political Economy of Media: Enduring Issues, Emerging Dilemmas*. New York: Monthly Review Press, 2008.

McRobbie, Angela. *The Aftermath of Feminism: Gender, Culture, and Social Change*. Los Angeles: SAGE, 2009.

———. "Post-Feminism and Popular Culture," *Feminist Media Studies* 4, no. 3 (2004): 255–264.

Meehan, Eileen R. *Why TV Is Not Our Fault: Television Programming, Viewers, and Who's Really in Control*. Lanham, MD: Rowman and Littlefield, 2005.

———. "Why We Don't Count: The Commodity Audience." In *Logics of Television: Essays in Cultural Criticism*, ed. Patricia Mellencamp, 117–137. Bloomington: Indiana University Press, 1990.

Meeker, Martin. *Contacts Desired: Gay and Lesbian Communications and Community, 1940s–1970s*. Chicago: University of Chicago Press, 2006.

Minow, Newton N. *Equal Time: The Private Broadcaster and the Public Interest*. New York: Atheneum, 1964.

Mittell, Jason. *Television and American Culture*. New York: Oxford University Press, 2009.

Molina-Guzmán, Isabel. "*Modern Family*'s Latina Spitfire in the Era of White Resentment." *Flow* 17, no. 1 (2013).

Montgomery, Kathryn. *Target: Prime Time: Advocacy Groups and the Struggle over Entertainment Television*. New York: Oxford University Press, 1990.

Moore, Candace. "Having It All Ways: The Tourist, the Traveler, and the Local in *The L Word*." *Cinema Journal* 46, no. 4 (2007): 3–22.

Moraga, Cherríe L. *A Xicana Codex of Changing Consciousness: Writings, 2000–2010*. Durham, NC: Duke University Press, 2011.

Moraga, Cherríe, and Gloria Anzaldúa. *This Bridge Called My Back: Writings by Radical Women of Color*. 4th ed. Albany: State University of New York Press, 2015.

Moritz, Marguerite. "Coming Out Stories: The Creation of Lesbian Images on Prime Time TV." Paper presented at the seventy-first annual meeting of the Association for Education in Journalism and Mass Communication (Portland, OR, July 2–5, 1988).

———. "Lesbian Chic: Our Fifteen Minutes of Celebrity?" In *Feminism, Multiculturalism, and the Media: Global Diversities*, ed. Angharad Valdivia, 127–145. Thousand Oaks, CA: SAGE, 1995.

Mosco, Vincent. "Media Sociology and Media Workers." *Contemporary Sociology* 12, no. 2 (March 1983): 153–155.

Mukherjee, Roopali, and Sarah Banet-Weiser, eds. *Commodity Activism: Cultural Resistance in Neoliberal Times*. New York: New York University Press, 2012.

Mullen, Megan. "The Fall and Rise of Cable Narrowcasting." *Convergence: The International Journal of Research into New Media Technologies* 8, no. 1 (2002): 62–83.

Muñoz, José Esteban. *Cruising Utopia: The Then and There of Queer Futurity*. New York: New York University Press, 2009.

Nader, Laura. "Up the Anthropologist: Perspectives Gained from Studying Up" (1972). https://eric.ed.gov/?id=ED065375.

Napoli, Philip. *Audience Evolution: New Technologies and the Transformation of Media Audiences*. New York: Columbia University Press, 2011.

———. "Audience Measurement and Media Policy: Audience Economics, the Diversity Principle, and the Local People Meter." *Communication Law and Policy* 10, no. 4 (2005): 349–382.

———. "Media Economics and the Study of Media Industries." In *Media Industries: History, Theory, and Method*, ed. Jennifer Holt and Alisa Perren. Malden, MA: Wiley-Blackwell, 2009.

Nestle, Joan, ed. *The Persistent Desire: A Femme-Butch Reader*. Boston: Alyson, 1991.

Newman, Michael Z., and Elana Levine. *Legitimating Television: Media Convergence and Cultural Status*. New York: Routledge, 2012.

Ng, Eve. "A 'Post-Gay' Era? Media Gaystreaming, Homonormativity, and the Politics of LGBT Integration." *Communication, Culture and Critique* 6, no. 2 (June 2013): 258–283.

O'Connell, Michael. "'Modern Family' Considering a Gay Wedding after Supreme Court Rulings." *Hollywood Reporter*, June 27, 2013.

O'Hehir, Andrew. "Did TV Change America's Mind on Gay Marriage?." Salon.com, March 30, 2013.

Ortner, Sherry B. "Access: Reflections on Studying Up in Hollywood." *Ethnography* 11, no. 2 (June 1, 2010): 211–233.

Ouellette, Laurie. *Lifestyle TV*. New York: Routledge, 2016.

———. *Viewers Like You? How Public TV Failed the People*. New York: Columbia University Press, 2002.

Ouellette, Laurie, and James Hay. *Better Living through Reality TV: Television and Post-Welfare Citizenship*. Malden, MA: Blackwell, 2008.

Out.com editors. "The Power 50." *Out*, April 3, 2007.

Park, Pauline. "GenderPAC, the Transgender Rights Movement, and the Perils of a Post-Identity Politics Paradigm." *Georgetown Journal of Gender and the Law* 4 (2003): 747.

Parkes, Chris. "Teaching Queer History." *NOTCHES*, February 7, 2015.

Penney, James. *After Queer Theory: The Limits of Sexual Politics*. London: Pluto, 2013.

Perlman, Allison. *Public Interests: Media Advocacy and Struggles over US Television*. New Brunswick, NJ: Rutgers University Press, 2016.

Perren, Alisa. "In Conversation: Creativity in the Contemporary Cable Industry." *Cinema Journal* 50, no. 2 (2011): 132–138.

Pertierra, Anna Cristina, and Graeme Turner. *Locating Television: Zones of Consumption*. London: Routledge, 2013.

Ping, Jonathan H. *Middle Power Statecraft: Indonesia, Malaysia, and the Asia Pacific*. Aldershot: Ashgate, 2005.

Polikoff, Nancy D. *Beyond (Straight and Gay) Marriage: Valuing All Families under the Law*. Boston: Beacon, 2008.

Provencher, Denis M. "Sealed with a Kiss: Heteronormative Narrative Strategies in NBC's *Will & Grace*." In *The Sitcom Reader: America Viewed and Skewed*, ed. Mary M. Dalton and Laura R. Linder, 177–190. Albany: State University of New York Press, 2005.

Puar, Jasbir. *Terrorist Assemblages: Homonationalism in Queer Times*. Durham, NC: Duke University Press, 2007.

Ramisetti, Kirthana. "GLAAD Report Shows TV Is Tuned In to LGBT Diversity." *New York Daily News*, October 1, 2014.

Rauch, Jonathan. "Prop. 8 Ads' Invisible Gays." *Los Angeles Times*, October 26, 2008.

Rice, Lynnette. "DOMA Reaction: 'Modern Family' Considering Gay Marriage." *Entertainment Weekly*, June 26, 2013.

Roarty, Alex. "Kentucky Has a Gay Senate Candidate—Does Anybody Care?" *Roll Call*, August 24, 2016.

Rook, Erin. "'Grey's Anatomy' Star Sara Ramirez Comes out as Bisexual and Queer." *LGBTQ Nation*, October 8, 2016.

Rose, Lacey. "'Modern Family': USA Plans Unprecedented Syndication Rollout." *Hollywood Reporter*, September 18, 2013.

Rosenberg, Howard. "Core Conversations" panel participant. *Flow* Conference, Austin, TX, September 11, 2014.

Rubin, Gayle. "Thinking Sex: Notes for a Radical Theory of the Politics of Sexuality"

(1984). In *Social Perspectives in Lesbian and Gay Studies: A Reader*, ed. Peter Nardi and Beth Schneider, 100–133. London: Routledge, 1998.

Russo, Julie Levin. "Labor of Love: Charting *The L Word*." *Wired TV: Laboring Over an Interactive Future*, ed. Denise Mann, 98–117. New Brunswick, NJ: Rutgers University Press, 2014.

San Filippo, Maria. *The B Word: Bisexuality in Contemporary Film and Television*. Bloomington: Indiana University Press, 2013.

Sedgwick, Eve Kosofsky. *Epistemology of the Closet*. Berkeley: University of California Press, 1990.

Seidman, Steven. *Beyond the Closet: The Transformation of Gay and Lesbian Life*. New York: Routledge, 2002.

Seiter, Ellen. *Television and New Media Audiences*. Oxford: Oxford University Press, 1999.

Sender, Katherine. *Business, Not Politics: The Making of the Gay Market*. New York: Columbia University Press, 2005.

———. "Dualcasting: Bravo's Gay Programming and the Quest for Women Audiences." In *Cable Visions: Television beyond Broadcasting*, ed. Sarah Banet-Weiser, Cynthia Chris, and Anthony Freitas, 302–318. New York: New York University Press, 2007.

Setoodeh, Ramin. "How Sarah Kate Ellis Brought GLAAD Into the 21st Century." *Variety*, September 27, 2016.

Shen, Aviva, and Kira Lerner. "Ted Cruz Just Won The Iowa Caucus. This Is His Radical Agenda For America." *ThinkProgress*, February 1, 2016.

Signorile, Michelangelo. *It's Not Over: Getting beyond Tolerance, Defeating Homophobia, and Winning True Equality*. Boston: Houghton Mifflin Harcourt, 2015.

Skover, David M., and Kellye Y. Testy. "LesBiGay Identity as Commodity." *California Law Review* 90, no. 1 (January 2002): 223.

Smith-Shomade, Beretta. "Narrowcasting in the New World Information Order: A Space for the Audience?" *Television and New Media* 5, no. 1 (2004): 69–81.

Southern Poverty Law Center. "Hate Groups Increase for Second Consecutive Year as Trump Electrifies Radical Right." February 15, 2017. https://www.splcenter.org/news/2017/02/15/hate-groups-increase-second-consecutive-year-trump-electrifies-radical-right.

Spigel, Lynn. *Make Room for TV: Television and the Family Ideal in Postwar America*. Chicago: University of Chicago Press, 2005.

———. *Welcome to the Dreamhouse: Popular Media and Postwar Suburbs*. Durham, NC: Duke University Press, 2001.

Spigel, Lynn, and Jan Olsson, eds. *Television after TV: Essays on a Medium in Transition*. Durham, NC: Duke University Press, 2004.

Spradley, James P. *The Ethnographic Interview*. New York: Harcourt Brace Jovanovich, 1979.

Stacey, Judith. *In the Name of the Family: Rethinking Family Values in the Postmodern Age*. Boston: Beacon, 1997.

Stanley, Alessandra. "Sex and the Gym: 'Work Out' and the Gaying of Bravo." *New York Times*, July 19, 2006, section E.

———. "Women Having Sex, Hoping Men Tune in." *New York Times*, January 16, 2004, 2.

Stein, Arlene, "All Dressed Up, But No Place to Go? Style Wars and the New Lesbianism." In *Out in Culture: Gay, Lesbian, and Queer Essays on Popular Culture*, ed. Corey Creekmur and Alexander Doty, 476–483. Durham, NC: Duke University Press, 1995.

Steinmetz, Katy. "Laverne Cox Talks to TIME About the Transgender Movement." *Time*, May 29, 2014.

Streeter, Thomas. *Selling the Air: A Critique of the Policy of Commercial Broadcasting in the United States*. Chicago: University of Chicago Press, 1996.

Stryker, Susan. *Transgender History*. Berkeley: Seal Press, 2009.

Sullivan, Andrew. "The Case against the Case against 8." *The Dish*, 2014, http://dish.andrewsullivan.com/2014/06/23/the-case-against-the-case-against-8/ (accessed July 3, 2015).

Sullivan, Nikki. *A Critical Introduction to Queer Theory*. New York: New York University Press, 2003.

Tasker, Yvonne, and Diane Negra. "'In Focus': Postfeminism and Contemporary Media Studies." *Cinema Journal* 44, no. 2 (2005): 107–110.

Terkel, Amanda. "ACLU Pushes for Cam and Mitch to Get Hitched on 'Modern Family.'" *Huffington Post*, May 15, 2013.

Tropiano, Stephen. "*Flow* Favorites: Gaycoms in a Progressive Age? *Partners* and *The New Normal*." *Flow* 17, no. 13 (September 27, 2012).

———. *The Prime Time Closet: A History of Gays and Lesbians on TV*. New York: Applause Theatre and Cinema Books, 2002.

Turner, Graeme, and Jinna Tay. *Television Studies after TV: Understanding Television in the Post-Broadcast Era*. New York: Routledge, 2009.

Turow, Joseph. "Audience Construction and Culture Production: Marketing Surveillance in the Digital Age." *Annals of the American Academy of Political and Social Science* 597 (2005): 103–121.

———. *Breaking Up America: Advertisers and the New Media World*. Chicago: University of Chicago Press, 1997.

———. *The Daily You: How the New Advertising Industry Is Defining Your Identity and Your Worth*. New Haven: Yale University Press, 2012.

Vaid, Urvashi. *Virtual Equality: The Mainstreaming of Gay and Lesbian Liberation*. 2nd ed. New York: Anchor Books, 1996.

Valdes, Francisco. "Latina/o Ethnicities, Critical Race Theory, and Post-Identity Politics in Postmodern Legal Culture: From Practices to Possibilities." *La Raza Law Journal* 9 (1996): 1.

Valocchi, Stephen. "The Class-Inflected Nature of Gay Identity." *Social Problems* 46, no. 2 (May 1999): 207–224.

Villarejo, Amy. *Ethereal Queer: Television, Historicity, Desire*. Durham, NC: Duke University Press, 2014.

———. *Lesbian Rule: Cultural Criticism and the Value of Desire*. Durham, NC: Duke University Press, 2003.

Von Drehle, David. "How Gay Marriage Won." *Time* 181, no. 13 (April 8, 2013), 16.

Walker, Lisa. "How to Recognize a Lesbian: The Cultural Politics of Looking Like What You Are." *Signs* 18 (summer 1993): 878–79.

Walters, Suzanna Danuta. *All the Rage: The Story of Gay Visibility in America*. Chicago: University of Chicago Press, 2003.

———. *The Tolerance Trap: How God, Genes, and Good Intentions Are Sabotaging Gay Equality*. New York: New York University Press, 2014.

———. Interviewed by Francesca Rheannon, "The Writer's Voice." August 7, 2014, http://www.writersvoice.net/2014/08/suzanna-danuta-walters-the-tolerance -trap-alex-sinha-with-liberty-to-monitor-all/.

Ward, Jane. *Respectably Queer: Diversity Culture in LGBT Activist Organizations*. Nashville, TN: Vanderbilt University Press, 2008.

Warn, Sarah. "Introduction." In *Reading* The L Word: *Outing Contemporary Television*, ed. Kim Akass and Janet McCabe, 1–10. London: I. B. Tauris, 2006.

Warner, Michael. *The Trouble with Normal: Sex, Politics, and the Ethics of Queer Life*. New ed. Cambridge, MA: Harvard University Press, 1999.

Weeks, Jeffrey. *Sex, Politics, and Society: The Regulations of Sexuality since 1800*. 3rd ed. New York: Routledge, 2012.

———. *Sexuality and Its Discontents: Meanings, Myths, and Modern Sexualities*. London: Routledge and Kegan Paul, 1985.

Wells, Debbie, and Alison Zawack. "Lesbian Market Gains Strength with 2008 Consumer Survey." *Jane and Jane*, December 18, 2008.

Wheeler, Leigh Ann. *How Sex Became a Civil Liberty*. New York: Oxford University Press, 2014.

White, Patricia. *Uninvited: Classical Hollywood Cinema and Lesbian Representability*. Bloomington: Indiana University Press, 1999.

Williams, Linda. "*Personal Best*: Women in Love." *JumpCut*, no. 27 (July 1982): 11.

Williams, Raymond. *Television: Technology and Cultural Form*. New York: Schocken Books, 1975.

Wood, Peter. *Diversity: The Invention of a Concept*. San Francisco: Encounter Books, 2004.

Index

Page numbers in italics indicate figures.